WITHDRAWN

EUGÈNE SCRIBE

EUGÈNE SCRIBE

EUGÈNE SCRIBE

AND THE FRENCH THEATRE

1815—1860

BY

NEIL COLE ARVIN, Ph.D.

ASSISTANT PROFESSOR OF FRENCH IN THE
UNIVERSITY OF CALIFORNIA

Benjamin Blom
New York

First Published 1924
Reissued 1967, by Benjamin Blom, Inc., New York 10452
Library of Congress Catalog Card No. 67-18422

Printed in U.S.A. by
NOBLE OFFSET PRINTERS, INC.
NEW YORK 3, N. Y.

TO

M. M. A.

PREFACE

I DO not feel that it is necessary to offer any apology for
writing about a man now so universally forgotten.
For nearly fifty years Scribe was the most successful and
most popular dramatist, not only in France, but in all of
Europe, and the completeness of the oblivion, disrepute
even, into which he has fallen, cannot change that fact.
Then there must be some interest in attempting to discover what elements entered into his success, and what
forces concurred in bringing him into disesteem.

At the outset, it will be apparent that a study of his
plays can have little interest from a purely literary or
stylistic point of view; and any effort to account for his
tremendous hold upon the public for so many years must
be directed along different lines. It may be, though, that
as a social symptom, as a painter of contemporary life,
as a composite picture of the French bourgeoisie from
1815 to 1850, Scribe will repay study. Every textbook
and critic dismisses him with an impatient remark to the
effect that he had no style (a *cliché* made current by Jules
Janin and Théophile Gautier), but that he undoubtedly
was a clever technician who knew how to write plays.
And both these statements are very true. Only it is looking for noon at two o'clock to be concerned with his
style; his plays are not models of style, he did not intend
them to be; and that point did not preoccupy him and
had very little to do with the excellence or worthlessness
of his pieces. As to his skill as a constructor of well-made
plays, it probably amounted to genius. At any rate, he

invented the form, the model, which Augier, the younger Dumas, Sardou, Labiche, Octave Feuillet, and all the others employed and imitated, and which, developed to excess and fallen into less capable hands, became the *pièce bien faite* — the well-made play — whose conventions fell before those of the Théâtre Libre; for the revolt against convention engendered convention: the *comédie rosse* — the tough play, the *tranche de vie* — the slice of life, the pessimism of 1880–1890, were as conventional as the colonels, the stockbrokers, and the capitalists of Scribe.

No, it is for other reasons that Scribe's plays are interesting now. He was a perfect representative of the French bourgeoisie of the Restoration and of the July Monarchy, and a very good picture of the bourgeois of that period can be found in his plays. By reading them, and also by reading contemporary estimates of them, as found in memoirs, in his own voluminous correspondence, and chiefly in the dramatic criticisms written after the first performances, one finds that many plays which now seem the essence of respectability and of mediocre conservatism seemed to contemporary audiences startlingly advanced, free, and even scabrous. On the other hand, certain pieces, different scenes, which to us appear exaggerated, caricaturish, or risqué, were accepted as natural, true, and matter-of-course.

Such a study promised to be interesting and to repay the time spent on it, to ascertain, not only Scribe's treatment of the manners, the vices, and the follies about him, but the reaction of contemporary society to his picture of the period. In only one way could such a synthesis of contemporary opinion be made: by reading every criticism, every article devoted to Scribe, in the leading journals and reviews from 1810 to 1860, and by going through Scribe's correspondence (now at the Bibliothèque Nationale). For this purpose I went through the complete files of the following publications: "La Presse," "Le Journal des Débats," "Le Constitutionnel," "Le Moniteur Universel," "Le Figaro," "La Quotidienne," "Le Globe," "Le Siècle," "La Revue des Deux Mondes," and "La Revue de Paris."

In writing this book it has been difficult to avoid what may be an excessive use of French terms. Many words and phrases, most of them technical, cannot be exactly translated into English. A *vaudeville* is certainly not a vaudeville like that offered by Keith and Pantage; a *comédie* is frequently anything but what an American would expect to see at a play announced as a comedy. And so on. It has therefore seemed best to retain the French word, in cases where a convenient and exact translation was impossible, and to give in the foot-notes a definition of the term that would make its further use clear and justifiable. If I have yielded to the temptation to say *coup de théâtre*, *hors-d'œuvre*, *procédé de théâtre*, etc., in cases where an English translation might be possible, my excuse is that, in discussing anything connected with the French drama (but not the *drame!*), it seems permissible, and perhaps logical, to use the French technical terms.

I take pleasure in expressing my gratitude to Madame Paul Biollay, daughter-in-law of Eugène Scribe, who very kindly placed at my disposal all the many documents now in her possession; to Professor Abel Lefranc, of the Collège de France, whose excellent suggestions were of great help to me; to Professor Mathurin Dondo, to Professor Percival B. Fay, and to my brother, Newton Arvin, who cheerfully read the manuscript and aided in reading the proof; and the dedication of the book is at best a poor return for the help which my wife has given me.

BERKELEY, CALIFORNIA
August, 1923

CONTENTS

EUGÈNE SCRIBE

CHAPTER I

THE LIFE OF SCRIBE

AUGUSTIN–EUGÈNE SCRIBE was born December 24, 1791, in Paris, in a small house in the Rue Saint-Denis, near the Halles, and was baptized the following day in the church of Saint-Jacques de la Boucherie. Thus Scribe, like Villon, Boileau, Molière, and Béranger, was a true child of Paris, born in the heart of the commercial and industrial district, the quarter occupied by the hard-working bourgeoisie. At the time of Eugène's birth, his father, a merchant who had made a modest fortune by dint of hard work, owned a small silk shop bearing the sign "Le Chat Noir"; but in 1798 Jean-François Scribe died, leaving three children, Eugène, and an older brother and sister, both of whom were favored in the father's will to the disadvantage of the youngest child. Shortly after the death of her husband, Madame Scribe, selling her stock in trade, removed with her family to a house near the church of Saint-Roch.

Scribe's mother, whom he always loved passionately, was forced to live on a very small income and to suffer many privations in order to give her son the education she wanted him to have. Through her efforts the young boy obtained a scholarship at the Collège Sainte-Barbe, an ancient institution which had just reëstablished the study of the Classics, and which was then called the Collège des Sciences et des Arts. His record at Sainte-Barbe was one of the most brilliant; many times in succession the future dramatist stood at the head of his class — an attainment which occasioned a number of flattering letters from Delanneau, one of the directors, to Madame Scribe; and when he left Sainte-Barbe it was with the *prix d'honneur*, after having maintained his thesis in a very brilliant manner before Laromiguières. The only reproaches made by his masters were that he seemed to lack concentration and that his religious observances were "more or less perfunctory." His training and accomplishments at Sainte-Barbe are sufficient proof that he was not, as some of his bitter critics later accused him of being, ignorant of French grammar and of history. It was at Sainte-Barbe that he made the acquaintance of Casimir and Germain Delavigne. The friendship lasted for years, and resulted in literary collaboration between Scribe and the older brother, Germain, with whom he made his dramatic début in 1811.

Shortly before her death, in 1807, Madame Scribe, who wanted her son to study law, had chosen a celebrated lawyer, Monsieur Bonnet, a relative, to direct the lad in the career for which she had destined him. Bonnet advised his ward to enter a barrister's office, and to take private lessons from an instructor; at his guardian's suggestion, Scribe entered the office of Guyonnet-Merville, with whom Bayard and Balzac were later to show their inaptitude for the law. For a time the young Scribe applied himself to his work with some seriousness, probably out of deference to his mother's desires; but after her death, his natural inclinations asserted themselves, and already at this age he was drawn to the theatre by a precocious interest in all things theatrical. In the years between 1811 and 1815, while he was supposed to be studying law, he was in reality writing *vaudevilles*,[1] in collaboration with Germain Delavigne. However, his literary activities did not prevent him from receiving his degree of bachelor of law from the Imperial University in 1815.

From his early childhood he had sketched *vaudevilles* and scribbled *couplets*[2] in his copy-book, and on holidays would run to the pit of the Théâtre du Vaudeville in the Rue de Chartres. Germain had already had the good fortune to have one of his plays accepted at this theatre through the influence of his uncle, Lambert, a friend of Barré, the director of the Vaudeville, and thus had an author's free entrance to the theatre. The two friends now set about trying to obtain acceptance of one of Scribe's plays, so that Scribe himself, whose resources were rather slender, might also have free entrance and thus accompany his friend more frequently.

Not until 1811, however, was their desire realized. One of the most popular writers of songs and *vaudevilles* at this time was Henri Dupin, for whom the two ambitious young authors had great admiration, and whom they begged to examine their first dramatic attempt. Dupin, after complying with their request, told them that their play, although lacking maturity, was clever and well-constructed and contained pretty *couplets*. He promised that, if they would continue to work on *vaudevilles*, he would help them, and predicted ultimate success.

It was under the guidance of this master that in 1811 they made their first appearance. In that year Lambert obtained the reception of "Les Dervis," the first perform-

---

[1] "*Vaudeville:* Petite pièce de théâtre, mêlée de couplets." (Larousse.)

[2] "*Couplet:* Stance faisant partie d'une chanson." (Larousse.)

ance of which was given on September 2. This little play, which, although not a failure, was only a moderate success, was followed by "Les Malades par ricochets," "Une Nuit à Ispahan," "Hasard et Malice," and "Le Bachelier de Salamanque." For all these plays the director of the theatre of the Rue de Chartres proved less sympathetic, refusing them, or rather accepting them "subject to correction," which was equivalent to indefinite adjournment. At this, Dupin suggested that they leave the Vaudeville, and offered his collaboration to help them enter the Variétés. The two friends, once more encouraged by their guide, hoped again for success. But the pit of the Variétés proved as unresponsive as that of the Vaudeville, and not even the help of Dupin brought them the success they sought. Germain Delavigne then modestly withdrew from the combination, fearing that he had brought ill luck to their venture.

Dupin and Scribe continued their work together, returning to the Vaudeville, where "Barbanéra ou les Bossus" was offered to the public, which once more proved unsympathetic. At this point Dupin told Scribe that he would do well to continue his efforts alone. But the young writer was not discouraged. He remarked naïvely to G. Delavigne that, when he had completed the four or five plays for which he had the plans in his pockets, he would renounce the theatre. Needless to say, there never came a time when he did not have a number of manuscripts on hand.

This persistence brought him his first real success, in May, 1812, with "L'Auberge, ou les Brigands sans le savoir," which he considered to be really his first play, as he had composed it while he was still in grammar school. "L'Auberge" won the hearty approbation of the great aristarch of the day, Geoffroy, not so much for the subject as for the gayety and the originality of the details. Its author now took rank among the most popular *vaudevillistes* of the time and was applauded on the stage where Désaugiers, Barré, Piis, Radet, and Desfontaines were reigning.

In 1813 he produced alone his first *opéra-comique*, "La Chambre à coucher, ou une Demi-heure de Richelieu," which, partly because of the illness of the principal actress, Mademoiselle Regnault, was taken off the stage after the first month. It was only seven years later, at the request of Auber, that he again tried his hand at such work. In 1813 he produced also his first melodrama, "Koulikan," with Henri Dupin. Although the young authors had chosen Voltaire as collaborator, adapting his "Scythes," the success of their play was but mediocre. Another play of this same period, "Thibaut, Comte de Champagne," whose original title, "Marguerite de Valois," had been forbidden by the imperial police, was received with hisses of disapproval.

Scribe has often been reproached, perhaps with some justice, for being so little moved by the tremendous political and social upheavals about him. This comparative indifference to the great changes taking place in the very life of his country, his ambition to please the public, and his conception of the theatre as a financial institution, were elements in his make-up which to a certain extent excluded that comprehension of and sympathy with the fundamental truths and principles of life without which an artist cannot be really great. And yet in fairness to Scribe it must be said that he personally had no motive for admiring Napoleon at the time of his glory, or for missing him after his disappearance. To him, as to so many other young men of his day, the Napoleonic régime meant conscription, barrack-life, bloodshed; the Napoleonic wars, while adding to the military glory of France, practically annihilated for a time intellectual and artistic production, and many very patriotic Frenchmen could only regret that all the capabilities of the nation were being devoted to the prosecution of foreign wars. It is to be noticed that, although Scribe was no worshipper of Napoleon, neither did he flatter him in the plays written during the Empire; at that time he maintained his independence, as he did later during the Restoration and the July Monarchy. That he later contributed in no small way to the growth of the Napoleonic legend, with his colonels and captains, his *lauriers* and his *guerriers*, for which he probably cared little except for the exigencies of rhyme, cannot be considered particularly inconsistent.

Although he had by this time acquired a very enviable reputation as a writer of *vaudevilles*, he was not satisfied with what he had accomplished, and realized that so far he had really only followed the beaten paths. The following lines, written by Scribe at this period, show what ambitions the young author had; he was still only a *vaudevilliste*, but one who felt himself called to introduce real comedy on the secondary stages, while awaiting the opportunity of making himself known at the Théâtre-Français.

Une révolution donne à la société une face nouvelle; le vaudeville, seul genre auquel je me suis adonné, peut être envisagé sous un autre point de vue que l'on ne l'a fait jusqu'à présent. Au lieu de suivre les traces de mes confrères et de les imiter comme je l'ai fait, je veux tâcher d'être moi, d'avoir mon genre, mon style, mon

théâtre à moi. Il faut chasser du vaudeville les rôles banals comme
Picard les a chassés de la comédie. En un mot, je veux suivre
l'exemple de Molière et tâcher de peindre les mœurs de notre époque.
Je sais que pendant un an ou deux encore je peux végéter avant
d'arriver; mais j'arriverai, je m'en sens la force.

Whether or not he succeeded in painting the manners
of his time, it is clear that it was his ambition to do so.
The next few lines show that he realized also that an
author need not necessarily be indigent; that literary
ability and financial success are not mutually exclusive.

Je sais que dans la littérature on fait rarement fortune, et que
bien des auteurs qui valaient mieux que moi n'y ont trouvé que la
misère et l'hôpital. C'est qu'ils l'entendaient mal, il est possible
d'avoir à la fois talent et argent: l'un n'exclut pas l'autre; tous les
directeurs de théâtre sont riches, pourquoi les auteurs ne le seraient-
ils pas? pourquoi les directeurs ne partageraient-ils pas avec nous
l'or que nous leur faisons gagner? Cela doit être et cela sera, tant
que cela dépendra de moi, du moins.

When one realizes the extent to which Scribe was influential in ameliorating the financial condition of his
fellow dramatists, in obtaining for them that just recog-
nition of their labors which theretofore they had been
largely denied, and when one knows the noble use he was
later to make of his own fortune, one likes to see him
thus dreaming of wealth and glory.

At his majority he received from M. Bonnet, his guardian, an income of 1700 francs, the modest remains of
his mother's fortune. It was with these meagre resources
that he began the career that was to make him several
times a millionaire. For from the very beginning of his
literary activities he gave evidence of a business ability
second only to his dramatic talent. In 1817, after the
success of "Le Solliciteur" at the Variétés, he demanded
not only a payment for his manuscript, but a percentage

or royalty on the nightly receipts. In those days directors bought plays from the authors at ridiculously low
prices, and the dramatists had nothing more to expect,
even from a very successful play. Men like Désaugiers
and Brazier frequently received only twenty or twenty-
five francs for each act. The Théâtre-Français and the
Théâtre du Vaudeville were the only theatres which
paid on a percentage basis. It was entirely through
Scribe's efforts that these conditions were changed and
that a sort of dramatic commission was founded, a serious control over authors' rights established, and an
authors' league formed against the directors. The
younger and less popular writers now began to receive
more financial profit from their productions, an improvement which they owed to Scribe.

Not content, then, with continuing the old traditions
of the *comédie-vaudeville*, and determined to draw his subjects and types from the life about him, he decided to
turn to the generals and colonels of the Empire, and then
to pass from the soldier to the civilian; notaries, lawyers,
bourgeois, workmen, all were to be represented. That
popular institution, the *Garde Nationale*, furnished the
subject for one of his most brilliant successes, a play
which marked a change in the *comédie-vaudeville* and
inaugurated a series of charming pieces, which was to
lead eventually to the five-act comedy of manners.
"Une Nuit de la Garde Nationale," produced in 1814,
was the first of a number of triumphs at the Vaudeville
and at the Variétés, among which may be mentioned
"La Jarretière de la Mariée" (November, 1816), "Les
Montagnes russes" (December, 1816), "Le Comte Ory"
(December, 1816), "Le Solliciteur" (April, 1817), which

Schlegel preferred to the "Misanthrope," "La Fête du Mari" (December, 1817), "La Somnambule" (December, 1819).

It was "Les Montagnes russes" which stirred up the famous *guerre des calicots*. A satirical description of those ribbon-counter clerks who, in order to give themselves a martial appearance, wore the military moustache, the red boutonnière and the spurs of the Napoleonic soldier, aroused the ire of these gentlemen, who for a time threatened even to destroy the theatre if the play was not withdrawn. A very clever and good-humored play called "Le Foyer du Gymnase" poured oil on the troubled waters, and brought satisfaction to the offended gentlemen.

It was for Poirson, later director of the Théâtre du Gymnase, that Scribe wrote "Une Nuit de la Garde Nationale"; and the manner in which he came to write for this man, with whom he worked for many years and for whom he proved to be a veritable gold-mine, is interesting enough to deserve mention. Poirson realized that Scribe was destined for a brilliant future, and saw clearly what benefit he himself might derive from association with the promising young dramatist. He realized also, however, that Scribe needed two things — solitude and continuity of work; and in order to get the young writer away from the distractions of Paris, he persuaded Scribe to go with him, in the summer of 1815, to an attractive country house of some friends of his, near Paris. Four months were passed in serious work at this estate, and it was only some time later that Scribe learned that he had really been at a boarding-house, and that Poirson had been paying his expenses. It was this modest property of Séricourt which Scribe was later to buy and transform into a delightful summer house. He returned there again, in the summer of 1816, with Poirson, and with another friend, Mélesville, who became one of his most faithful collaborators.

He had at this time three other collaborators in Brazier, Carmouche, and Saintine. In fact, most of his plays were written in collaboration with another writer, or with two or three others. The bulk of the work, however, was always done by Scribe himself, and it was ever a matter of honor with him to give his associates full credit. Mirecourt, in his biographical monograph on Scribe, said, in speaking of his collaborators:

> Scribe n'est jamais sorti des bornes de la collaboration permise; il a toujours nommé ses collaborateurs. Il a partagé non seulement les recettes mais la gloire avec ceux qui lui sont venus en aide pour ses travaux techniques. Il est le plus honnête et le plus laborieux des collaborateurs. Non content de faire sa part de travail, il reprend en sous-œuvre la tâche des autres et transforme complètement les scènes. Celui qui les a écrites ne les reconnaît plus.

Reference has already been made to Scribe's desire to break away from the conventional methods and subjects, and to make of the *vaudeville* a new and more interesting genre. At the moment when he made his first appearance at the Théâtre du Vaudeville, that theatre was still offering to the public the shepherds and shepherdesses, the lambs and the pastoral ditties of the eighteenth century. Scribe felt instinctively that the provision of such material was practically exhausted and that another kind must be sought. He quickly abandoned the thatched cottages, the trellises, lawns, and thickets, and drew his material from the street, the salon, and the shop. Little by little he dropped –the conventional figures of the bucolic *vaudeville*, with their patois and jargon, and took up the men and the follies which he found close at hand. So successful was his substitution that by 1820 he was by far the most popular of the furnishers of French gayety. "Une Visite à Bedlam" (1815), and "L'Hôtel des Quatre Nations" (1818), were among the most successful plays of those years; the former celebrated the coming departure from France of the allied armies, and the latter showed liberals as well as royalists congratulating the dynasty upon having rid the country of the foreigners. In 1819 he produced "L'Ours et le Pacha," a piece which may be considered a masterpiece and model of the buffoon genre. The same year witnessed the production of "La Somnambule," whose success at the Vaudeville was scarcely diminished by the assassination of the Duke de Berry by Louvel at the Opéra, which resulted in the demolition of that theatre, and the closing of all the others for two weeks during the carnival season. Whereas in 1812 his productions brought him 540 francs, in 1819 he earned 17,500 francs. This enabled him to join the Delavigne family in renting an attractive country house at Conflans, and, the next year, to take a very beautifully furnished apartment in the Rue Bergère.

In December, 1820, the Théâtre du Gymnase was founded, and this date may be taken as a decisive moment in Scribe's career. Thirty years of age, well broken to his trade, already an indefatigable worker, having as yet no fixed preference as to the manner in which he should frame and present on the stage his observations of society, he was free to take any route he chose. Delestre-Poirson, who had obtained the lease of a new

theatre, realized what a fortune it would be for any house
to have Scribe as its principal author, and was eager to
attach to his own establishment a collaborator whose
importance he was in a position to realize. He therefore
bought — at a high price — the support of his literary
associate. He bound him by a contract which forbade
Scribe to write for any theatre whose rivalry with the
Gymnase was direct. By the terms of the agreement,
Scribe was permitted, consequently, to write for the
Théâtre-Français. Moreover, Poirson also assured him
many advantages, inventing for his benefit that payment
called the *prime*, given to an author for each play before
the first performance. In a short time Scribe, inexhaustible and richly paid, had assured not only his own
fortune, but that of the theatre, whose Providence he
proved to be for the next ten years.

In 1821 began a series of *comédies-vaudevilles* which
forms a special genre in his works. That year saw fourteen of his most brilliant successes, among which may be
mentioned the famous "Michel et Christine" (December,
1821), and "Philibert marié" (December, 1821), on the
title-page of which Scribe attributes the honor of his
success to Picard, who had invented the main character,
and to Closel, the actor, who had created the rôle in
Picard's play at the Odéon. During these years at the
Gymnase, Scribe trained and formed many of the actors,
several of whom — Gontier, Perlet, Bernard Léon,
Madame Théodore, Mademoiselle Fleuriet, and Léontine
Fay — acquired wide popularity. Between 1820 and
1830 he wrote for the Gymnase more than a hundred
plays, the most important of which were: "L'Ecarté"
(1822), "La Loge du Portier" (1823), "Les Adieux au

Comptoir" (1824), "L'Héritière" (1824), "Le plus beau Jour de la Vie" (1825), "La Charge à payer" (1825), "Le Charlatanisme" (1825), "Le Mariage de Raison" (1826), "Une Visite à Bedlam" (1826), "La Demoiselle à marier" (1826), "Le Diplomate" (1827), "Le Mariage d'Inclination" (1828), "La Manie des Places" (1828), "Avant, Pendant, et Après" (1828), "Les Actionnaires" (1829), "Une Faute" (1830), "La seconde Année" (1830).

There is scarcely one of these which does not add a little touch to the dramatic picture of the manners of the Restoration society; a society which, some critics have maintained, was invented by Scribe, while others have reproached him for portraying it too faithfully, now flattering it in its prosaic enervation, now gently attacking it with rose-water epigrams. His attitude toward the government of the Restoration was independent. He had no cause for complaint, but, having no political ambition and aspiring to no favor, he devoted himself completely to the hope of realizing his dream of social independence and of enjoying the comparative liberty granted him by the *Charte* in writing his plays and in widening the scope of the more or less limited genre of which the secondary theatres had the privilege. Poirson recognized his indebtedness to Scribe, as the following letter, written in 1829, shows: "Je te dois tout, ma fortune, ma position, mon bonheur enfin. Cela vient de toi. A peine si j'ai pu y ajouter quelque chose."

Although he himself sought no favor, he was besieged by directors soliciting new plays, by composers requesting libretti, by artists aspiring to favorable rôles, by dramatists begging the privilege of collaborating with him. He had already begun to show himself the rival of the masters of comedy, of *grand opéra*, of *opéra-comique*, and of the ballet. Between the founding of the Gymnase and the Revolution of July, Scribe's popularity was at its height. The Gymnase, frequented from the first by the wealthy bourgeoisie of the Chaussée-d'Antin, soon received the august patronage of the Duchess de Berry, changed its name to Théâtre de Madame, and soon became the favorite theatre, not only of the Chaussée-d'Antin but of the Faubourg Saint-Germain as well. Scribe, as sovereign of the Gymnase, was applauded to the skies night after night, and constantly entertained and sought after. Many young apprentices in the art looked upon him as a kind of superhuman being who was to be approached only with fear and trembling, and considered themselves fortunate to be able to give him a suggestion or an idea.

Although permitted by the terms of his contract with Poirson to write for the Théâtre-Français, Scribe, realizing that the atmosphere at that theatre was not favorable to him, that disdain and rebuff might greet his efforts, did not use his privilege for some time. One should hardly consider "Valérie," presented at the Théâtre-Français in 1822, as his début at that theatre. This play, written especially for Mademoiselle Mars, and one of the chief elements in her early success, was originally a *vaudeville* in one act, with *couplets*, intended for Léontine Fay; and although changed for the Rue de Richelieu into a comedy in three acts, it remained really a *vaudeville*, differing in no essential from those at the Gymnase. It was only after seven years of popular and uncontested rule at the latter theatre that Scribe went on the first stage of the country with "Le Mariage d'Argent," a real comedy in five acts, without *couplets*, written without collaboration, its value residing in its dramatic interest, in the unity of the subject, the naturalness of the dialogue, and the truth of the moral lesson it contained. However, in spite of its unquestioned merits, the piece was not a brilliant success: the audience found it too similar to the author's lesser plays. Unfortunately also, at the first performance one of the actors, Cantigny, had a lapse of memory which caused him to omit an entire scene, thus rendering unintelligible an important situation and seriously compromising the success of the play.

In 1823 Scribe added another department to his already multitudinous activities, making his début as a writer of *opéra-comique* in "La Neige," for which Auber composed the music. The happy transformation which the *vaudeville* owed to Scribe, the *opéra-comique* was to undergo also, thanks to his activity and talent. Instead of following Sedaine, Marmontel, and Hoffmann, Scribe realized that it was necessary to make the action more animated, and, at times, more pathetic. His subjects were well chosen, the plots interesting, the dialogue natural. The *opéra-comique* thus renewed became a sort of complement to the comedy which he had inaugurated at the Gymnase. The charm of beautiful music was added, for Scribe placed his unusual dramatic ability only at the service of eminent composers, such as Cherubini, Meyerbeer, Rossini, and Hérold. It was in collaboration with Boïeldieu that in 1825 he wrote "La Dame Blanche," a play which marks an important date in the history of the *opéra-comique*. This charming play created a tremendous sensation in musical circles, and was heralded as an innovation, really an invention, of the greatest interest and importance. It is certain that "La Dame Blanche" contributed largely to the rejuvenation and enlargement of the *opéra-comique*.

Scribe's position was now consecrated, not only at the Gymnase and the Opéra-Comique, but at the Opéra as well, for "La Muette," written with Auber in 1828, placed him at the head of the suppliers of the Royal Academy of Music. This play, furthermore, marks in the history of the *opéra* a date as important as that of "La Dame Blanche" in the *opéra-comique*. Before Scribe, the repertoire of the Opéra consisted chiefly of ancient tragedies turned into libretti: Iphigénies, Alcestes, Œdipes, taken up in turn by different musicians, left the librettist only the merit of elegant versification. "Robert le Diable," "Les Huguenots," "La Juive," "Le Prophète," were works whose equal was unknown before Scribe. He made a subject of real art out of a genre which had hitherto been exceedingly monotonous; he did with romantic drama what Quinault in his time had done with tragedy, and made of it a new kind of *opéra*, rich in romantic color and passion, renewed by the study of a truer kind of history and one nearer his own time. He added, too, something that was largely lacking in romanticism: the theatrical instinct, the sense of appealing situations and of natural and probable *péripéties*. The character of Robert, in "Robert le Diable," is a most poetic creation; "La Juive," with its marvelous coloring, its romantic appeal to eye and ear, its historic evocations, shows to what extent he possessed the art of creating an operatic poem, meeting all the requirements of variety and of *mise en scène*. It is certain that Scribe was, of all the dramatic authors of the nineteenth century, the one who best understood the *opéra*, excelling in the creation of interesting musical situations which met the needs of the composer and which were adapted to his genius.

The following letter from Meyerbeer to Scribe shows how important was the librettist's part in the success of an *opéra* or of an *opéra-comique:*

J'ai dîné aujourd'hui chez Auber. Toute la table était composée de vos collaborateurs: Auber, Caraffa, Halévy, Planard. Tout le monde regrettait l'absence de l'inépuisable génie auquel nous devons tous tant de reconnaissance, pour tout ce qu'il a déjà fait pour nous et pour ce qu'il daignera faire.

Adam writes to him:

Vous êtes de ceux qui sont mieux en raison de ce qu'on les aide moins; avec vous je serai sûr d'avoir une pièce avec des scènes dramatiques, avec des paroles dont la musique est toute faite d'avance.

At the time of his first years at the Gymnase he had a vigorous constitution which seemed to resist the very serious strain put upon it by his habits of work. By five o'clock in the morning, winter as well as summer, he was at his desk, and before lunching had accomplished at least four hours of work. He would go out at noon to superintend rehearsals, returning home in the middle of the afternoon and working another two or three hours; at times, when he was hurried and overwhelmed with requests, he would devote his evening and even a part of the night to his work. In a few years, however, this régime began to tell on his health, and early in 1826 he became seriously ill. His physician ordered him to take a complete rest, and advised a trip to Switzerland, which he made with his friend Mélesville. He had promised

not even to talk theatre, and his companion had no reason
to believe that Scribe was indulging in any literary work
more serious than that of keeping a diary of their travels.
One day, however, Poirson, director of the Gymnase,
arrived unexpectedly at Geneva, and to the astonish-
ment of Mélesville told Scribe that he had received his
letter and asked him if the *play in question* was ready.
The guilty patient, in his embarrassment, could at first
find nothing to say, but finally stammered to Mélesville:
"Oh, c'est une petite pièce en deux actes que j'ai faite,
en me promenant, pour me distraire." The little play
in two acts was "Le Mariage de Raison." Many years
later one of his critics remarked that a man who could
write "Le Mariage de Raison" in view of the Righi and
the Jungfrau, and who could detach himself sufficiently
from the emotions aroused by such surroundings to de-
scribe the love of Bertrand for Suzette, would naturally
be incapable of strong passion and deep emotion. However that may be, his record of the trip is proof that, far
from being insensitive to the beauty and the grandeur
of the scene before him, he felt a poet's joy at the wonders
of nature among which he was living. Upon his return
from Switzerland he appeared to be in much better
health; but his illness declaring itself again, his physician
persuaded him to pass the winter quietly at Versailles,
where, although he did not give up writing, he continued
to improve. A trip through southern France in the summer of 1827 brought a complete recovery.

Such was Scribe's position at the moment of the Revolution of 1830. The change of ideas brought about by
this great event, the foreign dangers, the parliamentary
struggles, the conspiracies and uprisings, all gave new

interest to political questions, and gravely affected the attachment of the public to the rose-water comedy of the Théâtre de Madame. And in the midst of the post-revolutionary disturbance Scribe, recently so idolized, was for the moment forgotten. This neglect was not to last long, however. For although Scribe had not taken sufficient account of the interest of his spectators in the existence and action of new forces about them, he soon realized the situation and remedied it by giving to the public the kind of plays it demanded. Of the sixteen plays produced from July, 1830, to July, 1831, all were very well received and one, "La Famille Riquebourg," achieved great popularity.

The political struggle interested him less than that between Classicism and Romanticism. He was apprehensive of the effect that the invasion of the Romanticists might have upon popular taste, for it seemed that the public was going to desert all that it had appreciated and loved until then. Whereas during the Restoration, the vices and defects of which he did not spare, he had been admired and fêted by all, not only by the opposition but by the government as well, — at least by that part of it capable of understanding the tact and the good taste of his satire, — he now found himself attacked from all quarters, especially by the press. Scribe, who since 1815 had been classicist and liberal, was now called *arriéré* and *rococo*. However, he let the torrent unloosed against him and against the Gymnase pass by, following the line of conduct he had laid out for himself, that of common sense. His later successes prove that the healthy part of the public remained faithful to him. In fact, by 1833 the majority of theatre-goers were tiring of the dramas of bloodshed, adultery, and incest, and were returning to mental habits of decency and good taste.

It was at about the time of the appearance of "Bertrand et Raton" (1833), that this counter-revolution took place, caused partly by the very success of this comedy. A reaction had set in against the literary innovations as well as against the political agitation. The public was tired of insurrections, and of dramatic excesses as well. "Bertrand et Raton" was both a lesson for would-be conspirators and a return to the simple traditions of comedy. Commenting upon his successes of 1833, Scribe wrote in his diary:

> Je ne m'abuse pas de mon triomphe de cette année. Les dévergondages du genre romantique ont amené une réaction dont j'ai heureusement profité. Je relis les journaux et ils sont tous bons pour moi. Voilà au moins du bon ton, du bon goût.

His success at the Théâtre-Français with "Valérie" and his effort with "Le Mariage d'Argent" had opened for him the doors of that theatre. "Bertrand et Raton" confirmed his position there, and six or seven prose comedies in five acts, without *couplets*, gave him rank as one of the most successful writers for the *première scène*. "L'Ambitieux" (1834), "La Camaraderie" (1837), "La Calomnie" (1840), "Le Verre d'Eau" (1840), "Le Puff" (1848), "Adrienne Lecouvreur" (1849), and "La Czarine" (1855), are evidence of his ability to achieve success not only in *vaudeville*, in *opéra*, and in *opéra-comique*, but in real comedy of manners and in political and historical comedy.

To offset the depression of the period, caused first by the revolution and later by the terrible epidemic of cholera, theatre directors frequently resorted to means that were questionable morally no less than æsthetically. It must be admitted that Scribe also took advantage of the immunities of the new style. "Dix Ans de la Vie d'une Femme" (1832) can be classed, as to its subject, with those plays whose theme was furnished by the relaxed morals of the time. The dénoûment of the play, however, is moral, for Scribe maintains the laws of society by refusing to accord one moment of happiness to the woman who, influenced by evil advice and by her own vanity, is faithless to her duty. The severe criticism of this play by Alexandre Dumas, the author of "Antony" and of "Mademoiselle de Belle-Isle," seems at least inconsistent. Of the fourteen plays added to Scribe's repertoire in 1832, "Dix Ans" is the only one which makes any sacrifice to the prevailing taste.

In 1836 he was called to occupy in the Académie Française the chair left by Arnault. As early as 1830 he had presented himself; but, although his candidacy was vigorously supported, the vacant chair had been allotted to Pongerville. It was asserted that the clerical members of the Academy voted against him because of the irreligious character of some of his plays, "Madame de Sainte-Agnès," for example. His reception speech was very poorly received. The critics of the press treated it with bitter scorn; and their scorn was really unmerited, for, like most of Scribe's work, it is very clever. It develops the paradox, contradicted by his own example, that comedy, in order to be successful, does not have to resemble society, as if his plays for the Gymnase had not been a portrait, slightly flattering, it is true, of society during the Restoration. He was received by Villemain, who made generous use of epigrams, but who rendered full justice to the fertile and many-sided talent of the new-comer.

By this time Scribe has become a writer of international fame; his plays are given on the leading stages of Germany, Austria, England, and Italy; even at Tromsal, a small town in northern Scandinavia, "La Marraine" and "Le Mariage de Raison" are given each winter, and others of his plays are produced in eastern Russia. In Germany the leading theatres make every effort to procure his plays for production, and the competition between directors is so great that, when a new play by Scribe appears in Paris, the German translations are immediately announced, often before the play is printed. The director of the Royal Opera of Berlin begs him to write an opera in five acts, the music to be composed by a distinguished young musician who inspires great hopes, Mendelssohn by name. The King of Holland makes a personal request for an *opéra-comique* libretto to serve as a basis for a musical competition established by the throne. The Count de Piolay constructs a new theatre in Turin, and asks permission to call it the Théâtre Scribe, recalling the many comedies, *vaudevilles*, *opéras*, and *opéras-comiques* with which Scribe has entertained the Italian public. At the amateur theatricals given at the châteaux of the aristocracy of France, it is the repertoire of Scribe which supplies the material. Adolphe Karr, founding a daily newspaper at Nice, seeks the help of Scribe, urging him to add his name to those of Lamartine, Hugo, Ponsard, Legouvé, and G. Sand. Buloz, of the "Revue des Deux Mondes," asks him to counteract, by contributions to that paper, the socialistic tendencies then becoming pronounced. In 1835 he is made an officer of the Legion of Honor, and in 1848 commander. Emperor Don Pedro, the King of Holland, and the King of Belgium name him commander of their orders.

In 1839 he married Madame Biollay, the widow of a wine merchant who had been one of his friends. In his estate at Séricourt, a delightful domain near La Ferté-sous-Jouarre, he was a veritable châtelain, adored by all the villagers. In addition to Séricourt, he possessed a house in Paris and a villa at Meudon.

In spite of his manifold activities and the demands made upon his time by the exigencies of his work, he was always ready to help others with valuable advice and suggestions, and never refused a worthy request for financial help. His generosity was inexhaustible, and his kindliness proverbial. Scarcely a day passed that he did not receive from some old college friend, from a struggling author, from a needy mother, a request for help, and he seemed never to be too busy to respond graciously to these calls. His friends unite in praising his unselfishness and the delicacy which characterized all his good actions.

A certain elderly schoolmistress brought to him one day the manuscript of a *vaudeville* entitled "Les Empiriques d'autrefois." Scribe's first movement was one of good-natured impatience, for he was at that moment overwhelmed with work; but seeing that the authoress was insistent, he finally agreed to read the manuscript and to add any touches he might think necessary. The next day he learned that the author of the *vaudeville* was in urgent need. At once he left all his other work, took the manuscript of "Les Empiriques," arranged, corrected, and recast the play, took it to the Gymnase, and succeeded in getting it played — all in six weeks. Unfortunately the play was but moderately successful. The schoolmistress now brought to Scribe two other *vaudevilles*, from which she hoped to get more money than from the first one. A little alarmed at her disconcerting fertility, Scribe called Guyot, one of the two agents charged with the collection of authors' royalties, and gave him orders to have "Les Empiriques," whether it was played or not, bring in 1200 francs of author's rights each year. In this way he created for the poor schoolmistress a pension of 600 francs, hoping that he might thus be left in peace. But his hopes were illusory. The very delicacy of his aid exposed him to daily calls from the author of "Les Empiriques," and the deluge of manuscripts increased rapidly. "Let us keep on working, Monsieur Scribe, my part of the royalties is very satisfactory; consequently our play must be successful. Last month the receipts of ' Les Empiriques ' were greater than those of any other piece played in the provinces." The schoolmistress never knew the secret of the affair, and until the day of her death received regularly her share of the royalties — and yet she was irritated at seeing Scribe write forty or fifty plays with Mélesville and only one with her.

One of his best comedies, "La Camaraderie," and one of his most popular *opéras-comiques*, "Le Domino noir," were written in 1837. The fundamental idea of "La Camaraderie" is to be found in "Les Femmes savantes," but it had been developed and applied to contemporary literature by Henri Delatouche in the "Revue de Paris," in 1829. Delatouche was a bitter satirist who had been conspicuous among the precursors and reformers of Romanticism, but who had refused to enroll himself among the high priests of the small ultra-romantic cult. In 1837 the unfriendly critics of Scribe's plays did not dare resist the popular current and assail him bitterly; but a few, some expressing the rancor of the coteries which Scribe had satirized, the others inspired by mercantile interests, showed a spirit of hostility which was never disarmed, and which had been aroused by Scribe's courage in writing "La Camaraderie."

In 1839 he made a journey to Italy, and it was there that he wrote "La Calomnie." In taking for his hero an unusually honest, upright cabinet minister, Scribe was perhaps too honest himself, forgetting that at that time the sympathy of the public was with the Opposition and its spokesmen. Indeed, he owed part of his own reputation to the Opposition, for his *vaudevilles*, always somewhat *frondeurs*, had spared neither the *gardes-champêtres* nor the *gendarmes*, neither the prefects nor the ministers themselves; it was a little late to attribute to the representative of supreme authority that delicate loyalty, pure disinterestedness, and grandeur of soul, which make of Raymond a second Malesherbes.

One of his most successful plays, "Le Verre d'Eau," was written in 1840. "Le Fils de Cromwell" (1842) was only half successful, and for Scribe this was equivalent to a failure. Nevertheless he wrote good-naturedly in his diary: "Non seulement j'ai fait mon propre bonheur en 1842, mais encore j'ai fait des heureux par mes échecs." The winter of 1846–1847 is important in his literary career for the production of a long historical novel, "Piquillo Alliago," the scene of which is laid in Spain, and which shows clearly the influence of Sir Walter Scott. For some years he had been writing novels and short stories for the "Revue de Paris," the "Siècle," and the "Constitutionnel"; although to-day this part of his work is practically unknown, his fiction enjoyed a wide popularity at the time of its publication.

The Revolution of 1848 was a difficult period for Scribe as for all the other dramatists; the theatres were almost empty, the receipts fell very low, and the directors were forced to ask help from the government. Scribe had no great confidence in the improvised republic, and regretted the disappearance of the constitutional government; for the august victims of the Revolution he had the most respectful pity. In 1848, as in 1830, the ministers were most considerate of him, and consequently he could only wish that they had been less short-sighted. "Le Puff," written during this period, transfers to the stage the society of the mid-century with all its vices, satirizing the unscrupulousness of the journalists, the absurdities of the blue-stockings, the duplicity of the charlatans. The play reveals an independence and a fearlessness which do credit to Scribe, and which won him the hearty approval of all those who were not too jealous of his enormous success to recognize his achievement. Bizet went so far as to assert that since "Tartuffe" no play had appeared in which vice was treated so boldly as in "Le Puff." Merville, his old law professor, told him that not since his childhood days, when he had the pleasure of seeing or reading Molière, had he so enjoyed a play for the boldness and justice of the ideas expressed, the strength of the reasoning, and the cleverness of the dialogue; and he added: "Je dis de vous ce que Montesquieu disait de Voltaire: ' Vous êtes l'homme du monde qui ɔ le plus de l'esprit que tout le monde a.' " The play was withdrawn from the Comédie-Française to make way for Étienne Arago's "Les Aristocraties," although the latter comedy was no less direct in its attack on the aristocrats and the financiers.

The director of the Royal Opera of London had for some time been urging Scribe to write a poem for an opera based on Shakespeare's "Tempest." Scribe finally agreed to this request, and in May, 1850, in company with Halévy, went to London to direct the performance of the new play. For four months he was the lion of English society, fêted and entertained by the literary world and by the aristocracy. It was during this visit to England that he spent several weeks as the guest of his former sovereign, Louis-Philippe, with whom he collaborated in the writing of an opera, "Henry VIII." Shortly after his return to Paris, his friend Guizot wrote to him that some English visitors were very anxious to meet the celebrated author, and added: "Vous êtes plus européen que vous ne croyez." Charles Dickens, the guest of Amédée Pichot, requested his host to arrange a dinner in order that he might meet Scribe.

Although he had never taken a keen interest in politics, Scribe was well-disposed toward a régime which had suggested to him some of his best works; and when, in 1860, Napoleon III inscribed his name upon the list of members of the municipal council of Paris, he felt that he could not refuse this purely honorary position. Indeed he devoted himself most seriously to his new duties, and accomplished them with an active and kindly zeal which won him the esteem of all who knew him.

His last years were somewhat saddened by the increasing violence of the attacks made upon him by certain journals and critics. Without doubt, a large part of this abuse was quite unmerited, and was the result of jealousy and exasperation at his long-continued success. It became *de bon ton* to mock at Scribe's plays, at his style, and at the lack of literary value in his productions. Though some of this criticism was sufficiently just, the excessive malevolence of his adversaries reveals itself in the stupidity of their broadsides, for it was nothing less than ridiculous to attempt to make Scribe an unprincipled profiteer, coldly barring the way to all the younger writers of the day.

The following note written to Scribe by Augier in 1845 is only one of many he received from fellow writers whom he had aided with his counsel and his prestige:

J'ai besoin de vous remercier de vos applaudissements et des bonnes paroles que vous avez prononcées pour moi. Il sied à un homme de votre talent de montrer aux nouveaux venus cette sympathie encourageante et de tendre la main du haut de l'échelle.

His death in February, 1861, was wholly unexpected. He had taken a carriage to drive to the home of Maquet, director of the Porte-Saint-Martin, and when the coachman stopped, he discovered that Scribe had died on the way. At his funeral, held from the church of Saint-Roch, were representatives of the court, of the Académie Française, of the Club of Authors and Dramatic Composers, and of the state theatres. In the procession were actors from the Opéra, the Opéra-Comique, and the Gymnase, all of which were closed for the evening. In spite of a heavy rain, at least three thousand persons took part in the funeral services, accompanying the remains to Père Lachaise. In this gathering, composed of poets, philosophers, savants, novelists, diplomats, and ministers, there were hundreds of workingmen in their blouses, and doubtless it was they who mourned him most; for many times, in the galleries of the Vaudeville or the Gymnase, they had been able to forget their cares and sorrows, entertained by one who was himself an indefatigable worker.

CHAPTER II

THE COMÉDIES-VAUDEVILLES

IT IS a commonplace of dramatic criticism that Scribe was the greatest technician in the history of the French drama, and that all the dramatists of the nineteenth century who aimed at excellence of construction profited, consciously or unconsciously, by the new methods which he gave to dramatic art, and show his influence in the invention and arrangement of interesting plots. It is perhaps less clearly realized that he first displayed and exercised his technical skill in the *comédie-vaudeville*, for which he practically invented a new form, raising it to a level it had not reached before, and making of it the canvas for a light sketching of manners. Scribe's best five-act comedies are, so far as technique is concerned, no more than highly developed *comédies-vaudevilles*. The comedy of manners of Augier, the thesis-play of the younger Dumas, the drama of Sardou, derive their form and construction from the comedies and the *comédies-vaudevilles* of Scribe. These plays are interesting, not only because of their importance in the development of technique, but also because of the completeness and fidelity with which they depict the French bourgeoisie during the Restoration and the July Monarchy. In spite of the wholly undistinguished style in which they are written, these little plays have nevertheless the charm of an old album; for in them are gracefully sketched many of the figures that made up Parisian society during the first half of the nineteenth century.

A rapid glance at the history of the development of the *comédie-vaudeville* will show what changes Scribe wrought in this eminently French genre, and how he succeeded in making of it an almost new literary form. Originally the *vaudeville* was merely a popular song, composed and sung, as a rule, to celebrate some event or to ridicule some well-known personage. As a matter of fact, the Provençal troubadours of the twelfth and thirteenth centuries may be called the first *vaudevillistes*, for it was they who first in France satirized the follies of their contemporaries. From Provence the art and love of singing spread to other parts of France, notably Normandy and Picardy. The name *vaudeville* is probably derived from *vaux-de-vire*, the name given to the songs of Olivier Basselin, a cheerful singer of Vire in lower Normandy, who used to entertain with his ditties in Vire, and in the neighboring district of Val. Although it has lent itself to the expression of many feelings,—joy, despair, patriotism, tenderness, and anger, — the *vaudeville* is preëminently satirical. It has always been a courageous member of the Opposition.

> D'un trait de ce poème en bons mots si fertile,
> Le Français, né malin, forma le vaudeville.

Later, in the seventeenth century, the term *vaudeville* was applied to short comedies, usually of one act, written about contemporary events or based upon anecdotes and bits of scandal. Again, many comedies, in verse or in prose, contained *couplets* sung by the various actors, and these *couplets*, unrelated to the action, were called *vaudevilles*. Songs of this kind are to be found in some of the comedies of Legrand, Fagan, Dancourt, Dufresny, and Lesage, and in the plays of those who imitated them, like Beaumarchais, Collin d'Harleville, and Picard.

Comedy with songs interspersed has a long history, which goes back to Adam de la Halle's "Jeu de Robin et Marion," written in 1285. Not until the time of Molière, however, is there any evidence of a real development in the *comédie mêlée de chants*. There had, indeed, been a tendency to introduce music into dramatic compositions earlier, notably in "Le Ballet comique de la Reine," written in 1581 by Baltasarini and La Chesnaie, with music by Beaulieu, and in "La Finta Pazza," a spectacular melodrama produced in 1645 by Torelli for Mazarin. The next important stage is reached with the comedy-ballets of Molière, who inserted songs into the *entr'actes*, later weaving the songs into the story so as not to interrupt the unity of the action. In the "Ballet du Mariage forcé," songs are for the first time introduced into the ballet.

For a number of years after Molière's death it was the *opéra* [1] which, with its libretti, inspired imitation by writers of *vaudevilles*. The Italian actors of the seventeenth century in Paris soon began to add songs to their comedies, and under their influence French writers composed plays like Dancourt's "Opéra de Village," in which an actor could go from song to declamation without disturbing the auditor. In "Vénus justifiée," written by Dufresny in 1693, we can begin to see the difference in the various modes of dramatic expression: prose being used in the ordinary passages; verse in the scenes of more elevated tone, or in the satirical passages; the *vaudevilles*, or airs already known, in the buffoonery; and the orig-

---

[1] "*Opéra:* Poème dramatique mis en musique, sans dialogue parlé, et composé de récitatifs et de chants soutenus par un orchestre, quelquefois mêlés de danses. *Grand opéra*, celui dans lequel l'action est tragique." (Larousse.)

inal airs in the emotional scenes. Thus the *comédie mêlée de chants* is developed, ready for its subdivisions into *comédie-vaudeville* and *opéra-comique*.[1]

It was at the fairs of Saint-Laurent and Saint-Germain that the *comédie mêlée de chants* received its next impulse. Lesage, writing for the fair from 1712 to 1738, developed the plot of these plays and raised them to the dignity of a genre. "La Princesse de Carizine" (1718) has a very skillfully developed plot, with well-handled romanesque elements. "La Ceinture de Vénus" (1715) contains an *ingénue* rôle which foreshadows Favart. To the ingenious scenes and bright satire of Lesage, Favart added a grace and vigor, an originality of conception, and a skill of characterization which justly give him the rank of the greatest *vaudevilliste* of the fairs. In his hands the *vaudeville* received a double development: one form, with its original music and with the prose subordinated, leading to the *opéra-comique;* the other, with adapted songs and developed plot, to the *comédie-vaudeville*.

We next find the *comédie-vaudeville* in the boulevard theatres of Nicolet and Audinot and their imitators and followers. These plays are for the most part licentious or, at least, risqué, with very poorly developed plots, and an excessive use of *lazzi* [2] and other burlesque features. The Revolution, the Republic, and the Consulate of course supplied the *comédie-vaudeville* with ample material for comment and satire. There is at the same time a tendency to present little pictures of real life and manners,

---

[1] "*Opéra-comique:* Pièce moitié sérieuse, moitié comique, dans laquelle le chant alterne avec le dialogue parlé." (Larousse.)

[2] "*Lazzi:* Pantomime comique, dans le théâtre italien. Par extension, saillie bouffonne, plaisanteries moqueuses et souvent un peu libres." (Larousse.)

exaggerating the virtues of the good man and the vices of the villain. The technique remains slipshod, with a perfunctory and conventional exposition, usually in soliloquy form, with improbable accidents and a dénoûment which merely brings the play to an end without settling anything. What most interests one now, perhaps, in these plays, is their brisk and stinging satire, and the compelling *actualité* of their transcript of current manners — characteristics which were to reveal themselves so definitely in Scribe's *comédies-vaudevilles*. But the popularity of these compositions rested even more securely, one may be sure, on their broad and gay buffoonery, on the animation and the pertinence of their farce. "Les Désespoirs de Jocrisse," by Dorvigny, is typical enough and entertaining enough to be worth mentioning.

The *comédie-vaudeville* of the eighteenth century, then, was characterized by technical inferiority, literary worthlessness, and lubricity. Since the days of Lesage, Favart, and Panard, it had followed two courses, tending to be either the rehandling of some anecdote or incident, or a satirical criticism of the vices and follies of the day. In either case its greatest charm lay in its gayety, its rapidity of action, and the more or less farcical handling of the situations. It remained faithful to its origins, always smacking of the fair, and possessed to a high degree the two essential elements of the farce — topicality and general satire. During and after the Revolution of 1789 the *comédie-vaudeville* flourished as it never had before; and yet, though in the hands of Bouilly, Radet, Piis, Desfontaines, and Barré it began to show evidences of greater literary worth, it remained for Scribe to make of it a true literary genre.

The first step in the revolution which Scribe brought about in the *vaudeville*, at the first of the secondary theatres, was a purely external one — one of costume, so to speak: notaries, bailiffs, and magisters giving way to stock-brokers, to judges of the inferior court, to tax-collectors, and to the bankers of the Chaussée-d'Antin. He was the first to give contemporary professional names to stock characters conventional in all ages. This kind of local color proved attractive at once. He was well served by circumstances also; at the time of his first successes, the Théâtre-Français was dependent upon two actors for its hold upon the public; the Opéra was slowly going to ruin amid the débris of its former glory; a vicious administration was ruining whatever chances of success the Opéra-Comique might have had; the *vaudeville* theatres were invaded by a host of rhymesters who for ten years had been rhyming *les lauriers de nos guerriers*, and who during the Allied occupation had exploited the memory of French victories; and even melodrama was falling into discredit, for the public had begun to demand that Pixérécourt should at least make his characters speak intelligible French.

Seeing into what hands the sceptre of the *vaudeville* had fallen, Scribe resolved to take possession of this artificial but amusing genre, to regenerate it, and to raise it to a higher level in public esteem. His efforts were successful beyond his expectations, and his name upon the bill-boards soon became a drawing card which never failed to attract the crowd. "Une Nuit de la Garde Nationale," "La Somnambule," "Une Visite à Bedlam," these and other plays raised the receipts of the Vaudeville far above those of the other theatres. Society flocked to the Gym-

nase, for there only did it find the language of its drawing-rooms, those delicate shadings of sentiment and
character, and that indecision and uncertainty of manners which characterize all new societies. Scribe desired
above all to attract and amuse large audiences, and
realized that he could best do this by giving them light
pieces with brilliantly developed plots, full of complications and *quiproquos*, enlivened by witty dialogue and
graceful verses. A public worn out emotionally by the
horrors of the Revolution and by the disasters of the
Empire could best be entertained if its curiosity was
aroused by a skillfully prepared plot, if its interest was
held by a brilliant development of this plot, and if its
expectations were satisfied by a logical, even a predictable, dénoûment. If there were two qualities which
Scribe possessed in the highest degree, they were clearness
and logic; and he employed those qualities in the realiza-
tion that to hold his public he must be clear, and that, if
he was to be clear, he must so order his action and plot
that the spectator could follow easily and with pleasure
the different courses of the action.

Among the gifts with which Scribe was more highly
endowed than any other dramatist of the nineteenth century was that theatrical instinct which enabled him to see
at a glance the essentially dramatic elements of a situation. He lived, moved, and had his being in things theatrical; the incidents of everyday life were to him dramatic
possibilities, and he saw in everything material for the
stage. The most ordinary situation, the most unpromis-
ing anecdote, the scene least likely to suggest theatrical
possibilities to one less gifted with this sense of the theatre, gave him ideas which he would immediately trans-

late into dramatic action. Perhaps no one has ever had more than he the ability to see instantly which side of a situation would be most interesting when set before the public; no dramatic author has excelled him in the power to discover theatrical combinations of new and striking effect. And he was able, not only to discover these dramatic situations, but to translate them instantly into stage pictures; he did not have to develop and perfect them slowly. This fecundity of dramatic invention explains in part his extraordinary popularity during the twenty-five years in which he reigned supreme in the four or five best theatres in Paris.

For many years, ever since Théophile Gautier began his merciless attacks upon his popular contemporary, and ever since Théodore de Banville called him *Mossou* Scribe, it has been customary to dismiss Scribe with a word, as being simply a dramatic carpenter, as one devoid of all those higher qualities of the dramatic author, as a mere mechanician. Yet the fact remains that not many dramatists have had his genius — it comes to that — for making people see things in a certain way which, if not necessarily the true way, is at least the way which the dramatist must, for the moment, represent as inevitable. To do this one must be gifted with a native sense of perspective and of dramatic values, which enables one to sketch a character or a passion in a word.

Scribe's originality and fertility of invention are conspicuous in his handling of stage conventions. To a certain extent the plot of a *comédie-vaudeville* is necessarily conventional; the obdurate father, the sentimental heroine, the selfish and the noble-hearted lover, the scheming valet or soubrette, love-quarrels, jealousy, mistakes, and disguises — all those things by which the machinery of a plot is kept in motion, remain in substance the same. Scribe shows the greatest ingenuity in varying these combinations whenever it is possible; when it is not, he presents them under an aspect which gives a new direction to our sympathies, and boldly takes the side of the parent against the lover, of prudence and calculation against rashness and extravagance. Indeed, it is when he goes against the established current of theatrical sympathies that he is most successful. His championship of reason against romance, his defense of common sense as opposed to sentiment and passion, are resources by means of which he endeavors to impart new aspects to hackneyed and conventional stage themes. No less noticeable is his dexterity in handling a complicated plot. There are many of his plays the plots of which involve some absurdity or improbability, in which certain scenes hover on the brink of melodramatic exaggeration, and yet, by his discretion and by his constant command of effective dialogue, he disentangles himself from all his difficulties, just as the spectator is beginning to think the case is hopeless. No matter what the inherent weakness of a plot, he always manages to impart to it at least a temporary and artificial probability.

Scribe's dramatic theory, if indeed he had so clearly articulated his ideas and methods as to make of them a theory, was that one event may, by its influence, produce others, acting upon each other and mingling their effects until the impetus of the original event has been spent. For him the dramatic interest and value of a situation lay, not in the clash of characters and will that it may produce, or in the study of the passions causing it or arising from it, but in the combinations of circumstances and complexity of interests it may bring about. He selects some incident of ordinary life which to him seems curious or interesting. This fact is put into action; in its course it comes in collision with various obstacles placed artfully in its way, from which it rebounds until, after a certain number of recoils, it stops, its force of action having been spent. This conception of dramatic art by its very nature relieves the author of the responsibility of taking account of characters, sentiment, or passion.

Fertility of invention, dexterity in selecting the proper elements of a situation, and ingenuity in arranging them, were accompanied in Scribe's plays by a careful and effective planning of the various scenes of the play. Not content with presenting his scenes in a haphazard way, he trusted neither to luck nor to wit to redeem a badly constructed plot. The plan of a play was so important to him that he often said, "When I have finished my plan, I have nothing more to do." He insisted that every entrance and exit should be in its proper place, and that the scenes should follow each other in the clearest and most logical order. Scribe's chief desire being to entertain, he realized that to do this he must, first of all, be clear, so that nothing might be unexplained or misunderstood. To accomplish this he was first careful to see that in the opening scenes the subject should be well exposed, and that the audience should be in no doubt as to what the action was to concern. The expositions in his plays are nearly always clear and firmly handled. The different threads of the action are skillfully stretched, and the entire exposition is so enlivened with bright dialogue and pretty *couplets* that the machinery is cleverly disguised and the audience listens patiently.

But to be clear would not have been enough had the action moved fitfully, rapid here and lagging there; to hold the attention of the spectator whose interest has been aroused by a dexterous exposition, it is essential that everything shall tend, directly or indirectly, to hasten the solution of the difficulties encountered in the course of the action. If certain characters are digressive and retard the march of events, interfering with the play of the various forces upon each other, the spectator grows restless and the spell is broken. A constant, logical progression of events is characteristic of nearly all Scribe's *vaudevilles*.

Knowing that nothing is so certain to annoy an audience as an incident that occurs without warning, Scribe is always careful to scatter here and there in the early parts of the play words which at the time seem of no consequence, but which prepare the mind of the listener for the great event in the later scenes. Nothing is left to be taken cn faith by the audience; all that happens is the logical result of what has happened earlier, or what has been hinted at. No less responsible for his hold upon the public was his practice of taking the spectator into his confidence, of letting him know the things which were withheld from some of the characters in the play. In this way he succeeded in establishing a kind of tacit understanding between himself and his audience that certain situations which, if examined too closely, seemed improbable or farcical, were temporarily to be accepted. He realized, moreover, that it is human nature to enjoy being in a secret, and that the pleasure derived from watching the efforts of a character to overcome a certain difficulty — a difficulty which depends wholly on his ignorance of some condition which the onlooker understands — is greater than that of being kept in the dark and being made to wonder just what is wrong. The comic element in his plays is nearly always the result of the situations themselves, in which some of the characters are talking or acting with one object in view, while the others have something else in mind. In such scenes the actions are always at cross-purposes and the spectator is the only one who knows the secret of the situation.

Having thus clearly exposed the subject, arranged each incident and scene in its proper place, ordered the action so that it is rapid and constant and always sufficiently explained, he brings it to a logical, even inevitable, conclusion. He probably did not, however, work in the order just described; the dénoûment being the most vital part of a play, he always had it clearly in mind before the plot was fully developed. He was aware that a hastily accomplished dénoûment, convenient but not logical, would spoil the best play and disgruntle the most indulgent audience. That his dénoûment should be the only possible consequence of the combinations of characters and events which the play portrayed was a fundamental law with him, and in his most complicated pieces he never loses sight of what is to be the outcome of all the *péripéties* and *coups de théâtre* with which he complicates the action. Everything tends toward one end, which every element of the play announces and prepares for; and each scene makes the spectator more anxious to know the outcome.

"L'Ours et le Pasha," written in 1820, is a masterpiece of the buffoon farce, a kind of gay orgy of Momus, a mixture of clever jokes and farces which excite hearty laughter. Pasha Chahabaham has chosen as favorite a white bear; unfortunately this bear dies, and the entire seraglio

is in a state of the greatest consternation, for if good
Pasha Chahabaham learns of his favorite's death, he will
surely have fifteen or twenty heads cut off to appease the
shades of his bear. Luckily, La Gingeole and his friend
Tristapatte, two dealers in trained animals, arrive at this
juncture. They have left Europe with a rare collection of
very clever animals, all of whom have died *en route;* and
to repair this loss La Gingeole dresses up his comrade as a
bear and presents him to the Pasha, who, delighted at seeing Tristapatte dance and play the harp so well, promises
to make La Gingeole instructor to the children of the
harem if he can succeed in giving as brilliant a training to
his favorite bear. At this the seraglio is again thrown into
confusion; how can they inform the choleric Pasha that
the white bear is no more? La Gingeole, to rescue them
from this embarrassing situation, takes the fur of the
departed favorite and makes the grand vizier don it. The
vizier, thus disguised, meets the black bear, Tristapatte,
and as neither of them knows of the other's metamor-
phosis, they flee from each other in terror. In the precipi-
tation of their flight, their heads fall off; they recognize
each other and engage in conversation. Surprised by the
Pasha, they put on the wrong heads, the white bear taking the black one and the black bear the white one. The
astonished Pasha suspects some ruse, and to settle the
difficulty orders his executioner to cut off the heads of
both of them. The bears now disclose their identity and
implore grace; the Pasha, who is not cruel at heart,
grants pardon, but is angry when Tristapatte claims his
wages as a bear. "Comment, il m'en fait voir de toutes
les couleurs, et sa tête à la main demande son salaire!"
This little play can be taken as a good example of those

farcical *vaudevilles d'intrigue* which were so popular at that time, and with which Scribe made his first appearance as a dramatist.

The first *comédie-vaudeville* to break away from the old subjects and to show an attempt to give a little sketch of contemporary life is "Une Nuit de la Garde Nationale" (1815), in which Scribe utilizes that popular institution as the background for an amusing little comedy; though the plot is very simple, the pictures presented are, according to contemporary witnesses, strikingly lifelike, and the characters amusing but not overdrawn. One journal spoke of this play as a return to real genre; real genre it certainly is, but an arrival, not a return. The popularity of the play was so great that Scribe could not fail to see that such a piece appealed much more to the public than the *flonflons*, farces, and buffooneries which until then had been known as *comédies-vaudevilles*. The *vaudeville anecdotique* had, it is true, been a favorite form, but it had lacked careful development, its chief interest being, as I have said, its topicality. After "Une Nuit de la Garde" Scribe produced a succession of bright and amusing plays, in all of which there was a carefully developed plot accompanied by a picture of manners or a light satire of some folly or vice. The *couplet* still played an important rôle, but was becoming gradually more and more detached from the plot, more and more episodic; and finally it disappeared entirely, the final *couplet* being the one which was retained longest. Another type of *comédie-vaudeville* in which Scribe was eminently successful was that which may be called the sentimental *vaudeville*, in which the satire and the painting of manners are subordinated to the development of some tender, sentimental idea. One of the best known plays of that period, "Michel et Christine" (1821), is typical of this kind of *vaudeville*.

Stanislas, a Polish soldier, arrives after a long march at a village inn where he has once before fallen in love with a servant girl, Christine. The latter, having in the meantime received a sum of money from an unknown benefactor, has bought the inn and is now its mistress. Stanislas owns to being the author of her fortune — half of a purse which he received from his dying colonel he has sent to her. Her gratitude convinces Stanislas of her love, and he offers her his hand, only to learn that she is in love with an ungrateful cousin whose head is filled with grandiose ambitions. On his way to the city this cousin, Michel, stops at the inn, and falls asleep over a breakfast which Stanislas buys for him. Christine, furious at seeing herself deserted by Michel, offers her hand impulsively to Stanislas, stipulating that he shall at once pass for her husband. Michel, on seeing her married, as he thinks, expresses his regrets in so touching a way that Christine's love for him is reawakened. Stanislas at first plays the injured husband and offers to eject Michel violently, though the latter sues to be retained in the inn as a waiter. Christine, however, urges Michel to beg permission to love her, and the naïf villager, in spite of his fear of Stanislas, throws himself at the soldier's feet. Stanilas, moved by their love, withdraws magnanimously, leaving them the other half of the purse.

Scribe was eminently qualified to depict the follies, the vices, and the virtues of the society of the French capital. Born in the heart of commercial Paris, he was a true child of the Paris of the Halles, of the Marais, and of the Faubourg Saint-Denis. The ferocious attacks made upon him by Alexandre Dumas, by Théophile Gautier, and by others of their school, show him to be a representative of that class which was anathema to the Jeunes-France and their imitators. To the morbid and extravagant ideals of the Romanticists, he opposed the glorification of quiet optimism; to the undisciplined marriage of love, the marriage of reason. At a time when financial speculation and extravagance were rampant, he stood for order, industry, and economy. Despising charlatanism in all its forms, he showed that happiness comes to those who earn their living and win their rank through honest effort.

But although he may be called a moralist, he was no preacher. His desire was to interest and amuse his public; and, with his marvelous instinct for detecting the current of popular favor, he realized, soon after becoming attached in 1820 to the newly founded Théâtre de Madame as its official purveyor, that he could best attract and retain both the Chaussée-d'Antin and the Faubourg Saint-Germain by presenting light and amusing sketches of these two classes. If in many cases his inoffensive satire exposed and made harmless certain eccentricities, if occasionally the follies of the day were killed by ridicule, it was not because they were bitterly attacked. Political evils were not his concern. Instinctively avoiding extremes of opinion and emotion, he always preserved a moderate attitude, conservative, yet always inclining to the opposition when the government steered too close to reaction. Neither did he attempt to solve any of the great social questions of the day; at most he suggested that the way of the evil-doer is hard, and then passed on to pleasanter fields.

As the successful marriage and establishment of the child was the great preoccupation of the middle-class families, as all their planning, working, and saving had that for its object, Scribe, a faithful reflector of the period, if not its historian, could not refuse to marriage a predominant rôle in his plays. One is struck by the number of pieces with titles such as "La Demoiselle à marier," "Le Mariage de Raison," "Le Mariage d'Inclination," and "Le Mariage d'Argent." In some of the earlier plays, as "Les Adieux au Comptoir" (1824), and "La Demoiselle à marier" (1826), he shows that devotion to the solid, material side of life which, always characteristic of the French bourgeoisie, was particularly strong at that time. A moderate fortune, honestly earned, a comfortable home, and children well married, were all that an honest man should desire.

"La Demoiselle à marier" is a forerunner of Labiche's "La Poudre aux Yeux" and of the amusing betrothal scene in Brieux's "Les trois Filles de Monsieur Dupont." The play shows how the efforts of the parents to make an impression upon the suitor nearly succeed in driving him away. The observation which forms the basis of this play was not new; it had been several times adapted to the theatre, notably in "La petite Ville" by Picard, and in a play, "Marions ma Fille," by Francis and Brazier at the Vaudeville, which was a flat failure; it is to be found also in Auguste Lafontaine's "Tableaux de Famille," in the chapter on marriage. A girl in a provincial family is of marriageable age, and her parents are expecting a call from a very wealthy young aspirant. Before his arrival, great pains are taken to have everything in shipshape order — the whole house has assumed a very artificial air of festivity: an impressive luncheon is prepared, and all the members of the family have donned their finest clothes. The young man arrives; but, unfortunately, the great desire of the parents to make a favorable impression succeeds only in displeasing him. He judges the father to be false and calculating, the mother an unbearable flatterer, and the young girl insipid and uninteresting. As a consequence, he quickly gives up his matrimonial project. But as soon as the family is informed of this decision, everything changes: the father becomes cordial and frank, his wife an excellent, old-fashioned mother, the daughter a charming young lady. Now the young man's heart warms up, and he is only too eager to marry the girl whom an hour before he had disdained. While the characters are slightly forced and the young man's changes of plan insufficiently motivated, the sketch as a whole is delightful. The play would have been better had Scribe been less timid in tracing the plan, and had he divided it into two parts, with an interval of several days between the two acts; in that way he would have avoided many improbabilities, situations that seemed forced would have been more natural, and the brusque changes and precipitous succession of incidents would have come more in order.

The importance of the dowry and the sordid, even cynical view that many people took of it, are dealt with in many plays. A very clever and satirical treatment of the theme is found in "La Charge à payer, ou la Mère intrigante" (1825).

The first of his *vaudevilles* to deal directly with the marriage question was "Le Mariage de Raison" (1826),[1]

---

[1] Cf. *Globe*, 14 Oct., 1826; *Figaro*, 4 Oct., 1827.

in which, while indicating his own views, Scribe undoubtedly expressed also the convictions of many of his
contemporaries. The Count de Bremont, who had distinguished himself at Wagram, lives in retirement in his
château near Lyons. With him are Captain Édouard, his
son, a worthless young rake, gambler, and philanderer;
Bertrand, an old veteran of the Napoleonic wars; and
Suzette, a pretty young orphan, whom Madame de
Bremont before her death had taken into her home as
maid — for Suzette, although charming and refined, is
penniless and has been forced to accept this position.
Édouard has fallen madly in love with the young girl, and
to the general's amazement and fury wants to marry her.
In spite of Suzette's good qualities, her virtue, kindness,
and grace, she is not of noble birth, and although the
general's title is itself of very recent origin, and although
his wife had been a dressmaker, he absolutely forbids his
son to marry any woman not of high birth. To prevent
the marriage he persuades Suzette to marry Bertrand, the
old veteran, despite the great disparity in their ages, and
despite the fact that he has only one leg. After the marriage, Édouard for some time tries to persuade Suzette to
listen to his shameful proposals. She resists him, however, and the audience is given to understand at the end
of the play that she will eventually be happy with Bertrand, for, as her sister-in-law tells her, "on finit toujours
par aimer le père de ses enfants."

The success of "Le Mariage de Raison" was stupen-
dous. The dramatic critic of the "Figaro" called it an
aristocratic success, popularized by the acting and by the
charm of the details. The critics were practically unanimous in considering that the situation which forms the

basis of the play was one which was abnormal in 1826 and
could have been found only in a period like the Regency.
Had the play been written a hundred years earlier, these
critics said, it would have been an exact picture of the
manners of old France; had some spectator found the
character of the general false or odious, the reviewers of
the time would have replied that the author had carefully reproduced the customs and convictions of his
contemporaries. But it was considered unnatural that
a general of the Empire should be profoundly convinced
that a soldier like Bertrand was far beneath his worthless
son.

Voltaire also, in "Nanine," had put on the stage characters without fidelity to contemporary life, and although
"Nanine" is one of his worst plays, it had a great success.
Many a noble lady who had driven away her servant for
having lent a sympathetic ear to the proposals of her son,
applauded the countess in "Nanine" for preferring, as
daughter-in-law, not the brilliant baroness but the
daughter of an old soldier. Scribe has really transported
"Nanine" to the Gymnase, with a new dénoûment. Perhaps the success of "Nanine" as well as of "Le Mariage
de Raison" is accounted for by the fact that we do not go
to the theatre to be reproached for our vices or prejudices, but to find characters and situations which we
rarely meet in real life. If the stage were the exact picture
of society we should remain at home, and not need to go
to the theatre.

An interesting explanation of the success of "Le
Mariage de Raison" is found in the "Figaro" for December 14, 1826.

Qu'est-ce qui a fait le succès du Mariage de Raison? Le faubourg Saint-Germain, qui forme une secte au milieu de Paris. Les beaux messieurs et les belles dames qui ont l'honneur d'habiter la rue de l'Université et les environs, ne sont pas doués d'un esprit supérieur et d'une intelligence surnaturelle, mais ils ont des hôtels, des cuisiniers, des équipages, et du bon ton; aussi en matière de théâtre et de littérature le jugement de ces faubouriens doit-il prévaloir. Interrogez M. Poirson, chevalier de la Légion d'Honneur. Il vous dira, en versant des larmes de reconnaissance, que c'est grâce à l'intérêt que la cour a bien voulu témoigner à son entreprise qu'il peut arrondir la bourse de M. Scribe, auteur-économiste. Visitez les cent cinquante loges qui composent la salle du Gymnase, et dont les portes sont décorées de l'éternel écriteau: Louée. Vous verrez des toques à plumes, des chapeaux garnis de marabouts, des cachemires, et des élégants en bas de soie. Parcourez les corridors. Partout vous entendrez, retentir des noms titrés: monsieur le comte, madame la marquise. Jetez un regard sur le Boulevard Bonne-Nouvelle; voyez cette longue file de landaus, de calèches armoriées; considérez, sous le péristyle, ces laquais en livrée, ces grands chasseurs à l'air impudent, ces cochers sentant la noblesse à une lieue à la ronde; . . . pénétrez dans le salon où le *de* est encore dans toute sa gloire, et vous remarquerez que depuis l'émigré aux cheveux poudrés, jusqu'au président de 1760, on ne dit plus "ma loge à l'Opéra, aux Français, aux Bouffes," mais "mon huitième de loge au Théâtre de Madame." On ne chante plus que le génie incomparable de M. Scribe. Après ces observations générales, ne demandez plus pourquoi le Mariage de Raison compte déjà plus de cinquante représentations. Vous devez savoir pourquoi cette comédie, conduite d'ailleurs avec beaucoup d'art et de talent, est presque toujours peu naturelle, maniérée, fausse et pénible à voir. Ce n'est pas un tableau de fantaisie: l'original de ces mœurs-là est au faubourg Saint-Germain.

Augier in "Gabrielle" was no innovator. Twenty years earlier Scribe, setting his face against the sentiment prevailing on the stage, had shown the superiority of matter over intelligence, of prose over poetry, of reason over the heart, of comfort over noble aspirations, glorifying the bourgeois comfortably installed before the fire after a hearty dinner. While his predecessors had never had the temerity to suppress the love plot, which had been the soul of all dramatic action, Scribe, laughing at youth and its enthusiasm, its nobleness, and its constancy, found the secret of making all Paris weep at two plays in which he scoffed at love: "Le Mariage de Raison" and "Le Mariage d'Inclination."

The action of "Malvina, ou le Mariage d'Inclination" (1828) takes place in 1815. M. Dubreuil, a retired merchant, has for years planned to marry his daughter to her cousin Arved, an officer in Napoleon's army. Malvina, however, during a stay in England, where her father had sent her at the moment of the invasion of France by the allied armies, has contracted a secret marriage with a rascally adventurer by the name of de Barentin. Upon her return to France, this fellow accompanies her, and succeeds in working himself into the esteem and friendship of Dubreuil, who is far from suspecting that his charming guest is his son-in-law. When her cousin returns from the war, Malvina begins to suffer bitterly, for she realizes that she really loves Arved. Finally she becomes so unhappy that she confesses everything to her cousin, who assumes the responsibility of acquainting Dubreuil with the facts. Her father's anger and grief, upon learning the truth, are terrible. Malvina sees nothing but unhappiness in store for her, for de Barentin has now deserted her and Arved has fallen in love with Dubreuil's niece, Marie, and has asked her to marry him. The unhappy Malvina is thus left alone with her old father. The emotional effect produced by this drama was so real that at the end of the first performance a woman wrote to Scribe that her daughter had just confessed to her that she had been on the point of eloping, but that the terrible example of Malvina had saved her from that fatal step.

Never up to this time had Scribe been so successful in treating an interesting subject. It is impossible not to recognize his talent, for although the subject was one that had been tried a score of times, and several times happily, yet Scribe's play was immediately received with enthusiastic applause. He doubtless owed much to a novel by Van der Velde entitled "Armed de Gyllenstern"; but there are in "Le Mariage d'Inclination," particularly in Act II, situations which belong to Scribe alone. This version of the secret-marriage theme left far behind it all the dramatic works previously based on that subject. An element in this play that is really new is that because de Barentin is a rascal Malvina can never be happy, even after her marriage has been legitimatized by her father's pardon. The exposition in Act I is somewhat long, but the author needed to prepare the principal situations of his play with great care; moreover, in order that the spectators might realize clearly the difficulty of Malvina's situation in Act II, it was necessary that they see her first receive her young cousin coldly, when he reminds her of their parents' plans for a marriage between them, and then see this feigned indifference disappear gradually, giving way to a passion whose violence she could no longer conceal, when she learns how unworthy of her love is the man she has married. In order to shade this development of Malvina's love skillfully, Scribe had to force the audience to listen patiently to scenes which seem purposeless, but which lead to a catastrophe of the greatest dramatic interest.

There was always skill, and frequently art, in the manner in which Scribe drew certain characters which, parasitical in the earlier plays, later became the heroes. De Barentin is not the least daring of his conceptions, and there is evidence of a profound knowledge of the stage in the success with which he renders this brutal husband endurable. "Le Mariage d'Inclination" is in reality more than a brilliant, clever *vaudeville;* it is a comedy, in which Scribe depicts true and natural characters, in which the difficulties inherent in the characters are skillfully overcome, and in which the action proceeds victoriously to the moral lesson suggested at the dénoûment.

A reading of these two plays makes it clear why Scribe should have found such favor with the greater part of the upper and middle bourgeoisie. He was defending, against the attacks of the Romanticists and against intriguers and adventurers, the solid virtues of the home, the authority of parents, the sanctity of the marriage relation. In his plays there is no glorification of passion and guilty love; there is indeed no acceptance of the idea that a marriage can be a happy one when based merely upon love, no matter how pure. The prerequisites of a happy marriage are a satisfactory dowry, good dispositions, mutual esteem, and equality of social rank and education. After marriage it is order and economy, together with the desire to help each other, that make the husband and wife realize the joys of domestic life. "Le Budget d'un jeune Ménage" (1831) is a lesson in domestic economy, containing good-natured criticism of those young couples whose tastes and social ambitions lead them into extravagance and cause them to live beyond their means. The same theme is found, less well developed, in an earlier play, "La Pension bourgeoise" (1823).

Throughout his plays one finds pictured the sorrow that inevitably comes from infidelity and the happiness that strong and quiet love can bring. The disastrous effects of indifference, which often leads to infidelity, are described in "La seconde Année, ou à qui la Faute?" (1830). Derneville, a banker of the Chaussée-d'Antin, has been for a year happily married to a charming woman, Caroline, but at the end of that period he begins to weary of his happiness and to seek distraction elsewhere — chiefly among the *danseuses* of the Opéra. To his friend and confident, Edmond de Saint-Elme, he proposes to sell one of his best horses for four thousand francs, to make up the sum of ten thousand francs destined to soften the heart of a nymph whose virtue cannot be overcome at a lower price. To guard against Caroline's suspicions, he proposes that she go driving with Edmond in the Bois de Boulogne on the morning when he is to be visited in his office by his mistress, and that she go with Edmond, also, to a ball at her aunt's on the evening when he is to have dinner with the same young lady.

At this juncture, the discovery of a love note written by Edmond to Caroline apprises Derneville of his friend's love for her, and reawakens his own slumbering affection. To struggle with this rival, then, he begins to shower attentions upon his wife, to bring her new music, of which she is very fond, and to compose love poems for her. When she surprises him in the act of writing one of these, he declares that he has never written poetry except for her, but that as a youth he often wrote prose letters to his sweethearts, and even composed many for his friends, including Edmond. The style of these letters was, he says, always of one type, and he quotes phrases from Ed-

mond's note as examples — a ruse which succeeds in
arousing Caroline's resentment against Edmond. She
goes driving with him as planned, however; while Derneville breaks off relations with the *danseuse*, only to find
upon returning that Edmond has betrayed his secret to
Caroline. He attempts to dissuade her from going to the
ball with Edmond; but she is now not to be moved by his
protestations, and he has the chagrin of waiting while she
dresses for the ball. During this time he learns that she is
discontented with the jewelry she has to wear, and he
seizes the opportunity to send her the diamonds, worth
ten thousand francs, which he had intended for the
danseuse. This touches her heart, and when he reminds
her affectionately that this is their anniversary, she finds
herself melting and confessing her "unjust" suspicions —
all of which brings Derneville to the point of confessing his
own infidelity, when Edmond appears to take Caroline
to the ball. Won over by this time to her husband, she
dismisses Edmond summarily, and he sees that he need
not continue to court her. "Les amants s'en vont," as
one of the reviewers said, "les maris restent: c'est la
morale des bons ménages, c'est aussi celle de la pièce."

The greatest concord, moreover, is found in those
homes in which it is neither the husband's will nor the
wife's caprice which rules, but where the direction and
responsibility are shared. The husband should submit
himself to the same moral code he would have his wife
follow; for, as one of the characters in "La Cour d'Assises" (1829) remarks: "Quand monsieur trompe madame, madame trompe monsieur." Having in "La
seconde Année" suggested the certain results of indifference, in "Une Faute" (1830) he goes further and shows

that even the most virtuous wife is subject to temptation
when left alone for a great length of time, and that, no
matter what excuse there may be for proving faithless to
the marriage vow, such infidelity is always punished by
lifelong remorse and sorrow.

As love and marriage play so important a part in the
life of the middle class, Scribe, thoroughly bourgeois in
taste and principles, made these the most prominent elements of his plays. According to the laws of nature and
society, marriage is the complement, or ultimate object,
of love; but Scribe, although too completely imbued with
the principles of bourgeois orthodoxy to maintain the
contrary, firmly believed that one can exist without the
other. He put reason, interest, and desire for luxury in
the place of passion, and used them as motive forces
which influence the choice in marriages where the heart
is not consulted. At the Gymnase, love is not represented
as being that paroxysm of violence and fury which con-
sumes Hernani, Didier, and Antony, but as a quiet, gentle
emotion, suffering in its own modest way, perhaps, with
tears, sighs, and tender effusions. Love in Scribe's *vaudevilles*, unlike the love of the Romanticists, is not, *per se*,
the motive force in the action; it is always preparatory
to marriage, and it is marriage which interests him and
which he makes the main theme of the story. Antithetic
himself to all that is *romanesque*, Scribe painted the world
as he saw it, with its sorry realities, its prejudices, and
social conventions, which he respected and did not pro-
test against. And while this earned for him the scorn of
many idealists, he had on his side the great mass of the
spectators, the parents especially, who were delighted to
find an argument and safeguard against the raptures and
temptations of youth.

Second in importance only to love and marriage in these plays, and in many ways interwoven with them, is the subject of money. Scribe paints an interesting picture of the fierce struggle for financial preëminence which characterized the July Monarchy, and which accompanied the great industrial and commercial growth of France during that period. He notes the power of money as a factor in social life, and deplores the prevalence of gambling and speculation; he satirizes the *noblesse d'argent*, and, considering money a worthy object of effort, comes out strongly for the nobility of work, asserting that honest labor ennobles the worker.

A play written in the middle of the reign of Louis-Philippe, "Le Veau d'Or" (1841), contains the following lines:

Apprends donc, mon garçon, que de nos jours il existe peu de principes, peu de religions: il en existe une cependant que tout le monde professe. Une divinité devant qui chacun se prosterne. N'as-tu pas entendu dire qu'autrefois les Juifs adoraient le Veau d'Or? Eh bien, notre siècle est un peu juif, et la seule idole qu'on encense c'est l'or!

Although such a statement may have been somewhat extreme, it was doubtless essentially true. The bourgeois suffered from the universal weakness which makes men fawn upon the rich and powerful, which tempts one to cultivate the acquaintance of wealthy persons, and which, when once one has acquired wealth, makes him forget the friends of former days, and turn to those whose wealth exceeds his own.

With his mania for moderation, regularity, and economy, Scribe delights in ridiculing those who, through extravagance or gambling, dissipate fortunes built up by hard work. It is certain that during the July Monarchy

the gambling fever reached an intensity not often sur-
passed in French history. The gambler, consequently,
was one of the most prominent figures, not only in
Scribe's plays, but in other comedies and melodramas as
well. Moreover, the great development of industry and
the subsequent national prosperity soon gave rise to a
passion for speculation unequaled since the days of Law.
A reflection of the extravagance prevalent early in the
reign of the Citizen King, and of the dishonesty occasionally discovered in high places, is found in a number
of the *vaudevilles*, notably in "Le Voyage dans l'Appartement, ou l'Influence des Localités" (1833).

The gambling vice is vividly portrayed in two plays,
"L'Écarté" (1822), and "Le premier Président" (1832).
In the former the card mania is only lightly satirized; the
gambling scenes are handled with great dexterity, and
with an attempt to portray life with bits of realism which
anticipates the card scene in "La Dame aux Camélias."
Here he not only depicts the ruinous effects of gambling,
but shows also that this evil had caused a deterioration in
social life, driving out the older and more refined pleasures and introducing a general coarseness of manners.
The play is really only a series of pictures, for there is no
very complicated plot. It represents any one of those
drawing-rooms where card-playing was the favorite pas-
time. We find the parasite who seems indispensable to
all social gatherings, who is at all the banquets but never
pays his share, who receives without giving, who, as one
of the characters in the play says, "traverse sans payer le
fleuve de la vie"; the old woman who plays only ten
sous and will not accept any advice; the young clerk who,
not content with losing his month's salary, risks also the

money he owes his tailor; and, finally, the good-natured uncle who has taken up gambling to repair his nephew's follies.

"Le premier Président" is a far more vigorous treatment of the theme, practically unrelieved by any comic touches. The play, which is pure melodrama in the style of Ducange's "Trente Ans, ou la Vie d'un Joueur," sets before the audience, logically and emphatically, the fatal effects of gambling, the crime and suffering it frequently entails.

Another widespread vice of the time, that of speculation, which furnished the theme for many of the comedies of the Restoration and of the July Monarchy, is taken up by Scribe in "Les Actionnaires" (1829), in which, due allowance made for the forcing of tone legitimate in such a genre, there is a good picture of this frenzy of speculation. The moral to be drawn from the play — and it was *de rigueur* to draw one — is the moral that terminates "L'Agiotage," by Picard and Empis: "Anathème à l'agiotage, honneur et respect à l'industrie." "Les Actionnaires" is the story of an incredible charlatan, Piffart, who organizes a large stock company of credulous investors without having any definite enterprise in mind. At a stockholders' meeting, however, some such enterprise must be outlined, and Piffart explains to them a scheme for converting the sterile plains of Les Sablons into pasturages — an undertaking which requires only the digging of great artesian wells. Unfortunately no water can be struck, and Piffart's scheme is unworkable. He is on the point of blowing out his brains in despair, when he is approached by an old Breton nobleman, gullible but unscrupulous. From this Monsieur

Kernoneck, Piffart purchases, for 700,000 francs, a dilapidated old château and its surrounding forest. The château he proposes to convert into a factory, and sells it to the stockholders for two millions. In five minutes Piffart makes a fine fortune, but it remains to be seen whether the stockholders are ruined.

The stockholders' meeting in this play is clearly imitated from the meeting of the creditors in Picard's "Duhautcours" (1801). The critic of the "Journal des Débats" thought there were too many details. Des Granges, in his interesting book, "La Comédie et les Mœurs, 1815–1848," finds this remark interesting as showing that the play was perhaps too realistic for the audience, who preferred certain scenic illusions in these "business-comedies."

When it is remembered that Scribe was born of hardworking, thrifty parents, and that he was highly endowed with the ability to make money and to keep it, one is not surprised to find such importance given to money in his plays. Moreover, had he not laid stress upon the advantages of wealth, he would not have been painting a faithful picture of French society in those days; if the dowry, if legacies, gambling, speculation, indebtedness, and bankruptcy seem to hold too often the centre of the stage, it is because those were the things about which people thought most earnestly. There is this to be noted in his *vaudevilles*, as in the comedies of Picard, Empis, Mazères, and Casimir Bonjour: that the money question is treated as a real question. For while in many of his plays a lost fortune, or an inheritance, is simply one feature in the development of a complicated plot, in most of them it is presented as having a practical relation to the

life of the characters. The spectators, among whom
there were few who did not know the sordidness and
pettiness of the constant striving for a livelihood; who
did not know, either by experience or hearsay, the cost of
a lawsuit; who did not wonder whether hard and constant labor would result some day in comparative ease —
these spectators could feel the reality of this wealth which
they did not possess. Or if the play portrayed figures
from the upper financial world, again there was a real
appeal to a large part of the audience. It is interesting to
find Scribe dealing so frequently with the money question
before it is treated by Balzac.

Considering the number, the suddenness, and the importance of the political changes during Scribe's lifetime,
one would expect to find a very noticeable reflection of
them in his plays. But when the importance of political
problems, as they are presented in his *vaudevilles*, is compared with that of marriage and of the money question,
it is found that, in spite of the profound revolutions of
political and social life which he witnessed, he was not
sufficiently moved by them to use them frequently as
dramatic material. In seeking an explanation of this
fact, one must remember that Scribe, always careful of
the feelings of his spectators, and never forgetting the
fact that to draw large audiences he must not antagonize
them, preferred not to run the risk of losing the affections
of his public by attacking or ridiculing any political institution or party. This shrewd practice, together with
his naturally pacific disposition, is responsible for the
meagre interest he seemed to have in the political life of
his time. He was neither a reformer nor an agitator,
merely a good-natured writer trying to amuse his au-

diences. The very nature of his public, moreover, composed as it was of the two nobilities, those of the Chaussée-d'Antin and of the Faubourg Saint-Germain, made him avoid any extreme partisanship; for he could not have aligned himself with one class without losing the support of the other. He always trimmed his sails to meet the wind of public opinion. Legitimist during the Restoration, when the Bourbons were driven out he espoused the cause of the Orléanists, feeling sympathy no doubt for the Roi-Citoyen. Even during the July Monarchy, however, his liberalism was not advanced, for, like the majority of his class, he was by nature conservative.

One of the first of his *vaudevilles* which may be called a sketch of manners, "Le Solliciteur" (1817), depicts that mania for job-hunting which was to become such a plague throughout the first half of the century. Although one finds neither a profound study of the question nor a bitter satire of solicitors in this play, the author does from time to time attack those in power as well as those who bend the knee to them. The Revolution had created, not only armies of soldiers, but also armies of clerks. There was a time when there was a government employee for almost every voter, and a collector for almost every tax-payer. The facility with which places could be obtained through intrigue kept many people from making a position for themselves through work; their education was limited to their ability to write; and with the recommendation of some great lord or with the help of some pretty woman's eyes, they succeeded in becoming useless to society and a burden to the state. As everyone, of course, wanted a position, this universal ambition engendered intrigue, cupidity, and jealousy. A writer in the "Débats" said:

La multiplicité des emplois est un fléau pour la morale et pour les nations, car ils ne s'achètent qu'à force de bassesse et ils ne se paient qu'à force d'impôts. Le temps et le ridicule peuvent seuls faire justice de cet abus.

In "Le Solliciteur" Scribe took the initiative and directed a number of well-pointed arrows at these solicitors. The critics united in declaring that the play was a delicate and piquant criticism of manners. The character of the hero, L'Espérance, is quite well described in the following verses:

En mai comme en janvier,
Que le ministre change,
Lui, rien ne le dérange:
Il est, sur l'escalier,
Ferme comme un pilier.
On le voit aux finances;
Il est aux audiences,
Et trouve encore du temps
Pour nos représentants.

For five years he has been soliciting a tobacco concession. He carries about in his pockets nine or ten petitions; he slips one into the lodge of the ministry concierge under the wrapper of the "Moniteur"; he hands them to the Swiss guards, to the office-boys, to the supernumeraries. He knows better than anyone else the methods of getting ahead of the line: with No. 399 he gets in first; he brings in his dog, and while the Swiss is chasing it with his halberd, he slips into the antechamber. If these methods fail, he leaves his hat in a neighboring café, and enters the office boldly, with his pen in his mouth, and his papers under his arm as if he were an employee of the ministry.

But having once penetrated to the minister's salon, he still has to get into his office. At this juncture the cook brings in the minister's lunch; but as someone calls him out and he has to leave his tray for a moment on the table, L'Espérance at once picks up the waiter's napkin and the platter, and walks into the office. It was this play which Schlegel preferred to the "Misanthrope"; and without sharing such ridiculous enthusiasm, one can see that there is in this *vaudeville* in the author's first manner a real comic feeling absolutely lacking in the *landérirette* and *landérira* of his predecessors and imitators.

The satire is more definite in "La Manie des Places, ou la Folie du Siècle" (1828), in which he aims a more direct blow at politicians eager for power and at the office-seekers who pursue them. He directs his attention also to the follies resulting from the recently introduced parliamentary régime. The government had just granted new privileges to the secondary theatres, which allowed them to treat certain subjects hitherto forbidden. In "La Manie des Places" Scribe used this liberty with all the joy of recovering it, yet with the moderation dictated by the fear of losing it. A light, gay, and ingenious plot furnished him the occasion to touch lightly upon a number of administrative and political follies. Monsieur Berlac, whose brain has become addled as a result of thwarted ambition, thinks he is one of the cabinet ministers, and leaves his country home to come to Paris and take charge of his affairs. He puts up at a hotel in the Rue de Rivoli, where his apparent sincerity and his kindliness win him the esteem of all those whom he meets. He promises positions to everyone, intervenes successfully in a family marriage council, and is recalled to earth only by the arrival of his future son-in-law, who, in order to get him away, tells him he has been appointed ambassador to the Sublime Porte. The character of this monomaniac is really a very original and amusing creation; Berlac is at once gay and serious, joking and imposing, and his wild imagination does not prevent him from having periods of philosophical reflection.

Lines of social distinction being still closely drawn at this time, in spite of the Revolution of 1789, the dramatist could not fail to find material for sketches in these perpetual conflicts between pride and interest. And although he was very little concerned personally with questions of politics, or of strife between classes, and although he probably had no very strong or fixed convictions in such matters, Scribe realized clearly that for the dramatist there was in these parties, coteries, and castes, a real field for observation, keen criticism, and satire. One of the most interesting of his political pieces, "Avant, Pendant, et Après" (1828),[1] was written just at the time when liberalism was more and more gaining ground. The play, representing the three periods 1789, 1793, and 1825, is full of exasperating memories and allusions, and of cutting verses. It is a strange plot throughout, the first two acts irritating the most irritable set of people, the hotheads of both parties, who were willing to make no concession either to the upward march toward a better order of things, or to the necessity of a return toward order and refinement. However, after having laid bare in all their ugliness the vices of both the aristocracy and the democracy, the author succeeded in sending the entire audience away satisfied. Certain journals claimed that

[1] Cf. *Figaro*, 29 June, 1828; *Journal des Débats*, 25 Oct., 1828.

the noble inhabitants of the Faubourg Saint-Germain had objected to the representation of this play, which seems really to have been written in favor of the titled class. The dukes, counts, and barons of the old régime could scarcely criticize the author, for the most reasonable and the most interesting of all the characters is a nobleman. It is true that from the very first he is portrayed as being in opposition to the code of a caste grown old in a régime of privileges which were absurd when they were not odious; but it would seem from a careful study of this *comédie-drame-vaudeville* that the frightful excesses of the Revolution resulted from the abolition of those very privileges. The fact that at the end of the play we see the nobility reconciled to constitutional institutions is evidence that Scribe had entered into the manners of the time; but here, too, everything is in favor of the aristocrats. Although the Count de Surgy tells us that he is proud of having become a manufacturer, he seems after all only a noble, condescending to command a few hundred workmen. All the despicable or ridiculous characters of the play come from the untitled class: it is a man of the people who becomes a valet after having been a revolutionist; it is a wretch born of plebeian parents who, after being a Jacobin, turns Jesuit.

As a matter of fact, each party could find satisfaction in this play: the friends of the régime then in power were right in thinking that a light satire of the monarchy could not endanger the throne, and the republicans consoled themselves with the thought that in Act I the old régime is scoffed at and in Act III ridiculed. Strangely enough, the royalists were very much annoyed by " Avant, Pendant, et Après," and the august patroness of the Théâtre de Madame, the Duchess de Berry, frightened at seeing her theatre becoming a revolutionary centre, threatened to withdraw her patronage and her name. To counterbalance the revolutionary tone of the play and to obtain the clemency of the authorities, Scribe closed the last act with the following words:

Et nous, mes concitoyens, qui après tant d'orages sommes enfin arrivés au port, et qui goûtons, à l'abri du trône et des lois, cette liberté sage et modérée que tous nos vœux appelaient depuis quarante ans, conservons-la bien; nous l'avons payée assez cher. Toujours unis, toujours d'accord, ne songeons plus au mal qu'on a fait; ne voyons que le bien qui existe, et disons tous dans la France nouvelle: "Union et oubli."

Though Scribe occasionally censured and ridiculed the members of the old nobility, this honest bourgeois was most annoyed by the new barons and marquises, whose name had become legion since the days of the Empire, and it is their mania for titles which he most cleverly satirized. A number of plays, notably "Mon Oncle César" (1823) and "Louise, ou la Réparation" (1829), contain allusions to this new aristocracy and assert that honest labor is the most authentic claim to nobility.

Although Scribe usually deplored marriages between persons of different social rank, in "La Famille Riquebourg, ou le Mariage mal assorti" (1831) [1] the point is made that marriages between the nobility and the bourgeoisie were desirable, as they tended to break down the barriers between the classes. Riquebourg, a former shopkeeper in Marseilles, now a rich merchant in Paris, has been unfortunate enough to marry the daughter of a poor emigrant noble, who, although penniless, is far superior to her husband in training and education. The subject

[1] Cf. *Journal des Débats*, 10 Jan., 1831.

is that of "Georges Dandin," but it is treated seriously;
while in Molière's play the sanctity of marriage is somewhat violated, in "La Famille Riquebourg" it is treated
with all the consideration due to so respectable a bond.
Georges Dandin and those who surround him are either
villainous or ridiculous; the Riquebourg family is perfect. In Scribe's play the mésalliance results, not from
the fact that Riquebourg has married into the nobility,
but from the difference in training. Brought up in the
most fashionable convent, Madame Riquebourg dances
beautifully, plays the most difficult music, speaks Italian
and English, is strong in history and geography. Monsieur Riquebourg, a mere wine merchant, very clever in
his own business, but always confused as to grammar and
social customs, is a good fellow who adores his wife, anticipates her slightest desire, and places his immense
fortune at her feet. Riquebourg has a nephew, an
elegant young man with good social training and mod-
ishly inclined to tender melancholy, who has taken part
in the fighting of the Three Days. With so many bonds of
sympathy between them it would have been difficult for
the nephew not to love his aunt, and for the aunt not to
have felt a decided interest in her nephew.

Scribe, however, knew his public too well to allow himself to write any such heresy. The nephew is so distressed
at loving his aunt that Œdipus himself could have been no
more annoyed when he heard of his own misdeed. The
aunt is no less aghast at her adoration for her nephew;
she weeps and cries, and wants to leave for the country.
Finally the two lovers confess to each other the mortal sin
which weighs upon their consciences, but *en tout bien
tout honneur;* for the aunt demands that her too-charm-

ing nephew leave at once for Havana. He obeys, and when the coach has rolled away, Madame Riquebourg confesses all to her husband.

Des Granges remarks: "La Famille Riquebourg, c'est, si l'on peut s'exprimer ainsi, le vaudeville *cornélien*." The dénoûment is far from cheerful; but in order not to leave too painful an impression, the author gives us to understand that the male members of the Riquebourg family are not very long-lived, and that generally by the age of fifty they have gone to join their ancestors; as our hero is now forty-five, in four or five years the nephew and the aunt will be free to love each other at their ease. The journals pointed out that unfortunately the all-too-evident good health of Gontier, who played the rôle, was scarcely adapted to this illusion, in spite of his excellent acting.

From a reading of Scribe's *vaudevilles* one can get a good picture of the social life of Paris during the first half of the century: they are for the most part little comedies of manners depicting the essential qualities of the bourgeois, showing the part played in the social order by the military, satirizing charlatanism in its various forms, ridiculing the so-called *mal du siècle*, and lampooning political vices and follies. To one interested in the social history of France at this period these little plays are more instructive than one might suppose, forming, as they do, a series of sketches whose fidelity is attested by other comedies of the time, by the journals, and by writers of memoirs. By following the French bourgeois through the forty-odd years in which Scribe was putting him upon the stage, we find him to be a simple, practical man, satisfied with the pleasures of home and shop and street, prosaic and unimaginative until his common sense and mental balance are temporarily disturbed by too much reading of the *littérature cadavéreuse* which flourished for a time; a good friend and kind husband, putting family before all else, and proud of his profession because it enabled him to make his family happy. We see him bewildered for a moment by the excesses of the Jeunes-France, but find him quickly regaining his former placidity. Tempted by the opportunities which the new régime presents, he occasionally resorts to charlatanism and deceit in order to reach his goal. At times he is not above seeking advancement through the beauty and charms of his wife. For a number of years after the fall of Napoleon he looks upon the soldier as the most heroic figure in the country, and surrounds him with a tradition of chivalry and valor that falls away only when the nation turns itself wholly to the worship of money. In his leisure moments he visits and passes judgment upon the Vaudeville, the Gymnase, and even the Comédie-Française and the Opéra; if not always profound, his criticisms are most often shrewd and just, for he is quick to detect affectation and artificiality.

When one has thus followed the French family and French society through this period, one realizes that Scribe's *comédies-vaudevilles* are something more than mere exhibitions of technical virtuosity; that there is something more than a juggling of difficult situations and more than prodigious dexterity in taking care of these situations. The story of an interesting people is always interesting, and these plays help not a little in outlining and coloring a picture of those times.

Thus, beginning with the conventional *vaudeville-farce*, *vaudeville anecdotique*, and *vaudeville satirique*, Scribe, by early applying the formula of the intensive plot built upon a dovetailing of *quiproquos*, had before long developed the genre into a *vaudeville d'intrigue*. Having thus made of the *vaudeville* a more pretentious form by grafting it on the *comédie d'intrigue*, he gradually enlarged the new *vaudeville*, by weaving into it a sketch of manners, until he reached the real comedy of manners. In the transformation of the *vaudeville* into the *comédie-vaudeville de mœurs*, three stages may be remarked: first, there is a modification in the structure of the play, a more careful combination of the various elements, greater dexterity in building the framework, and more logical arrangement in the succession of scenes, in the action, and in the dénoûment. Second, the rôle of the *couplet* is gradually reduced until finally it disappears completely. Third, the later plays, while keeping their humorous and sparkling quality, become somewhat more sentimental in tone, more reserved and more restrained, than the lighter *vaudeville-farce*.

CHAPTER III

COMEDIES AND DRAMAS

BEAUMARCHAIS, in the eighteenth century, was the first to conceive of comedy as a dramatic genre worthy and capable of technical excellence, and his trilogy, particularly "Le Mariage de Figaro," is the first example of French comedy in which to character-study, or to painting of manners, to sentimentality or to indecency, is added the interest of a well-constructed plot. One would have to go back to Corneille's "Le Menteur" to find a comedy in which the development of the plot is a feature in the general excellence of the play; for from the Renaissance to the end of the eighteenth century [1] the treatment of the material action of comedy made very little progress. It is hardly necessary to point out that most often Molière makes no effort whatever to find a dénoûment; "Les Femmes savantes," which is probably his most skillfully constructed comedy, is brought to an end in the most elementary fashion by the use of a fictitious letter. Regnard is scarcely more ingenious, and in Marivaux's plays there is practically no plot at all. Picard, arriving after the Revolution, when the public was jaded by bloodshed and horror, began to construct plots in which all the threads were first apparently entangled beyond hope and then skillfully straightened out;

[1] Excepting perhaps those French comedies of the Renaissance written in the Italian style, with imbroglios and farcical situations, and the Spanish comedies of Lesage.

plays like "Les Ricochets" and "Les Marionettes" are the reflection of the kaleidoscopic changes which occurred between 1789 and 1815. He alone of the late eighteenth-century writers can claim with Beaumarchais a share in the ancestry of the well-constructed play, which in the hands of Scribe, Augier, the younger Dumas, and Sardou, was to become the consecrated form of the comedy of the nineteenth century.

The society of the French capital of the early days of the Restoration had lived through the horrors of the Revolution; had seen the glory of France rise at Arcola, Austerlitz, and Jena, and sink at Leipzig and Waterloo; had tasted all the joys of victory and drunk to the dregs the cup of defeat. Exhausted emotionally, if not physically, by the Napoleonic campaigns, wearied of the business of war, the nation sighed for peace and longed for the opportunity to restore its lost fortunes. Yet, by a strange, although perhaps natural, inconsistency, Bonaparte had scarcely reached St. Helena before the Napoleonic legend began to take form. Forgetting the days of conscription and the terrible retreat from Moscow, the French had begun to tire of the prosaic dullness of the Restoration, and to idealize the colonels and the captains of the Empire. On the one hand, sensibilities, emotions, and passions were exhausted by the succession of crises between the Tennis-Court Oath and the return of the emigrant nobles; on the other, an evergrowing desire was developing to find an outlet for the patriotic sentiment so cruelly disappointed by the exile of the Emperor.

The mental, emotional, and moral state of French society in 1815 seemed to call for dramatic entertainment from light, well-constructed comedies of plot; while the organization of this society, or rather its lack of organization, and the absence of social standards, made it practically impossible for a dramatic author to present masterly pictures of contemporary manners. In this world of shifting contrasts and changing values — on the one side the returned nobles, with their old prejudices and their worn-out claims; on the other, the partisans of the Empire; and everywhere a humiliation of the national spirit — it was next to impossible to give a faithful picture of contemporary society.

Early in the reign of Louis XVIII the government took in hand a much-needed reform of the educational system, religion began to regain its hold upon the people, and industry showed signs of flourishing again. The courses offered by Guizot, Villemain, and Cousin were immediately and exceedingly popular; a clerical reaction, hastened by the return of the emigrant nobles, soon set in; and better fiscal legislation put the national finances upon a sound basis and restored the public credit. As a result of this latter improvement great enterprises, such as the building of the canals of the Marne and of the Somme, were undertaken, material comforts were multiplied, and the bourgeoisie, reassured by the ever-increasing prosperity of the country, began to engage in all kinds of commerce and industry. Before long, however, it became apparent that the government, if not the King, was reactionary. Louis XVIII was succeeded by the pious Charles X, under whose ministers, Villèle, Martignac, and Polignac, the monarchical and clerical parties gained the ascendancy. Dissatisfaction first, then ill-concealed rebelliousness, became manifest. Peace, ten years before so ardently desired, had by this time begun to pall upon the nation, and the memories of the glorious days of the Empire to rekindle the popular imagination.

With the fall of the Restoration, and the accession of Louis-Philippe in 1830, the bourgeoisie, which had been responsible for the overthrow of Charles X and his ministers, took its place in the saddle and became the leading force in the nation. The old orders and privileges, with the distinctions of class, having been suppressed, the nobility of birth was replaced by that of money, the new motto being: "Enrichissez-vous." The King, created and supported by the bourgeoisie, leaned exclusively on this class, consulted, flattered, strengthened it. Carried along by the great commercial and industrial movement, the French before long found that luxury, materialism, and coarseness of manners had replaced the quiet elegance, the good taste, and the essentially aristocratic ideas of the older monarchy.

Scribe began writing at the time when this new society was making its first appearance in the French political organization, replacing the military and imperial society of the Faubourg Saint-Honoré, which had itself replaced the aristocratic and legitimist Faubourg Saint-Germain. Since Scribe is a painter of *actualités*, we find the foreground of his pictures invaded by agents of the Stock Exchange, busy with their speculations; the middleground by the military, still thrilled by the memories of its own exploits; and the background by aged peers who had nothing at all to recommend them. The Théâtre du Gymnase was to become the favorite theatre of this society, occupying the middle rank of condition, intelligence, and culture; for, while the aristocracy of the Faubourg Saint-Germain came also to the little hall, its real public was the bourgeoisie, only recently accustomed to fortune, to elegance, and to influence. It was there that Scribe developed and perfected the technical skill which enabled him for so many years to reign in all the leading theatres of Paris; and it was the *comédies-vaudevilles* produced at the Gymnase which were to grow into the five-act comedies of the Théâtre-Français.

Although there is scarcely one of Scribe's comedies which is not essentially a comedy of plot, a *well-made play*, and although the portrayal of manners, the development of character, the political thesis, and the historical picture are always more or less built upon, if not subordinated to, the brilliant development of a complicated plot, it is quite easy for the sake of study to make a division of his plays into comedies of plot, comedies of manners, political comedies, and historical comedies. In the first class fall "Le Valet de son Rival" (1816), "Valérie" (1822), "Rodolphe, ou Frère et Sœur" (1823), "Le mauvais Sujet" (1825), "La Grand'mère" (1840), "Japhet, ou la Recherche d'un Père" (1840), "Oscar, ou le Mari qui trompe sa Femme" (1842), "La Tutrice, ou l'Emploi des Richesses" (1843), "Bataille de Dames" (1851), "Mon Étoile" (1854), "Feu Lionel" (1858), and "Rêves d'Amour" (1859). Several of these plays—"Le Valet de son Rival," "Le mauvais Sujet," "Japhet," "Mon Étoile," "Feu Lionel," and "Rêves d'Amour" — are really nothing more than *comédies-vaudevilles* in one, two, or three acts, without *couplets*, differing in no essential respect from the *vaudevilles* of the Gymnase. "Rodolphe, ou Frère et Sœur" is a clever imitation of a very lugubrious drama by Goethe; while the original play would have been quite unacceptable on the French stage, that of Scribe had a great success. "Oscar, ou le Mari qui trompe sa Femme," and "Bataille de Dames" are brilliant exhibitions of stage legerdemain; the latter play still retains its place in the repertory of the Théâtre-Français. "La Grand'mère" more or less cleverly develops the opposite of the *vieillard amoureux* theme; a young lad's infatuation for his sweetheart's grandmother being the somewhat difficult subject which Scribe develops successfully. "Les Frères invisibles" is the best example of his attempts at melodrama, — of which he made only two or three, — conceived in the classical formula for melodrama, with brigands, subterranean passages, conflagrations, red cloaks, the explosion of a castle, and all the other accessories; *les frères invisibles* are the direct descendants of Jean Sbogar, the hero of a play produced some time before at the Théâtre de la Gaîté. "La Bohémienne, ou l'Amérique en 1775," is a melodramatic comedy of plot, the scene of which is laid in Boston under British rule.

"Valérie," [1] with which Scribe made his début at the Théâtre-Français in 1822, was written especially for Mademoiselle Mars, and helped in no slight way to establish that actress's reputation. The subject of the play was taken from a novel by Auguste Lafontaine, a German writer, translated into French by Châlons d'Argé, who had also published a collection of stories entitled "Contes à ma Sœur," containing the anecdote of "La Fille aveugle." In Scribe's play Valérie is a young girl who, blind since early childhood, penniless and orphaned, has been received into the home of a cousin where she has

[1] Cf. *Journal des Débats*, 23 Dec., 1822; *Moniteur Universel*, 22 Dec., 1822.

been tenderly cared for. One day she is insulted in the street, and to her surprise finds herself defended by a young stranger who, as a result of his interference, is challenged to a duel. Trying to separate the two adversaries, Valérie herself receives a dangerous wound; from this incident is born the mutual love of Ernest and Valérie. Inspired by love and pity, the young man makes a courageous decision. Leaving sweetheart, family, and country, he goes to Paris to study under a renowned oculist, and there, toward the end of the three years of his study, the death of an uncle has made him sole possessor of an immense fortune. His studies completed, he returns and persuades Valérie to undergo an operation which is to restore her sight, an operation which he himself performs with great success, receiving the hand of the young girl as the reward of his constancy and of the great service he has rendered her.

The success of this sentimental little play was complete, and the story of Valérie drew forth many tears. But the question naturally arises at once: can physical suffering be made the subject of dramatic treatment? Physical infirmities, unlike moral suffering, are not instructive on the stage. Passion is always capable of rousing dramatic interest. But accidental physical suffering, independent of the will, whose existence and whose cure have no relation to our moral being, would seem to belong more to the science of medicine than to the art of the theatre. Probably the picture of physical infirmity can never furnish the subject for a good comedy. The public of 1823 warmly appreciated the play, however, and found as much entertainment in the sad and tender emotions it produced as in the outbursts of gayety aroused by other comedies.

But it is in his longer comedies, those in which he attempts to portray different sections of the life of the French capital as he observed it, that Scribe gives the best measure of his genius. For, though his great claim to success must always remain the tremendous impulse he gave to the development of dramatic technique, one must not lose sight of the fact that his contemporaries regarded him as a very faithful portrayer of the society of the Restoration and of the July Monarchy. Scarcely less interesting than his comedies of manners are his political and historical comedies; "Bertrand et Raton, ou l'Art de conspirer," may well be his masterpiece; and while the Romanticists were making much pother over their historical investigations, — the naïve results of which may well be observed in "Henri III et sa Cour," — Scribe was turning, though without prefaces and proclamations, to French and foreign history for interesting dramatic material. Yet, in spite of the popularity of plays like "Le Verre d'Eau" and "Adrienne Lecouvreur," his comedies of manners are the most interesting of his longer plays, for it is in them that we find pictures of the life about him.

THE COMEDIES OF MANNERS

"Le Mariage d'Argent" [1] (1827) was Scribe's first five-act comedy written for the Théâtre-Français. Three classmates from Sainte-Barbe find themselves acciden-

---

[1] Cf. *Constitutionnel*, 6 Dec., 1827; *Moniteur Universel*, 4 and 5 Dec., 1827; *Journal des Débats*, 5 and 7 Dec., 1827; *Globe*, 8 Dec., 1827; *Figaro*, 5 Dec., 1827.

tally reunited in society: Dorbeval, a banker, Olivier, a young painter, and a colonel, Poligny, one of the most inexplicable characters that Scribe has portrayed, and one of the most absurd. Dorbeval is married, and is several times a millionaire; Olivier is a poor but very industrious artist of sober habits; Poligny loves luxury and high society, and considers himself poor with an income of eight or ten thousand francs. Dorbeval, from selfish motives as much as from generosity, offers Poligny the hand of his ward, Hermance, with a dowry of five hundred thousand francs and an office at the Stock Exchange. This Hermance is a young lady without an idea in her head, who talks constantly (and absurdly) about marriage, dowries, wedding presents, and boxes at the opera; nevertheless, Poligny accepts Hermance's hand and her dowry. Meanwhile he cherishes the memory of a woman whom he has loved before her marriage, and whom, as a matter of fact, he still loves. This lady, Madame de Brienne, conveniently arrives in Act II from the depths of Russia, where Monsieur de Brienne had left her a widow, and Poligny's love for her is rekindled. At the same time, however, his fiancée's income maintains its hold over his heart. Olivier, the artist, is in love with this noble widow also, but when he asks her to marry him, she refuses.

At this juncture Dorbeval discovers his wife reading a letter from one Monsieur de Nangis, an invisible character who stays behind the scenes throughout the play, and to save her friend's honor Madame de Brienne assumes responsibility for the letter, declaring it had been written to her. When Poligny hears of this incident, he at once assumes that Madame de Brienne has been faithless to him, in spite of a very positive declaration by her to the contrary, and in spite of a fidelity which has withstood the snows of Russia. Madame Dorbeval, however, confesses to the colonel that the letter was really for her, and thereupon Poligny returns contritely to Madame de Brienne. But he is now a stockbroker and must pay for his office. Tossed back and forth between love and cupidity, and not knowing that Madame de Brienne, in good Gymnase fashion, has just inherited 900,000 francs, he suddenly declares to her that he no longer loves her and has decided to marry Hermance for her money. Madame de Brienne, when she sees that Poligny has sacrificed her love to his own selfish interests, indignantly offers her hand to Olivier, the artist.

The announcement of the production of "Le Mariage d'Argent" had created the liveliest interest among the theatre-going public. For several years Scribe had been making the fortune of the Gymnase and of the Vaudeville; had drawn back the public to the Opéra-Comique; had created at the Opéra a ballet whose programme, for the first time independent of the choreographic execution, could upon a mere reading claim the honors of an interesting and clever drama; and at the Théâtre-Français had made a trial in the touching drama of "Valérie." The first performance of "Le Mariage d'Argent" was consequently an event of the first importance, and everyone was eager to know what impression the play would make. Although the first two acts were received with unanimous applause, the author's luck changed with the third act, the parterre first making itself heard by murmurs of disapproval and later expressing its feelings by whistling and hissing. At the second performance, also, the theatre was packed. The diversity of opinion occasioned by the first performance had aroused great curiosity, real connoisseurs wishing to fix their opinion of a work which had been condemned with suspicious haste, and the social world, especially that of the Stock Exchange, eager to see for itself how well an ingenious observer had been able to draw a striking portrait, or to what extent he had failed. At this performance the audience was just, attentive, and impartial, criticizing in silence, approving by spontaneous applause; there was no cabal, either for or against the author, and the success of the play was as decisive as it had been the evening before uncertain.

The title of the play announced nothing very new, for in many plays, beginning with "Tartuffe," "Les Femmes savantes," and "L'Avare," we see marriages projected, successfully or otherwise, for financial reasons. All the intriguers and rascals who under various names have appeared upon the French stage are rascals chiefly because they exploit the imbecility of some rich Cassander, or because they are aiming at the fortune of some young heiress or some disappointed dowager. Scribe's play had the misfortune to come after "L'Agiotage," by Picard and Empis (1826), "Le Spéculateur," by Riboutté (1826), "L'Argent," by Casimir Bonjour (1826), and "Les trois Quartiers," by Picard and Mazères (1827); and though money was undoubtedly the idol of the day, people were naturally weary of hearing it discussed so frequently at the theatre. This circumstance of course had some influence upon the general effect of the new play.

The treatment of the subject of "Le Mariage d'Argent," however, gives evidence of great inventive power in the author and shows him to be extremely well-trained in his art. The subject is a very difficult one to treat, the greatest problem lying in the character of Poligny, whose conduct has to be motivated without being made odious. It is not clear why Scribe made him a military man, for it is generally supposed that the career of arms develops other habits than that of low cupidity. Other antecedents would perhaps have been more fortunate. And yet Poligny, sacrificing his real love to selfish interest, is at heart loyal and generous, a man who, as the result of a moment of unreflection and because of his imprudent desire to enrich himself quickly, is forced to be false to his principles, to sacrifice an honorable passion from which alone he could expect happiness, and to acquire the splendor of a huge fortune at the price of domestic happiness.

This situation inevitably produces in the play an atmosphere of constraint and a certain malaise. At the theatre one prefers clear-cut, pronounced characters; capitulations of duty to interest are always disagreeable. And yet, assuming that comedy is the mirror of society, it would be wise, before condemning the image, to see whether it is a faithful one. As a matter of fact, there seems to be a tendency to assume that a man can never subordinate his real feelings to the force of circumstances; to assume that because he is honest, he must be strong, and that, placed before the alternative of misery and dishonor on the one hand, and on the other that which can save him from both, he must, under the risk of encountering the disapproval of the audience, courageously embrace poverty. According to the rules of ethics, his choice is not doubtful. But on the stage a character should be neither totally vicious nor absolutely irreproachable. It is on this model that the character of Poligny seems to be drawn. He loves, and is loved in return; but caught in the net of speculation, he loses the woman who would have made him happy, marries one whom he can neither love nor esteem, and is thus punished by his own weakness.

Madame de Brienne is noble and interesting, her character well established and well sustained. There is evidence of much art and shrewd psychology in the author's portrayal of the successive impressions aroused in her by Poligny's coldness, his tenderness, his feigned jealousy, his artifice concerning his marriage, his selfish perfidy, and his disloyal conduct. But the author passes the limits of *vraisemblance* when he makes Olivier, Poligny's rival, his champion, and when he makes Madame de Brienne, with really excessive generosity, offer her entire fortune to Poligny, who is to marry Hermance, and give only her hand to Olivier, who adores her. Her generosity is open to criticism ethically, and is no less indefensible from a dramatic point of view.

The character of Dorbeval, the banker, is quite unreal. It is of course possible to make a fortune at the Bourse without being a man of genius, but Dorbeval's tone and manner are not those of his century. Whereas the banker in Picard and Mazères's "Les trois Quartiers" is vain and ridiculous, a real financier of the Restoration, Dorbeval is a financier of the Regency, a Turcaret, heavy, coarse, thick-witted. And yet Scribe makes him the mouthpiece of his wit, and his facetiousness is inexhaustible. It would have been permissible to make him as stupid as all financiers are on the stage, — that is a convention which is probably as good as many others, — but it was unnecessary to make him so fantastically vulgar and common. It was a clever idea, however, to portray a fool who succeeds in all his undertakings, and who at the end of the play has completely won his game.

His wife, who has some traits in common with the countess in "Le Mariage de Figaro," does not always display in the expression of her troubles and sorrows all the delicacy and restraint one would expect from such a rôle. Madame Dorbeval would be an entirely useless *hors-d'œuvre* if Scribe had not imagined for her an intrigue, the hero of which remains unseen, to excite Poligny's jealousy. Here the methods seem strained, and the invention unfortunate. The rôle of Hermance, the Dorbevals' young ward, is the sketch of a figure for which there may have been models; but it is too devoid of the charm which is frequently found in naïve coquettishness; it is clear that the author felt obliged to portray a young lady of very bad training, in order to show that she would make a poor wife. Des Granges, in "La Comédie et les Mœurs, 1815–1848," speaks highly of this character, however:

Étudiez encore le caractère d'Hermance, l'ingénue du monde financier, qui joue la comédie de société (et quelle comédie!), le rôle de Fanchette dans le Mariage de Figaro, et qui accepte l'inconnu de la veille, heureuse de penser qu'elle dominera son mari de toute l'importance de sa dot. Rien de forcé dans ce personnage qui est bien de son monde et de son temps.

This play is a dramatic conception which could have sprung only from a talent trained to overcome many difficulties. The subject is carefully studied in all its parts, and marked dexterity shows itself in most of the combinations. Yet after a few performances it inspired but little interest; the characters seemed overdrawn, the

plot not brilliantly developed, the "moral lesson" un-
apparent, and the cleverness scattered through the dialogue insufficient to conceal the excessive length and
inutility of certain developments. There is evidence of
the neglect of certain rules and exigencies from which the
Comédie-Française was not yet freed. There is more
talk than action; and action, in a five-act play, can never
be replaced by even the most delightful conversation.
The tone of the dialogue itself is not precisely that of real
comedy, for tirades and declamations abound and frequently stop the forward movement of the play, so that
one has the impression of being read to from a novelist or
a moralist. In a comedy the characters, not the author,
should do the talking. The exposition of the subject in
the first act is insufficient; Act II presents a new exposition which involves repetition; and it is only in the third
act that the action is engaged and complicated, and then
it is by means which, as I have said, seem too unnatural
for credulity. There is great art, however, in the manner
in which the dénoûment is prepared for and developed.
There was a revival of the play twenty years later, in
1847, and Théophile Gautier, writing in the "Presse,"
seems to think more highly of it than at the time of its
first performances: "Le Mariage d'Argent est la pièce du
spirituel et fécond vaudevilliste qui se rapproche le plus
de la haute comédie, de la comédie humaine et sérieuse."
Des Granges comes to the conclusion that in 1847 society
was better able to understand and appreciate the play
than it had been in 1827.

To those who had thought that Scribe, when he decided to do so, would be able to compose a good comedy
of manners and of characters, as Piron wrote "La Mé-

tromanie" after having composed songs for the fairs, this play was a disappointment. The public had hoped that in going from the Gymnase to the Théâtre-Français Scribe would completely change his manner. Unfortunately such a change is difficult, and in the nineteenth century rather rare; for, though "Le Cid," "Cinna," "Polyeucte," and "Nicomède" are conceived each one in a different system, and though Molière created or employed almost as many dramatic forms as he produced plays, the method of writers in Scribe's time was different. Scribe, in writing "Le Mariage d'Argent," had merely enlarged his framework, for the play is essentially a *comédie-vaudeville*. Yet this error of an adroit craftsman is easily explained. In remaining a *vaudevilliste* Scribe was perhaps yielding less to habit than to the demands of public taste. When he began his career, the better elements of the theatre-going public were tired of the *flonflons* of the Empire, and of the ineptitudes of the Théâtre Montansier; Scribe appeared and created a new genre, the *comédie-vaudeville*. At that time comedy, frozen by classical decorum or mutilated by the censorship, was dull, banal, and lifeless, and real comedy, or what most closely resembled it, was thus to be found only at the Gymnase. At each new sketch by the indefatigable writer, the audience exclaimed: "There is more real comedy in this play than in the tiresome novelties of the Théâtre-Français." And the audience was right. But the time had not yet come when Scribe was able to do more than force the tone of his *vaudevilles*, brighten the coloring, prolong the situations, and design the characters a little more vividly.

La Bruyère says somewhere that, if those for whom we weep after their death were to return to earth after a short time, they would be astonished at the welcome they would receive. The same thought is to be found in La Fontaine's naïve story of the matron of Ephesus, and in the charming little story of the Jeune Veuve, whose grief is apparently inconsolable, and who after a year says to her father: "Où est donc le jeune mari que vous m'avez promis?" "Les Inconsolables," [1] produced at the Thé-âtre-Français in 1829, is nothing else than La Fontaine's story, without the frank gayety of the fabulist. Late in the century, Hervieu developed the same theme in "Le Réveil." We see one of those lightning changes of affec-tion which delighted Marivaux, but in "Les Inconso-lables" there is neither the skillful preparation which characterizes "Les fausses Confidences," nor that rapid succession of accidents and tricks which forces Araminte to yield in spite of herself. A sentimental *comédie-vaude-ville*, "Les Inconsolables" cannot be said to add any force to Scribe's claims as a dramatist.

Scribe could scarcely have been expected not to try his hand at the kind of horrible drama which for some time had been popular at the Parisian theatres, as the result of an imperious demand for violent emotions. Plays like "La Tour de Nesle," "Antony," and "Lucrèce Borgia," are sufficient indication of the taste of the public at that time. Perhaps, also, Scribe was tired of hearing every-thing he wrote dismissed as pretty; he may have wanted to show that he could be as terrifying as the others. If so, it must be said that he was eminently successful in "Dix Ans de la Vie d'une Femme, ou les Mauvais Con-seils" (1832).[2] The thematic idea of the play is the same

---

[1] Cf. *Figaro*, 9 Dec., 1829.

[2] Cf. *Temps*, 19 March, 1832; *Constitutionnel*, 26 March, 1832; *Journal des Débats*, 19 March, 1832; *Revue de Paris*, vol. xxxvi, p. 257.

as that of "Les Liaisons dangereuses," a novel by
Laclos which was the complement of those of Crébillon
fils. Laclos's book was the history of the social degrada-
tion of an epoch, and a picture of its vice; moreover, it
was a sort of revelation of the future, and it was to that
fact, chiefly, and to the terror which it inspired, that it
owed its immense popularity. Scribe's attempt can
hardly be said to have had the same elements of success;
for the spectacle of manners which are definitely alien to
those of the onlooker can at the most create only an interest of curiosity; it cannot arouse passionate interest.

"Dix Ans de la Vie d'une Femme, ou les Mauvais
Conseils" is curious as the expression of a talent futilized
by the task of creating something foreign to it and beyond its powers. In this play we see a woman of the social
world, who, as the result of a domestic quarrel, punishes
her husband by being faithless to him, and who, after the
scandal of a separation, instead of repenting, prefers to
lead the life of a kept woman; who, sinking one stage
lower, joins forces in a house of ill-repute with a villain
who exploits the remains of her beauty; and who finally
dies of consumption brought on by "exposure to the
night air." In addition to this prostitute, there is another
woman, chosen from the same class of society, the wife of
a banker, who lends her apartments to adulterous rendezvous, and eventually takes up the same trade as her
friend.

Scribe's justification to the ethical mind is that vice was
never more cruelly punished than in this play. Yet not
for one moment is his Adèle interesting. In order to
appeal to the audience, she should have been really a
victim of bad advice, a victim to be pitied rather than

ostracized; and to make her "sympathetic," Scribe should have represented her as being very passionate and at the same time really virtuous. Instead, she is heartless, vain, selfish, passionless, and consequently not in need of evil counsel to bring about her débâcle. By nature she is so bad and so exceptional that her example is of no moral consequence. Manon Lescaut, whom the perverted eighteenth century considered scandalous, was a model of honor and virtue compared with Adèle, for she had at least one virtue, that of her love; she despised herself each time that through her horror of poverty she betrayed her lover. Madame de Merteuil, in Laclos's "Les Liaisons dangereuses," was at least energetic in her disorderly life, and was, besides, the victim of her violently passionate temperament. Even the eighteenth century, that period of disenchantment, never conceived the idea of a woman devoid both of virtue and of passion, debasing herself without pleasure and without emotion. (A real drama is found in Drouineau's novel, "Le Manuscrit vert," in which two sisters are described, one born with dispositions toward evil, but heroically correcting her own character; the other, with better instincts, degrading herself as the result of weakly following evil advice.) Madame Dorval, who played the part of Adèle at the first performance of Scribe's play, was so ashamed of her rôle that during the fourth act she left the stage, and it was only upon the insistent demand of the audience that she was willing to return, weeping. There is, however, one scene in the play which is really strong and dramatic. Adèle's family is assembled for tea; her husband quietly relates the story of a man basely deceived by his wife, and then asks each one what he would do in the husband's

place. Adèle's sister replies: "Je pardonnerais à ma
femme." The sister's fiancé says: "Moi, je la tuerais."
"Je lui ôterais tous ses cachemires," adds an old aunt.
"Et moi," says the father, "je la rendrais à sa famille."
"Eh bien! je vous la rends," cries Darcey; "c'est
Adèle." This scene is effective, and worthy of the elder
Dumas. The character of Adèle is in certain respects
similar to that of Séraphine in Augier's "Les Lionnes
pauvres."

An ancient truth which Boileau deplored, after Horace,
and which Pascal himself admitted as *une chose raison-
nable*, is that society is founded upon money, thinks only
of money, and that a little more or a little less money is
the only real difference between one man and another.
But because money is the greatest of social powers, it
does not necessarily follow that money in itself can furnish a dramatic idea; and in "La Passion secrète"
(1834) [1] Scribe made the mistake of thinking that, because it moves the world, it will suffice to fill the framework of a little comedy. How many *vaudevilles* and
comedies he had already constructed upon money! He
had studied the human heart in all phases of its reaction
to money; and when by chance he had not made money
the moving force of his comedies, he had replaced it by
the most positive personal interest, representing the en-
joyments money can procure. In "La Passion secrète"
there is no mysterious love, as the title might lead one to
expect, and the play should have been called "La Femme
de Bourse." Unfortunately he has selected an exceptional woman, and has attacked an individuality so rare
that it is not worthy of being put on the stage. Had he

[1] Cf. *Journal des Débats*, 15 March, 1834.

made of this folly a mere episode, the choice would have been defensible; but as the subject of an entire comedy it is impossible. Madame Dulistel finds that even after her marriage she still loves Léopold de Mondeville, and to cure herself of this love gives herself up to a passion for bouillotte, and later to playing at the Bourse. At first moderate and cautious, she soon becomes so entangled in her speculations, most of which have turned out unfavorably, that she finds herself in debt to the amount of 50,000 francs. Having no money herself, and not daring to confess the situation to her husband, she takes 40,000 francs which she holds in trust for her sister's dowry, and 5,000 francs entrusted to her by an old servant — an arrangement which very nearly prevents her sister's marriage; for at the contract ceremony she finds herself unable to present the 40,000 francs. Except for Léopold, who has sincerely fallen in love with the sister, to whom he has been betrothed, and who generously consents to give up the dowry, Madame Dulistel would have been the cause of her sister's life-long unhappiness.

The secret passion of Madame Dulistel, then, is the love of money, avarice disguised under the form of gambling at the Bourse; a passion absolutely foreign to the tender and noble sentiments of the human heart. For two hours the audience hears nothing but bouillotte, income, Spanish and Haitian loans. The stage requires convention, even exaggeration, and when an author represents love, hate, or vengeance, he may safely develop these passions to excess; for we accept violence and fury, even madness, when we are transported into a supernatural world, unrelated to the reality of human things, and when we are interested only in the dramatic truth.

But if an author bases his plot upon the most positive thing in the world, upon the object whose value is best known to everyone; if he talks to the spectator of that which constantly occupies his thoughts, which he acquires with the utmost difficulty and husbands with the greatest care; then he places before him a mathematical certainty from which he cannot escape. The author can no longer afford to exaggerate even the slightest detail. No one of the indispensable conventions is allowed him, for the spectator is no longer at the theatre, in an ideal world, but at home, before his bank-book, calculating. At each word the actor pronounces, the spectator tears to shreds the products of the author's imagination; and a man who would applaud the murder of a rival, loses his temper if the hero lends a large sum of money to an unhappy friend who has nothing but mortgages to give as security.

In "Les Indépendants" (1837) Dhennebon, an accountant, is tired of his work and longs for independence, while his wife considers that a certain amount of restraint and responsibility is not only salutary but necessary. A friend of Dhennebon, du Rouvrai by name, a radical deputy, persuades him to leave his office, to buy a certain number of railway stocks, and thus assure himself a fortune. Meanwhile Madame Dhennebon's sister Esther, who five years before has refused Edgar, a noble young soldier, and who has gone to Brittany to live with an old aunt in order to be independent, returns to Paris for no other reason than to hunt a husband, preferably Edgar. After many ups and downs a marriage is arranged between Esther and Edgar; Dhennebon, who has narrowly escaped losing everything in his speculation, is only too glad to return to his office; and du Rouvrai, who considers himself so independent, finds two mistresses and a spendthrift ward more expensive and exacting than a wife and family, and decides to marry.

In writing this play Scribe had clearly a serious object. He was trying to satirize, in all its many forms, one of the central evils of the period, that hatred of all restraint and of all law, which might almost have threatened the dissolution of society. He has pursued this evil in the political order and in the social world in the persons of the radical deputy and of the "free woman." There is no doubt that at the end of the play these two characters are badly battered, but it is doubtful whether he has conceived them as they really were, and whether the adversaries over whom he has triumphed resembled those whom the reader or the spectator might have expected him to attack. If radical tendencies in politics were represented only by individuals such as du Rouvrai, — quarrelsome, boasting, indiscreet, and innocent of ideas, — we should expect no government to attach the slightest importance to them. The marriage institution is menaced in this play by nothing more serious than the caprice of a young girl who, at the age of twenty, refuses a husband in a moment of vanity, and who before she is twenty-five already regrets her folly and is hunting one with all her strength and all her resources. A resolution to combat the "enemies of society" would have been no doubt most praiseworthy, but it can scarcely be said that Scribe has accomplished this object in "Les Indépendants." Certain critics remarked that as a defender of society Scribe reminded them of La Fontaine's lines:

> Rien n'est si dangereux qu'un imprudent ami;
> Mieux vaudrait un sage ennemi;

and that possibly George Sand herself had not done more harm to the marriage institution than Scribe in this play.

In one of his plays Molière suggests a number of portraits which are lacking in his comic gallery and which he intends to paint later. Among other subjects he cites calumny, a subject eminently dramatic and moral, in which the facts of private life can be mingled with the events of public life and combined for the interest and movement of the stage. Molière left this idea to his successors, and Scribe seized upon the precious legacy, which he treated with great success in "La Calomnie." This play, written in 1840, is based upon Bazile's famous definition of scandal:

La calomnie, monsieur! j'ai vu les plus honnêtes gens près d'en être accablés. Croyez qu'il n'y a pas de plates méchancetés, pas d'horreurs, pas de conte absurde, qu'on ne fasse adopter aux oisifs d'une grande ville, en s'y prenant bien. D'abord un bruit léger, rasant le sol, comme l'hirondelle avant l'orage, pianissimo, murmure et file, et sème en courant le trait empoisonné: telle bouche le recueille, et piano, piano, vous le glisse à l'oreille adroitement. Le mal est fait, il germe, il rampe, il chemine, et rinforzando de bouche en bouche, il va le diable; puis tout à coup, on ne sait comment, vous voyez la calomnie se dresser, siffler, s'enfler, se grandir, à vue d'œil. Elle s'élance, prend son vol, tourbillonne, enveloppe, arrache, entraîne, et tonne, et devient, grâce au ciel, un cri général, un crescendo, un chorus universel de haine et de proscriptions. Qui diable y résisterait?

The scene of "La Calomnie" (1840)[1] is laid at the Casino at Dieppe, where the members of the family of the Marquise de Savenay are gathered for the marriage of her niece and ward, Cécile, to Lucien, a talented and ambitious young deputy. Madame de Savenay, an old

---

[1] Cf. *Constitutionnel*, 22 Feb., 1840; *Moniteur Universel*, 24 Feb., 1840; *Siècle*, 24 Feb., 1840; *Temps*, 24 Feb., 1840; *Journal des Débats*, 22 Feb., 1840; *Presse*, 22 Feb., 1840; *Figaro*, 5 Nov., 1857.

dowager whose ideas are still those of 1814, and who speaks of the "usurper" and the "Corsican ogre," shares her guardianship of Cécile with Raymond, a friend of the young girl's father, who has recently become Prime Minister, partly because of his talent and partly as a result of the July Revolution. He himself loves Cécile, but his forty-five years and the demands of business and politics seem to him to be too great obstacles. Raymond has also a sister, Madame Guibert, a coquette, jealous and ambitious, whose only occupation is to tarnish the reputation of other women by her evil remarks. Madame Guibert takes precedence over her husband, who is really only her protégé, her broker, and her scandal agent, by business a banker, at present soliciting from his brother-in-law the portfolio of finance. Among the guests there is also the Viscount de Saint-André, a diplomatic apprentice, who studies his international law in drawing-rooms and actresses' dressing-rooms, a lion of the theatrical and social world, who has come to Dieppe for a rest from his conquests and pleasures, and to escape from his mistresses and creditors.

Cécile, overhearing a number of the Casino guests and employees attacking Raymond's character, accusing him, among other things, of mistreating his father, because of his humble origin, and of making money out of his brother-in-law's tenure of the Ministry of Finance, takes his defense so warmly and so eloquently that the idlers and gossipers spread the report that she is the Prime Minister's mistress, a report which Madame Guibert herself takes little pains to deny. When the Viscount de Saint-André is seen talking to Cécile, the rumor now arises that he too has been, or is, her lover, and Guibert, who enjoys being mixed up in gallant affairs, strengthens this supposition by saying that some time previously, at a hotel in Rouen, he has seen Saint-André coming out of Cécile's room early in the morning. Lucien, kindly informed of this report, asks the Marquise to explain the slander, telling her that she has been accused of tolerating her niece's guilty relations with the Prime Minister, receiving a handsome pension as the reward of her complaisance. This so outrages the Marquise that, instead of defending Cécile, she says that where there is smoke there must be some fire, and reproaches the poor girl violently for her thoughtlessness, frivolity, and indiscretion. Raymond, in Lucien's name, now demands an explanation from Saint-André; and although the young diplomatist at first refuses to discuss the matter, he finally admits to Raymond that, whereas he had told Guibert that it was Cécile's room he had been seen to leave, he had in reality been coming from an amorous rendezvous with Madame Guibert herself. Lucien, hearing this confession, which justifies Cécile but dishonors his friend's sister, hesitates to marry her, for fear of what people will say. Seeing Cécile thus threatened again, Raymond, in order to silence the slander, surprises everyone by asking her to marry him. As Cécile has secretly been in love with him for some time, she joyfully accepts this offer, and is thus justified in the eyes of all.

This play was received enthusiastically. The "Presse" relates that for several weeks before the first performance Parisian society had been discussing almost nothing else. The announcement of the first performance of "La Calomnie," postponed from day to day, upset social arrangements to such an extent that all invitations were conditional: if one was invited to dinner, he accepted only upon condition that the dinner should not interfere with the opening performance of the new play. Naturally, certain portions of the press were decidedly hostile. Théophile Gautier called the play "le néant le plus pur qu'on puisse obtenir"; but as usual his criticism reduces itself largely to a discussion of the style, "car sans style rien n'existe au théâtre, et le style de Scribe ne va pas au-delà de la conversation la plus lâche." He even said that Scribe ought to stop writing for the Théâtre-Français, "parce qu'il est entièrement dépourvu de style, condition indispensable pour un théâtre littéraire." The same critic advised him to quit writing for the Opéra, because he was totally ignorant of the mechanism of verse and of the laws of prosody; yet his unparalleled, almost incredible success as a librettist shows, as we shall see, that, in spite of constant difficulties occasioned by the demands of his musical collaborators, he was capable of composing dramatic and inspiring verses. Certain journals, however, notably the "Constitutionnel," the "Moniteur Universel," and the "Journal des Débats," were generous in their praise of the new play. The "Siècle" was interested chiefly in the political features of "La Calomnie," contending that, whereas political comedy had heretofore been a satire on government, Scribe had conceived it differently from Aristophanes, praising those in power "avec un zèle qui, en des jours moins rebelles aux dotations et aux subventions, serait digne de plusieurs croix d'honneur."

As political questions, before everything else, interested the public of the period in which Scribe wrote "La Calomnie," he has painted, from his point of view of

course, the political manners of the reign of Louis-
Philippe. There is no doubt that the success of the play
was due largely to its topical character, and that a recent
public scandal partly explains the interest it aroused.
The very title, significant but vague, had stimulated the
curiosity of the public. The spectators thought they
recognized Thiers, then in the plenitude of his powers, influence, and renown, in Raymond, this son of a wine-
grower, who had become Prime Minister; and certainly,
although Scribe has not painted a perfect portrait of the
man then in power, he has borrowed a number of striking
and characteristic features. Raymond, who, sprung from
the people, becomes Prime Minister; who is accused of
being an ungrateful son and of driving his father from
Paris because he is ashamed of him; who is suspected of
sharing the emoluments of the high financial position to
which he has raised his brother-in-law — this Raymond
was certainly taken from a story of contemporary politics
which had been published in a score of opposition journals and discussed in the corridors of both Chambers.
Des Granges considers the character of Raymond exceedingly well-drawn.

Où il faut louer sans marchander le talent d'observation de Scribe,
c'est quand il représente les tracas inséparables d'une situation
officielle sous un régime parlementaire. Aucune pièce contemporaine, que je sache, ne contient sur ce sujet un meilleur ensemble
de faits et de formules que le premier acte de la Calomnie. Insinua-
tions, délation, interprétation malveillante du passé, du présent,
d'un écrit, d'un geste; recherche minutieuse de tout ce qui peut
dégrader l'homme au pouvoir; plaintes de ceux qu'il ne veut pas
favoriser, exigences de ceux qu'il a déjà comblés de ses dons; en-
quête sournoise sur sa vie privée; ne vivons-nous pas dans un temps
où tout ce manège continue à se pratiquer? Scribe, en pleine monarchie de Juillet, assistait à l'organisation de ces mœurs politiques;
il pouvait voir un Guizot, un Molé, un Casimir-Périer, en butte aux

plus absurdes imputations; il constatait que l'opinion publique, loin de repousser la calomnie, l'acceptait avec joie, la multipliait par les bavardages de la presse et les conversations de café. La Calomnie — intrigue à part — est une belle, honnête et courageuse comédie. Qui sait si la Calomnie, représentée aujourd'hui devant des spectateurs qui lisent avidement chaque matin tant d'articles de diffamation et de chantage, n'obtiendrait pas un succès inattendu? Le type du ministre, Raymond, n'est pas du tout démodé; je vous affirme qu'il est tout aussi vivant que le Vaudrey de M. Jules Claretie.

The central idea of the play is cleverly followed out, and is developed in an entertaining plot. The slander which arises against Cécile is occasioned by two good actions: it is because she has so eagerly justified Raymond's probity, and because she has obtained from him a little financial aid for some poor sailors, that she is thought to be his mistress. Thus to give virtue itself as the origin of the calumny was a very happy idea. Though the first two acts are long and full of senile jokes, the real action beginning only at the end of Act II, the whole of Act III is very interesting; Act IV, in the scene of the viscount's revelation, in the misadventure of the banker forced to eat the bitter fruit of the slander which he himself has spread, and in the dramatic situation where Madame Guibert's guilt is revealed by accident, shows great dramatic resourcefulness; in Act V, the surprise and the striking effect produced by Raymond's proposal, ignorant of Cécile's feeling for him, are evidence of a keen sense of dramatic values. The dénoûment, conditioned as it is by Raymond's character, is simple and dramatic. "La Calomnie" recalls Marmontel's celebrated anecdote of the cup of chocolate and Gresset's "Le Méchant," as well as the two plays on "Le Médisant," Destouches's and Gosse's, and anticipates Hervieu's "Les Paroles restent."

The subject treated by Scribe in "Une Chaîne" (1841) had often tempted the novelist and the dramatist; from Benjamin Constant's "Adolphe" to Scribe's play, many dramas and many novels had been written upon this eternal weakness of the human heart, ashamed of a bond it cannot break. There must be in this episode of passion something profoundly real, for it has almost always happily inspired the authors who have treated it. "Une Chaîne" is a variant of the eternal triangle story. Emmeric, a young musician, falls in love with the wealthy woman, the Countess de Saint-Géran, who has helped him to his first success, and who becomes his mistress. Unfortunately for the countess, Emmeric's love cools, and the liaison becomes an irksome bond for him, particularly when he falls in love with his own cousin, Aline, whom, as a matter of fact, his family wants him to marry. After a period of deception, hesitation, and complications, he breaks with the countess, who, in spite of her unhappiness, finally is able to forgive him; and, thus released, he marries his cousin.

The exposition in Act I is well developed, showing us all the characters; in Act II the various threads of the story are interwoven; at the end of Act III the drama begins to develop, giving the spectator reasons to fear for the destiny of the real comedy, as the action for a time threatens to become miserably pathetic; and yet, although Act IV continues this unfortunate arrangement, the author succeeds, by the use of a simple and worn-out trick, in reëstablishing the real comedic character and

jovial humor of the play; Act V sums up touchingly all
the emotions of the drama, and the dénoûment is most
ingeniously and delicately accomplished. Two of the
characters are particularly interesting and well-drawn:
Baladard, the lawyer, who is constantly being tricked by
someone and who is always amusing, and the Admiral
Count de Saint-Géran, who, in spite of the fact that he
too is tricked, inspires esteem and fear. Scribe's skill is
apparent in the sympathy he gains for the admiral, making the audience love and honor this betrayed husband.
The character of the countess, save for a few traits which
appear early in the play, is decent and well-drawn; her
love and jealousy are touching without verging upon the
drame larmoyant.

Although it offered great difficulties, the main idea of
the play is just and dramatic. The subject was one which
could be successfully treated on the stage only if it were
developed with great delicacy, for the author had to ob-
serve all the proprieties without thereby altering the
morality of the subject and the force of the situations.
Although the difficulties have not been entirely overcome,
they have at least been glossed over. The struggle between an old passion and a new love, the hero's hesitation
between his feelings of gratitude and tenderness, on the
one hand, and the duties involved in marriage, on the
other, are presented in a touching and natural way.

A very interesting, and, for the period, very realistic
play by Mazères and Empis, "Une Liaison" (1834), had
dealt with the same theme; it was received with indifference, even disapproval, by the public. Mazères himself, many years later, in speaking of his play, of Scribe's
"Une Chaîne," and of "La Dame aux Camélias," said:

Une Liaison est venue vingt-cinq ans trop tôt. J'ose dire que nos jeunes imitateurs prêtent à leur héroïne un parfum attrayant, une auréole presque mystique, qui demandent en quelque sorte faveur pour ses vices, tandis que nous avons eu la brutalité de peindre la nôtre telle que sont toutes ses pareilles.

If there is one quality which cannot be denied to Scribe, a quality which is important for the dramatist, it is the address with which he could, at just the right moment, seize upon a vice or folly of his epoch and make it the object of satire upon the stage. He never ran ahead of his time in choosing subjects, but waited for them, and when the proper time came, attacked them boldly and triumphed over them with the hearty applause of the public. Instead of working for a cenacle composed of a few superior spirits who despised the *profanum vulgus*, — for he knew his art too well and had practised it too long, — he employed all the resources of his ingenious nature, fertile in theatrical combinations, in rendering to the public what he had borrowed from the public. "Le Puff, ou Mensonge et Vérité" (1848) [1] illustrates his method. The word *puff* expresses the charlatanism by means of which, in all classes of society, lies are sown by those who wish to acquire importance, and by means of which people are made to believe in something which does not exist. While the thing represented by *puff* had existed for a long time, the word itself, of Anglo-American origin, was imported into France toward the end of the reign of Louis-Philippe, where increasing publicity had brought it new fortunes. It was upon the false reports spread by *puff* that many people based all their hopes; by it some

[1] Cf. *Journal des Débats*, 24 Jan., 1848; *Presse*, 24 Jan., 1848; *Siècle*, 24 Jan., 1848; *Moniteur Universel*, 26 Jan., 1848; *Constitutionnel*, 24 Jan., 1848.

were raised to great heights, others brought low. It was the guiding spirit of office-seekers, who attributed to themselves qualities they did not possess. At times it was employed to attract attention to a person who, for some reason or other, had an interest in standing out from the crowd. One of the best definitions of the word is that of Jules Janin:

Le puff, l'œuvre immense de la blague européenne, le bruit de chaque matin, l'annonce de chaque jour, le mensonge flamboyant de tout ce qui se vend, de tout ce qui s'achète, de tout ce qui s'invente de puéril et de solennel, une comète et une chandelle. Le puff, c'est-à-dire la vapeur appliquée au succès de l'infiniment petit et de l'infiniment ridicule, un si laid métier qu'il ferait peur si l'on ne prenait pas le bon parti de rire aux éclats; un piège vil à ce point que l'on se pendrait de honte si l'on n'y tombait qu'une fois; mais comme on y tombe tous les jours, à toute heure, à chaque instant, comme le puff se respire dans l'air, dans le bruit, dans le silence, on s'en fiche et l'on se console en voyant la mine piteuse du voisin.

"Le Puff" is more than a comedy; it is a cruel and acidulous satire, without violence, it is true, but not without courage. Like most of Scribe's plays, it is exceedingly well constructed, and although long and complicated, it contains so many amusing incidents and unexpected *péripéties* that the spectator's interest never lags. Yet — and this is what gives the play its significance — the author has given more attention to the painting of manners and to the portrayal of character than to the development of the plot. From the point of view of dramatic art, "Le Puff" marks a transformation in his manner. Whereas in most of his earlier plays the follies and vices which figure therein serve chiefly as pretexts for dramatic situations, here the contrary is true: the observation is more important than the dramatic interest, and the subject dominates the action. Scribe directs his attacks on charlatanism chiefly against two characters: one an odious bluestocking, Corinne Desgaudets, an insolent, *galante* spinster, a combination of harpy and poetess — Cathos, Madelon, Bélise, and the Countess d'Escarbagnas all in one; the other, the Count de Marignan, a would-be statesman and literary impostor, who has published under his own name the memoirs of a general of the African wars. Grouped around these two frauds are a number of lesser tricksters, the three most interesting being Corinne's father, who has acquired money, renown, and social standing, merely by a skillful pretense of being wealthy; a young broker, whose dubious transactions dissipate his sister's dowry; and a venal publisher, of doubtful probity.

Scribe's heroine, Corrine Desgaudets, is one of his most successful characters. Out of the *femme savante*, the ridiculous type scourged by Molière, a sickening mixture of the evil passions of man and the vanity of woman, out of the bluestocking satirized by Byron, he has succeeded in making a portrait which is at once lifelike and acceptable. A grotesque and curious conception, which would have frightened anyone but Scribe, it is one of the boldest portraits he has ever traced, and one which is most to his credit. While Corinne is a very cleverly portrayed personality, she is one which defies any attempt at identification, for even in his most excited moments Scribe never deals with personalities; his kindliness and urbanity would have refused any such easy success.

At the end of the play Corinne has married her count, whom she has pursued relentlessly through five acts; the unprincipled editor has been made a knight of the Legion of Honor; the young gambler is an esteemed millionaire;

and the literary impostor and would-be statesman has been received into the Académie des Inscriptions, the Académie des Sciences Morales, and even the Académie Française ("la seule qui compte," — says Scribe, with fitting and pardonable pride). And they all owe their happiness and advancement to persistent and well-organized charlatanism.

Never had Scribe been bolder than in this play. It is at once an interesting comedy and a Satire Ménippée. He combined enthusiasm and invention, biting irony and good-natured criticism, caricature, and portrait. He said what he had to say frankly, boldly, and simply. He seems a different Scribe from the one who wrote "La Demoiselle à marier" and "Les premières Amours," and yet we recognize his adroitness and his good sense. He asserted here his right to speak his mind, a right which he had acquired by years of success and by virtue of the many beautiful scenes and touching lines he had written. An author who speaks the truth can afford to be bold, for he will win the attention, the interest, and the unanimous applause of the public.

The following letter written to Scribe by Bizet shows the extent to which the play was topical, and how audacious the conception seemed to a large portion of the literary public.

ILLUSTRE MAÎTRE: Savez-vous que vous avez fait là un acte d'un grand courage et presque une action téméraire? Mettre l'actualité de la société en scène, placer les vices à la face des vicieux, dire aux journalistes, aux auteurs, aux bas bleus, aux spéculateurs de toutes les sortes qu'ils sont d'infâmes menteurs, d'abominables charlatans, et le prouver, si cela n'est pas une action téméraire, je ne m'y connais plus; mais je dirai et proclamerai par-dessus les toits que c'est l'action d'un parfait honnête homme, d'un homme de cœur et de courage, d'un homme qui a le courage de ses opinions (la chose la plus rare de nos jours), d'un profond philosophe, à qui le ciel a longuement accordé le difficile talent de resserrer les observations de sa philosophie dans les bornes étroites d'un drame, où tout doit avoir de la vie. Une vieille chanson dit que la comédie est un miroir; ce qui me faisait remarquer à notre ami Saintine, placé à côté de moi à la représentation: "Ne vous semble-t-il pas ce soir que ce théâtre est une glace, dans laquelle se reflètent toutes les passions des personnes réunies dans cette salle?" Mais votre comédie n'est pas un miroir, car dans un miroir les figures sont fugaces et disparaissent pour ne laisser qu'une glace avec son étain; on dit que vous avez fixé les images de notre actualité en daguerreotype: elles resteront éternellement dans leur cruelle vérité. On disait, on a dit, on dit encore, que Lesage a merveilleusement tracé quelques ordures dans son Turcaret, auquel on donne encore le nom de chef-d'œuvre. Mais pour être juste, que dira-t-on de votre Puff? Pour mon ̌compte je lui décerne le titre cent fois mieux mérité qu'à l'œuvre de Lesage. J'ose dire que depuis l'apparition de Tartuffe, je ne sache aucune pièce ou les vices ont été mis plus hardiment en scène que dans votre dernier ouvrage.

The popularity of the play was enormous. While Scribe had known more brilliant success, he had never won a more difficult battle. Most of the critics received the play very favorably, although some of them found the subject too unimportant for a five-act piece; even as late as 1848, there still existed a prejudice against Scribe whenever he went beyond the limits of a two-act *vaudeville*. Théophile Gautier found the theme "invraisemblable, fausse et stérile," and was angry because in Act IV Antonia and Corinne dine with Monsieur de Marignan at his home: "et il est garçon." Also he objected to "j'ai été" for "je suis allé." The very shallowness of such criticism nullifies it. He also declared that the play was completely lacking in idealism and enthusiasm. True; but Gautier's reproach itself proves, as Des Granges says, that Scribe has painted the manners of his time, and that his comedies instruct us as to the *état d'âme* of his con-

temporaries. Hippolyte Lucas drew attention to the fact
that while Scribe might have made the mistake of trying
to write "Le Puff" as a political comedy, he made it instead a social comedy, a keen study of manners. The
same critic found that the portraits and pictures were
lifelike and true, and did not hesitate to place "Le Puff"
among the most estimable pieces of the time as a criticism
of manners. Even Scribe's implacable enemy, Jules
Janin, was completely disarmed and made honorable
amends for his past attacks by giving almost unstinted
praise to this piece. "Le Puff" naturally makes one
think of Pailleron's "Cabotins"; but Scribe's play was,
for its period, a better one.

There is in "Les Doigts de Fée" (1858) no particular
interest either of plot, character-drawing, or painting of
manners. It is the story of a poor orphan of noble birth,
neglected and ill-treated at the home of the aunt who has
brought her up, who goes to Paris and earns her living by
dressmaking, later saving her aunt from bankruptcy.
The play called forth a torrent of bitter criticism, almost
abuse, of which the following lines by Jouvin in the
"Figaro" are typical:

M. Scribe est dans son droit. Ce n'est pas à un académicien sur-
mené par l'appât du gain que la critique doit s'en prendre de ce qui
arrive; c'est à l'auditoire qui se fait proxénète en se rendant coupable d'excitation à la débauche sur la personne d'un vieillard. J'ai
assisté à la troisième représentation, j'ai pu me convaincre que la
pièce etait fort goûtée par la très grande majorité du public auquel
elle s'adresse. Le théâtre de M. Scribe est l'expression de la société
bourgeoise du dix-neuvième siècle; ce théâtre subsistera aussi longtemps que la bourgeoisie en littérature sera la forme de l'esprit moderne. Un peuple a toujours la littérature qu'il mérite.

Political and Historical Comedies

Among Scribe's more serious and pretentious plays there are a number in which he satirizes the political manners of his time; others in which he deals with certain historical personages or events, developing ideas which may be taken to represent his philosophy of history; and others in which he uses the historical subject merely as the basis for a complicated plot. "Bertrand et Raton" and "La Camaraderie" are his two political comedies; in "L'Ambitieux" and "Le Verre d'Eau" he illustrates his historical theories; while "Le Fils de Cromwell," "Adrienne Lecouvreur," "Les Contes de la Reine de Navarre," "La Czarine," and "Les trois Maupins" are historical comedies in the style of "Henri III et sa Cour," "Marie Tudor," and "Le Roi s'amuse."

> Bertrand dit à Raton: Frère, il faut aujourd'hui
> Que tu fasses un coup de maître. . . .

These lines of La Fontaine teach us that those who burn their fingers playing with the fire of a revolution are not those who profit most by it, and that bourgeois, artisans, and workmen are very silly to mix in quarrels between political parties: for them the results are broken shop-windows and pillaged counters. Such is the moral of "Bertrand et Raton" (1833).[1] The historical facts upon which the play is written are the following. A sister of George III of England, Princess Caroline Matilda, had married Christian VII of Denmark. Caroline was young, beautiful, pure, and gentle-minded, while her husband, the King, was an abject wretch verging on imbecility.

---

[1] Cf. *Moniteur Universel*, 17 Nov., 1833; *Constitutionnel*, 16 Nov., 1833; *Journal des Débats*, 19 and 22 Nov., 1833. See also Weiss: *Trois Années de Théâtre*, vol. i, pp. 85 *ff*.

During his travels he had attached to himself one Struensee, then a physician at Altona, handsome and talented, whom in a short time he appointed Prime Minister. Under the circumstances this appointment gave Struensee absolute power over the kingdom. In such a state of things it was natural, even necessary, that Matilda should have frequent communication with him on matters of public interest. But her enemies, of course, then spread the report that she was faithless to the King. While these accusations were doubtless false, it is certainly true that she was imprudent. Struensee, soon after his rise to power, entered upon a course of such violent and arbitrary measures that a secret league, having the King's mother, the dowager Queen Juliana, at its head, was formed against him. This league at once proceeded to organize a conspiracy, the time for its execution being fixed at the close of a masked ball to be given at the court on January 16, 1772. Just before the ball a number of the conspirators burst into the King's room and assured him with well-simulated zeal that his life and throne were in peril and that his wife was plotting to overthrow him. The stupefied monarch signed the papers that were laid before him, ordering Struensee and his coadjutor Brandt to be seized and cast into a dungeon, and Queen Matilda to be arrested and hurried away as a conspirator to the Castle of Cronenburg. A few days later Struensee and Brandt were executed.

Such are the outlines of an incident which had already been treated in the novel and on the stage when Scribe used it as the basis of his political comedy. The tragedy of Struensee had been arranged for the theatre some thirty years before by Duval; but the Danish ambas-

sador had intervened, and Duval's play was never produced. In 1828, at the theatre of Munich, Michael Beer,
a brother of Meyer Beer, had produced a violent and
horrible tragedy on Struensee. Three weeks before the
première of "Bertrand et Raton," a play by Gaillardet,
"Struensee," was presented at the Théâtre de l'Ambigu-
Comique. It is possible that Scribe had read the memoirs of Falkenskield, translated into French by Secrétan
in 1822. He borrowed from the story of Struensee merely
the period, a few characters, and the outcome of the
revolt, and used his material to write a comedy dealing
with the events of his own day, directing his sarcasm,
irony, and satire at these events, their causes, and their
effects, at the government and at the people, at the fool,
the intriguer, the workman, the lord, and the merchant
seeking power.

We learn in the first scene, from M. de Koller, colonel
of the regiment on service at the palace, that the im-
becile King has just conferred on Struensee the highest
powers, really investing him with his own royalty; all of
which is distasteful to Koller, still more so to Rantzau,
one of the most powerful members of Struensee's cabinet,
and jealous of him, and still more so to the dowager
Queen, Marie-Julie. The latter, an energetic woman,
easily finds a remedy for this evil, which is to seize upon
all the ministers in person the following noon, at a dinner
to be given by Falkenskield, the War Minister. While
this project meets with the ready approval of Koller,
Colonel of the Guards, who is ready for anything provided there is something to gain, Rantzau refuses to
listen to the proposal, which seems to him to be in bad
taste, brutal, and, above all, perilous.

To help him accomplish the same object with greater safety, fate sends him two unsuspecting agents: one, Eric de Burkenstaff, who is soliciting a lieutenancy, and who is promised what he seeks; the other, Raton de Burkenstaff, his father, a rich and conceited merchant, ready to sacrifice even his money to his pride, which is saying a great deal for a bourgeois. Now, as it happens, Raton is furious; he has come earlier in the day to bring certain materials to Queen Mathilde, who has made him wait with his cloth, and then, without even receiving him, has dismissed him. Rantzau fans the flame of Raton's anger, pretends to sympathize with his wounded pride, and encourages him to make a few rather free remarks about the Queen, which he quietly repeats in the following scene to the Minister of War, also quietly demanding the arrest of this rascally merchant, a demand which seems to the minister an act of high justice and of no less high politics.

The second act shows us Monsieur and Madame Burkenstaff in their shop. We already know Bertrand's aspirations; Madame Burkenstaff is just the opposite of this fool; living for their shop, seeing only as far as the counter, having no ambitions beyond the safe, she is a clever, sensible woman. This character is true and well conceived, although lacking perhaps that strength, sharpness, and good-humor which make the wife of the Bourgeois Gentilhomme such an original creation.

But a really new and most amusing character is found in Jean, another member of the Burkenstaff household. No counter-jumper ever had a more profound knowledge of the science of insurrection than this young clerk; not that the poor boy is really malicious or hostile to kings —

Jean considers the insurrection only from the material, physical point of view; noise, uproar, mud-slinging, broken windows, wrecked street lights, are for him the *nec plus ultra* of enjoyment. And he sees still one more advantage in an insurrection — a holiday; his reasoning is as follows: when there is a disturbance, the shops are closed, there is no more work to do, and that gives us an extra Sunday.

As a matter of fact Jean does not have to wait long for an occasion to show his zeal; two consecutive insurrections break out, both caused by Burkenstaff the elder, who has been warned by Eric, his son, that the War Office has heard of his remarks about Queen Mathilde, and that he is to be arrested. As this worthy merchant is first and foremost a coward, he has asked shelter of one of his friends; but while he is crossing the palace square, two soldiers notify him politely that the Minister of War is most anxious for his presence. At this Jean, as can easily be imagined, does not stand by with folded arms, but begins to shout so loudly and to make so much noise that all the children in the neighborhood run up, then the men, then the women, and finally all the riff-raff. This time the law is the weaker, and Monsieur Raton Burkenstaff is freed by his fellow-citizens.

While these things have been going on off-stage, the audience has had to listen to two somewhat long and uninteresting scenes. In the first, Eric tells his mother of his love for Mademoiselle Christine de Falkenskield, daughter of the Minister of War; tells how this passion came while he was the minister's secretary, how he has a rival in the person of M. de Goelher, and how, having been insulted by this rival, he has asked for a lieutenancy so as to be able to challenge Goelher to a duel. In the second scene we see Christine led on to the stage by the happy lieutenant, who has saved her from being insulted by the crowd, and who takes advantage of this situation to tell her of his love.

Meanwhile Raton has not only been set free by the crowd, but has been led to the palace and pardoned for everything. The disturbances seem to have quieted down; and they would have done so except for Rantzau. As his projects are somewhat upset by the public peace, he makes a call upon Raton, who is proud of his new popularity and of the celebration which his fellow-citizens are arranging for the evening, a celebration which his modesty will not allow him to refuse. Alas! he will have to forego his triumph, however, for at the very moment when he is making preparations for this celebration, when he is in the cellar getting the wine for the ovation, the wine destined for his friends and liberators, Rantzau closes and locks the cellar door upon him, and our hero finds himself lost among his wine casks. This dramatic device is weak and unsatisfactory, as it depends upon mere chance; while the accidents of real life are often matters of hazard, those of the drama, on the contrary, should be the result of calculation.

Meanwhile, after Rantzau has turned the key upon Raton and put it in his pocket, the crowd, which has come to get the unhappy merchant for the triumphal celebration, fails to find him, and Rantzau spreads the report that Raton has been arrested by order of the court. At this the uproar begins again and the insurrection is revived, more windows and lamps are broken, first of all those of Raton's shop, which is then pillaged, his silks being torn to shreds and his velvets burned. As he is the hero of the occasion and has given hospitality to the malcontents, it is perhaps just that they should ruin him first of all.

The third act takes place at the residence of the Minister of War, the Count de Falkenskield. In the first scene Christine and the Count de Goelher, whom her father wants her to marry, are talking together. This scene would not be worth mentioning were it not for the rôle played by Goelher, a rôle which seems to me a very bad one, for Goelher is related to the play only by a very slight incident: his future marriage with Christine, a marriage which does not interest the public, to whom it makes little difference whether she marries Eric or Goelher. Scribe doubtless thought it was necessary to add a love interest to the play; and while he may have been right, the love of Eric and Christine would have been sufficient, perhaps even superfluous; consequently there was no need of adding this Goelher, a cowardly, odious, and ridiculous character. The third act, as a matter of fact, has really only two scenes. Raton has been found in the cellar, and while the crowd is delighted at having found him, the War Office is angry and intends to act rigorously. Two men have been arrested, Hermann and Christian, two agents of Colonel Koller, who in the first act had promised Queen Marie-Julie to arrest the ministers at Count de Falkenskield's dinner. Koller, fearing these two agents will reveal the plot, calls a meeting of the council, and declares himself head of the conspiracy in the interest of Struensee and the Queen. In the other scene the ministers, informed by the confessions of Christian and Hermann, and particularly by Koller's revelations, that they are to be seized and arrested during their dinner, have the approaches to the house guarded and give orders that entrance shall be free to all. One man alone appears, Eric, who has not come to arrest single-handed all the ministers, but to challenge Goelher, who is his rival and who has insulted him. Having been recognized and pursued by the guards, he takes refuge in Christine's room, at her entreaty. Here he is found and arrested, and although he knows nothing about the real conspiracy, he declares to Rantzau, in order to save Christine's honor, that he is the agent of a conspiracy. As a result he is led to prison.

The council has decided that Eric, having confessed himself guilty of conspiracy against the authority of Struensee and of an attack on the liberty of the ministers, shall be put to death. Rantzau refuses to sign the decree, convokes the courts of justice, talks about the rights of the people, and even resigns, thus creating such an influential position for himself that Koller, who had gone over to Struensee's side, bewildered by these changes and frightened by threats of hanging, decides to stand by Marie-Julie, on condition that she make him a general. This is the cleverest scene in the whole play.

Three elements which are really exterior to the plot — Christine's love for Eric, Madame Raton's love for her son, and the peril which this young man runs — occupy too large a place in the first part of Act V. But toward the end, when Jean returns, it begins to be entertaining again. Struensee and his party are overcome and Marie-Julie triumphs. The people have won this victory without knowing in whose interests they have acted, and Rantzau is the only real winner, for he is made Prime

Minister. Raton, although he has been imprisoned, beaten, pillaged, locked in the cellar, almost condemned to death, has been appointed furnisher to the Queen: is that not ample compensation? Only, as he himself says, before having been imprisoned, beaten, and pillaged he was furnisher to two queens; as he has helped dethrone one, he has lost fifty per cent.

The comic element in this play is lively and original throughout, and the dramatic situations impressive. The spectator has a real interest in the action, for it arouses his curiosity. There are few more animated, more life-like pictures that that of the second act, which takes place in the shop of Raton Burkenstaff, the ambitious but silly merchant whom Rantzau, the wily politician who overthrows Struensee, uses as his tool. As a matter of fact, this whole act is a masterpiece. The characters of the play are for the most part well drawn. Rantzau is the type of the witty courtier, with his finesse, cunning, dignity, and nobility. His sarcasm is bitter, his repartee sparkling. Calmly conscious of his superiority, he works the marionettes surrounding him with cynical facility. He has been compared with Nepomucène Lemercier's Pinto, but the comparison is scarcely just. One is interesting because he is always in action, the other because he never acts; it is hard to tell which is the cleverer — both are very intelligent. Madame Burkenstaff is one of those wise and simple women whom Chrysale in the "Femmes Savantes" speaks of; although her ambitions go no further than her household, and the training and happiness of her children, this gentle mother is beautiful in her strength and energy, when her son's life is threatened.

The rôle of Jean, the noisy little clerk who finds nothing more amusing than a revolution because, when the crowd is in the street, he does not have to work, is a true and original creation. He is the young man who, at the trial of the ministers after the Revolution of 1830, was the noisiest in clamoring for their heads, not through rancor or hatred, but merely because he enjoyed a disturbance. Raton is scarcely more than a good copy of Mathieu in "Une Journée de la Fronde," and of the "Bourgmestre de Saardam." Koller serves as a pendant to Raton, conceited, ignorant, and poltroonish. It would seem that, in creating Colonel Koller, Scribe wished to reply once for all to the epigrams against "les colonels de M. Scribe," as they were called. He has shown us an absolutely new one: the most weak-willed person imaginable, never knowing what to do and always doing the wrong thing. In these two characters Scribe has portrayed the stupid pride of the bourgeoisie and of the nobility.

In "Bertrand et Raton" Scribe has tried only to write a comedy representing the follies and the vices of the society of 1830, and has not attempted to give a warning or point a moral, unless it be that the best conspirator is the one who does not conspire. And yet he was too highly endowed with the *esprit comique* not to know that the spectator likes to find a moral lesson in what he sees and hears, even though he does not take advantage of it. Consequently, in most of his comedies we find the exposition of certain practical truths: in "Le Mariage de Raison" he develops the maxim that in the choice of a wife one should depend upon the experience of his parents rather than upon the impulses of his own heart; in

"Le Mariage d'Inclination" he shows the terrible consequences of a first mistake; in "La seconde Année,"
"La Famille Riquebourg," and "Les Malheurs d'un
Amant heureux," he is a moralist who has seen of society
more than its exterior forms, its language, its style.

As far as the historical side of "Bertrand et Raton" is
concerned, it may be said that, beyond the date, the
costumes, and a few proper names, nothing is historical.
There is no trait of manners or of character which belongs
essentially to the place, the time, and the characters of the
drama, and the scene could just as well have occurred in
Paris as in Copenhagen; the Maréchal d'Ancre, as well as
Struensee, could have furnished a palace revolution.
Scribe merely put French society on the stage with
foreign names and costumes. But is Raton really the
type of the French bourgeois of 1830? Certainly there
were many who were as naïve in politics and in revolutionary activity; but it is possible that they were not
numerous enough to furnish a type recognizable by its
general features. At any rate, Scribe has succeeded in
exposing the low, the repulsive, and the amusing features
of every revolution. He has proceeded in the manner
dictated by his own nature, that of a smiling philosopher
professing for his fellow men a gentle, temperate scorn,
moderated by his incurable belief that, among those
whose ambition is lawless and faithless, among the
shameless intriguers and tricksters, the villains and the
fools, there are still a few honest people.

But it is not revolution in general which he has represented; it is the under-side of a certain revolution, which
he had seen with his own eyes in 1830. In reality the play
deals with the Duke d'Orléans and with those who put

him on the throne. We are not in Copenhagen in 1772, we are in the Paris of 1833; we see the disillusionment, the bitter disappointment, the indignation of a host of heroes, of noble-hearted citizens, of energetic politicians, and of busybodies, who had staked their all on the attack on the former government, and who are duped and neglected by the new one; who have left everything, domestic happiness and fortune, to realize their political dream, and who have failed. And although in the play nearly all the action occurs before the revolution, the moral of the piece is directed to its aftermath. The morning after, the culmination of the drama, is at the same time sad and amusing when Raton, having lost his fortune, run the risk of imprisonment, endangered his son's life in the service of Marie-Julie, receives from the victorious Queen, as a reward for all his sacrifices, a scutcheon to put on his sign and a diminution of his royal clientèle; when Koller, who has struck the decisive blow, finally after much difficulty becomes colonel-general, which he would have become without conspiracy or revolution, while Rantzau, who in the heat of the struggle has not risked a single hair of his head, inherits Struensee's power and takes for himself the fruit of the danger run by the others. All the general currents and fundamental types of a revolution are found in Scribe's play except the element of idealism, except the good citizen in whom is incarnated thirst for justice, hatred of oppressors, and love of country. But this current and this type did not belong to the subject. Three principal figures in the personnel of a conspiracy or of a revolution belong to the domain of comedy, those represented by Raton, Rantzau, and Koller.

"Bertrand et Raton" is the only real political comedy written in France between "Le Mariage de Figaro" and Lemaître's "Le Député Leveau." What is particularly interesting in the play is that in it Scribe sets forth, not only his own views and ideals, but those of the contemporary bourgeoisie, with its worship of success, its devotion to material interests, its selfish desire for positions, for social distinctions, for money and for power.

The very form of such plays as "Bertrand et Raton" shows that Scribe realized to what extent the public was weary of the shamelessness of the contemporary theatre; weary of adultery without passion, of incest without fatality, of the hangman, of assassins and prostitutes. Well aware that this libertinism of action and dialogue was nearing the end of its days, that the good sense of the public would sooner or later break with such things, he sought to hasten the rupture. He proved to the public that, after all, decent people could be entertained at the theatre without an outrage to their modesty in every scene and a violation of decency of language in every phrase. He reconstituted good society at the theatre. All the critics of 1830, even those most hostile to him, unite in pointing out the part he played in this regeneration, and the critic of the "Journal des Débats" sums up the situation by saying:

Le public à la première représentation de cette pièce m'a semblé un jeune homme dont le cœur n'a été jusque là troublé que par d'impures amours; tout à coup le ciel lui envoie une honnête femme; il admire qu'avec moins de bruit et de désordres on goûte une volupté plus douce, et revient à la vertu. Que béni soit le dieu du Théâtre-Français! Sa colère à la fin s'est apaisée. Il a eu pitié de nous et de nos longs ennuis; il nous a rendu la comédie amusante, spirituelle; le drame sans débauche et sans dégoût; non pas cependant cette comédie forte et puissante par la peinture des caractères humains et

des passions sociales, telle que l'a faite Molière, non pas encore le
drame lié à triple nœud, serré à triple intrigue que nous a montré
Beaumarchais.   Mais enfin, avant-hier pendant quatre heures, nous
avons ri, nous nous sommes amusés, et ce rire était franc, ce plaisir ne
coûtait rien à la morale la plus réservée; nous avons retrouvé Dancourt avec plus d'action, Picard avec plus d'esprit, ou du moins un
esprit plus relevé.

"L'Ambitieux" (1834) [1] is difficult to class. It is a
political comedy and a character-study together; and
both the portrayal of characters and the political satire
are accompanied by the dexterous development of a complicated plot. There is, moreover, an historical element
and interest, the scene of the play being laid in the England of George II and Sir Robert Walpole. But when one
takes account of Scribe's penchant for looking to the
events and tendencies of his day for dramatic material,
one is inclined to consider the play primarily a political
comedy, developed by means of character portrayal.

"L'Ambitieux" was greeted with applause by the
greater part of the press; and although certain critics
found the two main characters false, the action weak, the
style dry and uninteresting, the play was recognized as
the outcome of a notable effort to compose a real comedy,
one in which by the mere development of a strong character the author had attempted to excite interest, curiosity, and laughter, leaving aside the easy methods
which a complicated plot might suggest and all those
theatrical devices which he knew so well — in a word, as
a return to the traditions of Regnard, of Dancourt,
Lesage, and Destouches.

[1] Cf. *Journal des Débats*, 29 Nov., 1834; *Moniteur Universel*, 28 Nov.,
1834; *Temps*, 4 Dec., 1834. See also Rolland: *Les Comédies politiques de
Scribe*.

Few passions are so ubiquitous as that of ambition in all its various forms. It would seem, then, that for the dramatist ambition would be a fruitful source of combinations, of effects, of contrasts, and of observations comprehensible even to the most unintelligent spectator. Yet such has not been the case in the history of the drama; this passion, which animates and vivifies society, seems cold and lifeless when analyzed by comedy, fails to interest, and seldom even amuses.

The action of "L'Ambitieux" is conducted by six characters: Sir Robert Walpole, Lord Henry, Dr. Newborough, Marguerite (his daughter); Cecile, Countess of Sutherland, and the King, George II. Throughout the play Walpole makes one think of the reply made by Philip of Spain to one of his courtiers: "Sire, il y a juste un an que l'empereur Charles-Quint abdiqua sa couronne." — "Monsieur, il y a juste un an qu'il s'en repent." Walpole surrenders his portfolio for only a few hours, and is in despair. While this situation is natural, it is hardly sufficient; in a play entitled "L'Ambitieux" one would have liked to see the hero acquiring and preserving his power rather than bewailing the power he has lost.

Robert Walpole, Prime Minister of England, is urged by his friend and physician, Dr. Newborough, to resign his position and give up the direction of public affairs, if he would retain his health. To this counsel Walpole replies that nothing would please him more, but that the King refuses to accept his resignation. Newborough, meanwhile elected to the House of Commons as member for Southwark, has become an almost intimate friend of George II, and succeeds in persuading his sovereign to replace his friend and patient. When he hears of the King's decision, Walpole, instead of being grateful, is only angry at losing his portfolio, and immediately begins planning a method whereby he may remain minister in fact if not in name, thinking of his nephew, Lord Henry, as his successor. While such a course is not necessarily impossible or implausible, Scribe should have represented Lord Henry as being influential in and highly esteemed by both Chambers. This he has not done, for in the play Lord Henry has no greater merit than that of being loved by two women, scarcely a sufficient reason for being made Prime Minister. The King finds a handkerchief belonging to his mistress, the Countess of Sutherland, and in this handkerchief is tied a passionate love-letter, in which George recognizes Henry's handwriting. At this the King becomes angry at the Countess and at Lord Henry, which is quite natural. But it is contrary to English law and custom for him to order Lord Henry's arrest merely because he is loved by the King's mistress. Finally, however, George's anger cools off, he restores Lord Henry's liberty, and even insists that he remain Prime Minister. But this the young man refuses to do, as he has seen his uncle's grief and despair at no longer possessing that power which was his for years. And so, at the end of the play, as at the beginning, Walpole is in power.

Had this comedy been played three months earlier, a general cry of disapproval would have arisen, and the author would have been charged with grossly exaggerating the ambition of Walpole, on the ground that no man ever existed who clung to power like an oyster to the rocks. Three months pass, and Scribe, always fortunate in his speculations, finds in contemporary events a ready-made proof to justify his comedy. That thirst for power, that mania for honors, which he has analyzed, was written in the history of the three preceding weeks, and printed in all the papers and reviews of the capital. It seemed almost as if the last ministerial crisis had occurred purposely to assure the success of "L'Ambitieux."

In this play, Scribe has widened the circle and enlarged the interest of his action, for his *ambitieux* is none other than Sir Robert Walpole; the scene, England. While it might seem that political manners, often very amusing in reality, can be made no less amusing on the stage, experience leads to the opposite conclusion. In any case, the political manners of a constitutional country adapt themselves to the stage less easily than those of any other country, for there everything is foreseen and decided, and nothing is left to the caprice of the individual. Intrigue naturally has its rôle in such states as in all human affairs, but it must be intrigue based upon real talent and ability, of which the people are judge, and not the king. The king of England, even in the days of George II, could not appoint a minister for his own pleasure; his appointments were controlled by a minister who directed his choice, and this minister was the people. In a word, the king did not choose, he ratified the choice of the majority. And so, if politics can be interesting in a drama, it is only when the government is an arbitrary one, when the will of the prince makes and unmakes — as at Versailles when Louis XV was king, Madame du Barry mistress, and Choiseul minister. But in England since 1688, as in France since 1814, affairs of state are too closely watched, too easily within the reach of all, to admit the fictions of the drama.

Scribe might have replied to such a criticism that in "L'Ambitieux" we are not really concerned with England, its Magna Charta, and its Cabinet, not even with Sir Robert Walpole, but merely with a man consumed by ambition. He might have said that in this minister, whatever his name, he has shown the disorders of this terrible passion — thirst for honors, necessity of rest coupled with imperious need of agitation. But the answer could be made that, after all, the spectator cannot at the author's will rid himself of his memories and impressions. If the dramatist shows us an *ambitieux* in a despotic government, we want to see him employing all the secret means which the form of government places at his disposal; if he shows us a minister in a constitutional state, we want to see him setting in action all the wheels of this other machine. Moreover, call the *ambitieux* Smith or Jones and we shall not demand a character which history does not attribute to him. But when an author places a Robert Walpole before our eyes, he promises, as it were, to revive him "in his habit as he lived." To Walpole's ministry is attached the notoriety of a corrupting and corrupted minister; we should like to see how corruption became such a powerful weapon in his hands. While we do not demand that the author give us an exact picture of English manners in the time of George II, we do ask him not to forget that he has laid the scene of the play in England, and not to outrage our ideas of history.

The *ambitieux* of Scribe says too often that ambition devours him, and too seldom puts into play the real springs of that passion; he proclaims his ambition but does not prove it. Tartuffe never claims to be a hypocrite and thereby never ceases to be one. Like Scribe, Destouches makes his *ambitieux* a Prime Minister, who has reached the highest point of brilliance and of fortune, but who, not content with having risen as high as a subject can rise, forms the rash project of allying himself with his master and sharing his power. There we recognize unbridled ambition, never satisfied, always aiming higher. When this passion remains stationary, it loses its essence, and becomes mere envy, restlessness, or jealousy. Yet it is thus that Scribe represents Walpole, whose only ambition is to be Prime Minister and to remain Prime Minister. The real *ambitieux* of the play is Newborough, for no sooner is he made minister than he aspires to replace Walpole and become the head of the government.

It is clear that in this play Scribe was aiming at the July régime over the shoulders of eighteenth-century England, and the *humeur frondeuse* of the Voltairean bourgeoisie is evident. In his three political comedies, "Bertrand et Raton," "La Camaraderie," and "L'Ambitieux," and in the *vaudeville* "Le Solliciteur," we see him both conservative and *frondeur* in politics; for there is in all these plays a touch of bourgeois liberalism; Scribe is upholding the throne, but at the same time ridiculing the Chambers and the ministers.

Literary coteries were nothing very new in France. Since the Hôtel de Rambouillet, which Molière has marked with ineffaceable ridicule in "Les Précieuses ridicules" and "Les Femmes savantes," many have sprung up and disappeared, overwhelmed by sarcasm. The Empire saw the birth of one which was more fortunate, — very well known at the time but by 1836 already forgotten, — called the *Déjeuner à la fourchette*. The members, unknown, obscure, worthless poets, or heavy prose-writers, made it a practice to compliment each other in public and to glorify each other's genius, the objective of this mutual admiration being the Academy.

When, about 1825, the new school, the Romanticists, bold, insolent, and often absurd, formed a similar union, at once the broadsides of the stage attacked the new phalanx. Scribe began the charge in a *vaudeville* entitled "Le Charlatanisme," one of his cleverest plays. In 1829 the "Revue de Paris" published an incisive article by H. de Latouche, entitled "La Camaraderie littéraire," which created a sensation, for at that time the clamor of literary disputes filled the air. Paris was an arena given over to the quarrels between Classicists and Romanticists; even political controversy was less interesting than that between the Racinians and the Shakespeareans, and the two schools occupied public attention more than the two Chambers of Parliament. Latouche had said:

L'amitié est une des calamités de notre époque littéraire. De jour en jour elle glisse en tous lieux sa partialité plus dangereuse, et peut développer au sein de quelques hommes, réservés peut-être à de brillantes déstinées, le sentiment le plus infertile qu'ils puissent cultiver: l'amour de soi. C'est aux seuls poètes que nous nous adressons. Il se sera rencontré une petite société d'apôtres qui se disant persécutés dans les pratiques d'un nouveau culte s'est enfermée en elle-même pour s'encourager. Les apôtres se seront aimés; ils se seront appuyés les uns sur les autres pour leur utilité réciproque. Mais le danger passé, l'amitié sera devenue une spéculation. Une congrégation de rimeurs bizarres est devenue un complot pour s'aduler.

"La Camaraderie, ou la Courte Echelle" (1837)[1] deals with a set of people who have taken as their motto the remark made by Armande in "Les Femmes savantes": "Nul n'aura de l'esprit, hors nous et nos amis," and continues de Latouche's attack on coteries. But whereas the clever article in the "Revue de Paris" had dealt chiefly with literary charlatanism, this play is really a satire on political manners, with, it is true, a number of clever digs at the Romanticists. Oscar Rigaut, a harebrained coxcomb, ignorant and fatuous, tells his naïve young friend Edmond de Varennes that he has scarcely any time to devote to his law studies now:

OSCAR: J'ai d'autres occupations qui me conviennent davantage. J'ai fait un livre de poésies.
EDMOND: Toi?
OSCAR: Comme tout le monde! Cela m'est venu un matin, en déjeunant — "Le Catafalque, ou Poésies funèbres d'Oscar Rigaut."
EDMOND: Toi! un gros garçon réjoui?
OSCAR: Oui, je me suis mis dans le funéraire . . . il n'y avait plus que cette partie-là; tout le reste était pris par nos amis, des beaux, des gants-jaunes de la littérature, génies créateurs ayant tout inventé; et ça aurait fait double emploi si nous avions tous créé le même genre. Aussi je leur ai laissé le *vapoureux*, le *moyen-âge*, le *pittoresque*; j'ai inventé le *funéraire*, le *cadavéreux*, et j'y fais fureur.

Scribe was taking innocent revenge here on Théodore de Banville, Théophile Gautier, Jules Janin, and others whom he had the gift of irritating. But this is only in passing. He is chiefly interested in ridiculing mutual advancement by quack means, whether in literature, medicine, economics, or politics; chiefly in politics. Ed-

[1] Cf. *Revue des Deux Mondes*, 1 Feb., 1837; *Revue de Paris*, vol. VII (Oct., 1829), pp. 102 *ff.*, and vol. v, third series, p. 279; *Constitutionnel*, 22 Jan., 1837; *Temps*, 23 Jan., 1837; *Moniteur Universel*, 24 Jan., 1837; *Presse*, 22 Jan., 1837; *Siècle*, 21 Jan., 1837; *Journal des Débats*, 21 and 30 Jan. and 13 Feb., 1837.

mond de Varennes, a very temperamental young lawyer
of real ability, finds himself balked at every step in his
career by the invisible and consequently potent hostility
of Madame de Miremont and her cohort of worthless
"comrades"; at their head is Dr. Bernardet, whose reputation she has established by her nervous spasms, which
only he has been able to cure. Madame de Miremont
had at one time been secretly in love with Edmond, and
his failure to respond to her affection accounts for her
present antipathy to him. This lady also dominates her
noble husband, the Count de Miremont, septuagenarian
peer of France — and it is in his person that Scribe prods
the members of the Upper House. Dr. Bernardet de-
scribes him thus:

> Ennemi des secousses et de tout ce qui pourrait entraîner un dé-
> placement quelconque, il est partisan de ceux qui se maintiennent,
> fanatique de tout ce qui existe, mais sans se montrer et sans se
> compromettre. Car, vivant obscur dans son illustration, il craint de
> faire parler de lui et se met au lit, deux mois d'avance, quand il doit y
> avoir quelque crise ou quelque procès politique. Je le sais, c'est moi
> qui le traite, et nous n'entrons en convalescence qu'après le pro-
> noncé du jugement.

Césarine de Miremont confines her husband to his bed
when his absence from the Luxembourg serves her purpose. And it is her hostility that is keeping Edmond
from accomplishing his ardent desire to be elected deputy
for Saint-Denis. For Agathe de Miremont, Césarine's
step-daughter, has delicately confided to him that her
father would not perhaps be averse to her marrying a
deputy. Clever as Césarine is, though, she is outwitted
by Agathe's friend, Zoé de Montlucar, whose husband is
a member of the *camaraderie*. When Edmond, who in this
Freudian day would be clearly recognized as a victim of

the inferiority complex, hesitates to run for Saint-Denis, Zoé urges him to do so:

ZoÉ: Il faut vous mettre sur les rangs.
EDMOND: Mon Dieu! y pensez-vous? Jamais!
ZoÉ: Pourquoi pas?
EDMOND: Une pareille ambition demande de si grands talents!
ZoÉ: Vous n'avez donc jamais été à la Chambre?

And Oscar encourages him, also:

Des députés? Nous en faisons beaucoup. De véritables députés, des députés qui votent; je ne dis pas qui parlent, mais qu'importe! Il y en a tant d'autres qui ne font que ça! Sois tranquille; nous te ferons nommer. Présenté par moi à nos amis, ils deviendront les tiens, à charge de revanche. Dès qu'on est admis, on a du talent, de l'esprit, du génie; il le faut, c'est dans le règlement. Tu les verras à l'œuvre!

Bernardet is won over to Edmond also — after Zoé has enlisted Césarine's support by persuading her that Edmond really returns the love she thought was spurned. Bernardet notices that his *cénacle* counts many great lights, but no deputy:

BERNARDET: Nous avons parmi nous de grands talents, de grands génies; nous n'avons pas de députés . . . et un député qui serait des nôtres . . . qui serait à nous . . . ça ferait bien.
CÉSARINE: Certainement! . . . ou du moins, si ça ne fait pas de bien, ça ne peut . . .
BERNARDET: N'est-ce pas? C'est ce que je dis.

And so the phalanx is put in motion. Its actions are described by Oscar:

OSCAR: Membre de deux sociétés littéraires, officier de la garde nationale, et maître des requêtes, j'aurai le mois prochain la croix d'honneur; c'est mon tour, c'est arrangé.
EDMOND [*still naïve*]: Avec qui?
OSCAR: Avec les nôtres — ceux qui, comme moi, sont à la tête de la jeune phalange; car ils sont aussi à la tête — nous y sommes tous; nous sommes une douzaine d'amis intimes qui nous portons,

qui nous soutenons, qui nous admirons; une société par admiration
mutuelle. L'un met sa fortune, l'autre son génie, l'autre ne met
rien; tout cela se compense, et tout le monde arrive, l'un portant
l'autre. Seul pour s'élever, on ne peut rien; mais montés sur les
épaules les uns des autres, le dernier, si petit qu'il soit, est un grand
homme. Il y a même de l'avantage a être le dernier — c'est celui-là
qui arrive.

However, in this case, it is only just to say that, although Scribe's *jeune premier* is elected deputy through
the help of the comrades, who are unwittingly made to
advance an outsider, almost an enemy, Edmond himself
is ignorant of their manœuvres and ingenuously attributes his success only to friendly help, aided by circumstance.

EDMOND: Ah! que j'étais injuste! . . . ce matin encore, je me
plaignais des hommes et du sort . . . j'accusais mon siècle de
partialité, d'intrigues, de cabale, et je vois maintenent (*regardant
Césarine*) qu'il y a encore amitié véritable (*regardant Bernardet*) et
désintéressée (*regardant les autres camarades*), qu'on peut parvenir
sans coteries, sans honteuses manœuvres.
Zoé (*le regardant avec compassion*): Pauvre jeune homme!
OSCAR (*à Zoé*): Eh bien! vous le voyez par lui, qui refusait notre
secours, on arrive quand on a des camarades.
Zoé: Oui, monsieur, mais on reste quand on a du talent!

The general idea of the play comports with the conception that every dramatist ought to have of comedy.
It is based upon a moral observation of follies and vices
whose existence could not be seriously denied and which
it was honorable to attempt to uproot. It would be unjust not to praise Scribe for his intentions. For a long
time the public had considered him only a frivolous and
indifferent, if very clever writer, but "La Camaraderie"
showed once and for all that he was capable of clear observation and of acrid satire, and that he could portray

the life about him with inexpugnable fidelity. One of the
journals in speaking of the play remarked:

Le temps est venu quand le vieillard éternellement assis au
parterre du Théâtre-Français, qui avait interpellé Molière à la représentation des Précieuses ridicules, qui avait souri à Picard, et
depuis lors se tait, quand ce vieillard doit se lever et dire à M.
Scribe: "Courage, monsieur, vous entrez plus profondément dans
le vrai."

Scribe's play is a satirical attack upon the two Chambers of Parliament, upon the methods employed in national and local elections, and upon the charlatanism and
advertising by means of which the members of an unintelligent and unprincipled coterie attempt to advance their
own and each other's interests.

As might naturally be expected, "La Camaraderie"
was a brilliant success at the Comédie-Française, received unstinted praise from certain critics, and was
severely mishandled by others. Jules Janin said:

Monsieur Scribe vient de donner dans le vide un de ces grands
coups d'épée destinés à des géants et qui ne tuent que des moutons.
Il n'était pas besoin d'une si grosse massue pour tuer ce petit cénacle;
il n'y avait qu'à le laisser mourir de sa belle mort, écrasé naturelle-
ment sous sa prose et sous ses vers. . . . L'animal annoncé n'y est
pas. Mais entrez toujours, Messieurs, on vous montrera mieux que
la camaraderie innocente de quelques faiseurs de vers, on vous montrera les deux grands pouvoirs de l'Etat, la Chambre des Pairs et la
Chambre des Députés, livrées pendant cinq actes à mille petites
railleries d'autant plus innocentes qu'elles ne sont pas nouvelles.

The gravest objection brought against the play was
that it held up to ridicule two bodies which because of
their prestige and their accomplishments should never
have been the objects of such satire. In another *feuilleton*
Janin compares "La Camaraderie" with "Le Charlatanisme," saying that, whereas the latter had made a

charming *comédie-vaudeville* for the Gymnase, the comedy presented at the Théâtre-Français was only an enlarged *vaudeville*, long, diffuse, depressing, developed by means of disreputable methods and horrible characters. Alexandre Dumas, in a spirited article in the "Presse," while finding that Scribe had failed to attain his object, considers three of the characters brilliantly portrayed: Oscar Rigaud, Monsieur de Miremont, and especially Dr. Bernardet; and says that Scribe deserves credit for not having once let the play become sombre drama.

Certes, s'il y avait à Paris un auteur dramatique qui pût traiter en toute conscience et en toute liberté un sujet comme celui-ci c'était Scribe. Scribe n'appartient à aucune faction politique, à aucun club artistique, à aucune coterie littéraire; il n'a jamais été poussé par la franc-maçonnerie d'une société mangeante ni par l'imitation d'un cénacle poétique, et cependant Scribe est arrivé jeune encore au but de son ambition, c'est-à-dire à un million de fortune, ce qui lui donne un aplomb social, et au fauteuil académique, ce qui lui donne une position littéraire. P. S. Succès d'argent.

[Later on in the same article he says]: Scribe est, quoiqu'on fasse et quoiqu'on dise, un des trois hommes placés à la tête de la littérature dramatique de notre époque, bien entendu que les autres sont Casimir Delavigne et Victor Hugo.

A letter written by Labrouste shortly after the *première* shows that the non-professional critics took a somewhat different view of the play:

La pièce a parfaitement marché, au milieu des rires et des applaudissements, et malgré la hardiesse de la satire. Les journaux, je crois, ne pourront pas en affaiblir le succès. Ce n'est pas seulement un bel ouvrage, c'est un trait de courage fort rare et fort honorable. Cette bonne Chambre des Députés qui devait représenter l'opinion publique la représente si peu, par bonheur pour l'opinion publique, que les traits lancés aux honorables ont été applaudis à deux ou trois reprises. On voulait crier, "Bis!" Nous avions près de nous Monsieur J. J.,[1] qui faisait la plus drôle de mine. Nous avions au-dessus

---

[1] Jules Janin.

de nous une loge remplie de messieurs à barbe pointue à qui le parterre faisait visiblement l'application de tous les traits du deuxième
acte.

One of the gravest defects in the play is that the development of the plot does not respond to the expectations aroused by the title and by the two first acts; for
after Act II we see nothing of the coterie until late in
Act V, when the "comrades" reappear, and then for no
apparent reason. The real subject of the play seems to be
an attack on the two Chambers and a satire on political
methods in general, illustrated by the elections at Saint-
Denis and by Césarine's manipulation of the ministry,
and at the same time a clever development of the disappointed love and the ambitions of Césarine. It is difficult
to share Dumas's enthusiasm for the portrayal of the
character of M. de Miremont; a senator and a peer of
France thus exhibited in his senile impotence and jealousy, and represented as still being a powerful figure in
politics, certainly cannot be representative of the states-
men of the day — at least not sufficiently representative
to serve as a type. Where did Scribe ever see an election
such as the one he has described? In what electoral
college could five or six clowns of the intelligence and
ability of those he has portrayed direct the actions of an
assembly in which no one takes his duties seriously, and
in which such intriguers are represented as adroit and
even intelligent?

And yet, although Scribe made a mistake in going to
such low classes of intriguers for his representatives of
political manners, it is nevertheless true that he has, in
general, given a faithful picture of the society of 1837,
and that the main interest of the play lies in that por-

trayal. Whenever a dramatist writes a comedy dealing with contemporary events of general interest, he is sure to engage and please the public, whatever may be the tone or color of his picture. In such sketches we like exaggeration and do not object even to caricature; the important thing is that the audience may be able to say: *Mea res agitur*. Modern comedy being based upon interests rather than upon passion, it matters little whether the story be plausible and whether the characters be intelligent or even clever. So great is the charm and attraction of topicality that "La Camaraderie" proved to be extremely interesting.

The enormous success of the play is partly explained by the fact that, for the first time, and notably the first time since the Revolution of 1830, a dramatist had obtained permission to treat on the stage the two most illustrious bodies of the kingdom, and to expose them, with moderation and good taste, it is true, to the laughter of the pit. As one of the greatest joys of a French audience is to ridicule and laugh at those in power, finding a sort of innocent revenge in such amusement, French dramatists have always attacked the vested authorities as much as they were allowed to, and have never failed to entertain the spectators. Molière, in attacking the court marquises with the permission of Louis XIV, appealed to the desires and tastes of his public. "Tartuffe," the masterpiece which struck a deadlier blow at the Holy Roman Catholic Church than the entire "Encyclopædia," was one of the boldest attacks ever directed against sacerdotal power. A large part of Voltaire's success as a dramatist was due to his constant and bitter opposition to all the established powers and to all accepted beliefs — an opposition which was clearly visible beneath the Greek and Roman costumes of his heroes. Beaumarchais, possessing few if any of the qualities which ordinarily make a great dramatist, was for a time more successful and popular than Molière and Voltaire together, because of the violence of his attacks upon the powers of society. "Le Mariage de Figaro," his engine of destruction, now that it has accomplished its work, has lost much of its interest. Comedy certainly has the right to attack those in power, and it is unquestionably true that the success of "La Camaraderie" was due largely to the attacks directed against the Parliament. One dramatic critic explains the popularity of the play by the fact that it dealt with questions of the day.

C'est une comédie du jour au point que Scribe a pris soin de la dater de décembre 1836. . . . Ce n'est plus Valérie, ce n'est plus le Mariage d'Argent qu'il fallait au public. La comédie de mœurs semblait finie. Quant à l'élégie dramatique en trois actes sur la Jeune Aveugle ou sur la Jeune Fille, il ne fallait plus y penser. Cela était bon de 1822 à 1825, en pleine Restauration, lorsque les recueils de poésies pullulaient et que tout Paris faisait et achetait des héroïdes et des stances chagrines. Mais en 1837 le public doutait de tout, s'inquiétait de tout. Il lui fallait de la satire et non de la comédie. Il ne s'attendrissait plus au larmoyant. Son humeur était sceptique, il voudrait rire ou pleurer franchement qu'il n'y réussirait pas.

The censor's report of the play is interesting.

Montrer la camaraderie comme une coalition de l'intrigue et de la mediocrité qui de nos jours enveloppe de son réseau le monde politique et littéraire, comme un pouvoir caché dont l'influence exclusive envahit toutes les positions de renommée et de fortune, tel est l'objet de cette comédie. Rendre l'esprit de coterie dupe de ses propres œuvres et faire tourner au profit du talent modeste les pratiques du charlatanisme et de l'ambition, tels sont à la fois la pensée comique et le but moral que l'auteur semble s'être proposés. [Then follows a synopsis of the play.] Telle est, monsieur le ministre, l'analyse de cette pièce qui se pose comme une satire contemporaine de nos mœurs politiques. Sous ce point de vue elle offre d'abord dans le style un assez grand nombre de traits dont la portée ne serait pas sans danger à la scène. Toutefois des modifications de détail seraient facilement praticable sans nuire à l'ensemble de l'ouvrage. Mais il est un point plus grave en ce sens qu'il est inhérent à l'action et qu'il nous paraît excéder les bornes de la critique dramatique. C'est la partie de l'intrigue relative à la feinte maladie d'un pair de France, haut fonctionnaire, dont la santé s'altère périodiquement aux approches des procès politiques et dont la succession préma- turée, livrée dans la chambre élective à un concours d'ambitions vénales, rallie une majorité douteuse et contribue ainsi à la confusion d'une loi. Ce moyen de comédie qui tend à attaquer le courage politique de l'un des premiers corps de l'état et la probité parlemen- taire de l'autre nous a paru de nature à être plus longuement dis- cuté.

"La Camaraderie" is reminiscent of Dorat's "Les Prôneurs," which was a frontal attack upon the Ency- clopædists, particularly d'Alembert. The satire was so direct and so telling that d'Alembert would not allow the play to be produced at the Théâtre-Français. Continu- ing the attack begun in "Les Précieuses ridicules," and continued in "Les Femmes savantes" and in "Les Prôneurs," "La Camaraderie" was in turn followed by "Le Monde où l'on s'ennuie."

After a revival some years later of "La Camaraderie," Regnier, of the Théâtre-Français, wrote to Scribe:

Grands applaudissements du public! Je lorgnais du coin de l'œil une personne assise à l'orchestre et qui me semblait prendre sa très grande part de la joie générale. Est-ce un retour, est-ce une con- version que vous avez faite? Je n'en sais trop rien, mais j'aurai peine à croire qu'après avoir paru si satisfait, Monsieur Janin n'abjurât pas ses feuilletons de 1837.

Historical Comedies

The revolution wrought at the beginning of the nineteenth century in the historical method — a change which did not, naturally, occur in one day — had its effects on the novel and on the drama. The new method came from Germany, where Herder had published his "Philosophy of History" in 1784, Wolf his "Prolegomena" in 1795, Niebuhr his "Roman History" in 1811. As very few Frenchmen knew German at that time, it was Madame de Staël's "De l'Allemagne," published in 1810, which initiated the French to the literature, the philosophy, and the historical method of their neighbors. The adaptation of the "Wallenstein" made by Benjamin Constant, and the remarkable preface which accompanied it, and later the translation of Schiller by de Barante, popularized German drama in France. In 1810 Pierre Lebrun achieved great success with a "Marie Stuart" imitated from Schiller. During the same years the novels of Sir Walter Scott, translated into French as into the other European languages, were enjoying enormous popularity in Paris. "Ivanhoe" was written in 1820; and while it is true that it was the transformation of historical method which renewed the novel, it is only just in return to recall that it was the novel of Sir Walter Scott which awakened in Augustin Thierry, according to his own confession, that profound interest in the past and that *esprit de divination* which characterize his historical studies. Moreover, during those fertile years when nearly all the intellectual work of the nineteenth century was taking its form, art and science, poetry and history, lent each other mutual help. The new criticism, at once severe and daring, did not hesitate to make use of imagination in its study of the immense domain it had just discovered. Guizot, a serious, methodical historian, who had none of the audacious fancy of Michelet or of Carlyle, was nevertheless a fervent admirer of Shakespeare. In 1823 he published his collection of memoirs relative to the English Revolution, and revised Letourneur's translation of Shakespeare, for which he wrote a preface.

This infusion of history into the novel, into poetry, and into the drama, was one of the essential and characteristic features of Romanticism. While the leaders, Hugo and Dumas, might play with reality and take such liberties with fact as Corneille, Racine, and Voltaire would never have imagined, it is none the less true that they very seriously intended to be historical in their own way and, while perhaps not very scrupulous as to the verity of facts, to paint more faithfully than the professional historians the spirit and the manners of past centuries. The great thinkers who had renewed history had gone on the principle that it ought to be a science, or at least to emulate the rigor of scientific methods. This idea was gradually making its way, and the consequences soon began to be felt, slowly at first, in the domain of art. Eugène Delacroix obeyed the new law, as well as Victor Hugo, Alfred de Vigny, or George Sand. Although Ponsard seemed for a moment to have dethroned the Romanticists, he was in reality following their precepts. Neither "Lucrèce" nor "Agnès de Méranie" nor "Charlotte Corday" is a tragedy of the classical age — they are romantic dramas without the genius, but also without the extravagances, of Hugo and Dumas.

Thus all the novelists and dramatists of the century,

even the mediocre and the less serious ones, had, unconsciously perhaps, and involuntarily, a conception of history definitely superior to that of the contemporaries of Racine and Corneille. In spite of the absurdities and the excesses of the Romanticists, the Realists, and the Parnassians, the nineteenth century produced no rhapsodies like "Clélie," in which Mademoiselle de Scudéry travestied Roman history in ten volumes. The nineteenth century was the century of history.

Casimir Delavigne and Scribe, like all their contemporaries, had undergone this influence, and to attract the public they put history into their plays, as Paul Delaroche put it into his pictures.

Scribe, in writing historical dramas, had numerous illustrious predecessors: Shakespeare, Schiller, Racine, Corneille, Voltaire. The Romanticists themselves, although they thought they were breaking away from the traditions of their predecessors, as a matter of fact were merely continuing them; the main difference between their historical plays and those of the Classicists is that they devoted to the exact reproduction of costume and furniture, and to the exterior features of the manners of a country or of a period, the attention which Racine and Corneille had given to understanding and painting the souls of men of former times. This difference of conception, objective, and treatment, resulted in plays like "Henri III et sa Cour," "La Maréchale d'Ancre," and "Marie Tudor." Thus, under the influence of the romantic movement, the old historic tragedy of Corneille and Voltaire was renewed, and this new conception of history, felt rather than understood, transformed the drama as well as the novel. Even those who resisted the influence of the romantic movement, or who made only timid concessions to the new ideas, were obliged to follow the current or find themselves abandoned by the public. Casimir Delavigne, in writing "Les Enfants d'Édouard," was writing a kind of boarding-school Shakespeare. Scribe, always on the look-out for novelties, extremely skillful in detecting the slightest changes in the taste and demands of the public, determined to join the ranks of the writers of historical dramas and comedies.

In "Avant, Pendant, et Après," a piece written in 1828, the historical element is no less pronounced than the political, and yet even Alexandre Dumas *père* took more pains to inform himself than Scribe did in writing this play. Historical sketches thus conceived add nothing to the psychology of the old aristocracy or to that of the Jacobins. The drama which Scribe produced the year following at the Gymnase, "La Bohémienne," is extraordinarily and joyfully fantastic. In order to enjoy the savor of the play, the reader must remember that Scribe has not borrowed his subject, like Shakespeare in the case of "Hamlet," from some old chronicle about a person who does not count in history, but has taken it from one of the most glorious episodes in the history of the world, the American War of Independence. It needed a strange confidence in the ignorance and credulity of the public to mingle with such familiar facts characters as fantastic as those of the spy Zingaro and his gypsy niece, Bathilde. The uncle and the niece capture the confidence of a young American patriot, Lionel Lincoln, colonel of the Virginia dragoons, who, because, of Zingaro's disguise, takes him to be a Baron de Courville sent by France to the help of the Americans. But Bathilde, falling in love with the brave and loyal young man whom she is to betray, reveals everything to him. Thus the English, who were confident of surprising the Americans, find them prepared; instead of winning an easy victory they are obliged to flee, and Lord Gage himself escapes death only through Lionel's intervention. To get rid of his heroine, who was rather embarrassing at the dénoûment, for he could not marry a former spy to the patriotic leader, Scribe has used a trick which, although not new, is ingenious: Bathilde learns that, instead of being the niece of Zingaro, she is Lord Gage's own daughter, kidnapped by gypsies in her childhood. At the end of the play, her father is obliged to return to England, and she departs with him, not without sorrow at leaving the young hero, who remains in America to continue the struggle. Neither Alexandre Dumas, nor Xavier de Montépin, nor even Ponson du Terrail, ever took such liberties with reality and with common sense.

I have spoken of these two plays chiefly to show the spirit in which Scribe treats history and the use he intends to make of it; they show that as to historical exactitude he is easily satisfied, and that he treats the most important events with a freedom at least equal to that of Alexandre Dumas.

Montaigne, in Book III, Chapter 20, of his "Essais," wrote: "J'ai vu de mon temps les plus sages têtes de ce royaume assemblées avec grande cérémonie et publique dépense pour des traités et accords desquels la vraie décision dépendait cependant en toute souveraineté des deviz du cabinet des dames, et inclination de quelque femmelette." Generalizing the skeptical Gascon's remark, Voltaire made a historical dogma of the generation of great events from small causes, and among other proofs of this theory explained the famous Peace of Utrecht by a joke between two women attached to Queen Anne: "Quelques paires de gants d'une façon singulière que la duchesse de Marlborough refusa à la reine, une jatte d'eau qu'elle laissa tomber en sa présence pour une méprise affectée, changèrent la face de l'Europe."[1] Helvétius taught this fantastic system *in extenso*. Then La Harpe took it up, leaving aside the quotations from the author of "L'Esprit" and concerning himself only with that from the historian of Louis XIV, and proved learnedly that the Queen's change of attitude toward the Duchess of Marlborough would have had no consequences had it not been for the change of public opinion caused by the war-weariness of the people and the exhaustion of the finances.[2] The interesting thing about this refutation is that Voltaire, although La Harpe had not noticed it, had already made it himself in the passage quoted, where, a few lines after those already transcribed, he says: "Les écrivains qui prétendent que Marlborough et son parti tombèrent quand la faveur de la reine ne les soutint pas, ne connaissent pas l'Angleterre." A striking example of the inconsequence of the great man.

Scribe in his turn takes up the theory, one dear to him, and one upon which his dramatic system was based, and for subject takes the incident mentioned by Voltaire. The historical facts of the situation are these. Marlborough's victories had exhausted France. Louis XIV, instead of choosing generals like Catinat or Villars, obstinately insisted upon confiding to incapable courtiers

[1] *Siècle de Louis XIV*, chap. 22.
[2] *Cours de Littérature*, part iii, book iv, chap. 3.

the task of restoring his shaken fortunes. The battle of Malplaquet, which destroyed all hope of revenge and spread consternation through the kingdom, forced the old conqueror to sue for peace. For a long time, however, Marlborough's ambition and cupidity delayed the success of the negotiations, as the war perpetuated his authority and influence and necessitated subsidies from which, it is said, he took a good part for himself. His wife, all-powerful with Queen Anne, whom she tormented and persecuted with her influence and her haughty pride, constantly fought the peace party at court and in Parliament. Louis XIV's envoys were repulsed, and through the duchess's intrigues denied entrance to the palace and access to the ministers. Louis, whose generals were vanquished on the battlefield and whose diplomats were rebuffed at court, thus seemed to be facing complete ruin, when an unexpected hazard, more powerful than the skill of his generals and his ambassadors, saved him from this extremity: the fall of the favorite saved the old monarch and, with him, France. Negotiations were begun, Marlborough was recalled, and the Peace of Utrecht was concluded.

The action of "Le Verre d'Eau" (1840)[1] takes place in a drawing-room of Queen Anne's palace. Louis XIV's ambassador, M. de Torcy, hands to Henry St. John a secret note addressed directly to Queen Anne. St. John, who in Parliament is the declared enemy of Marlborough and his party, promises to use all his influence to obtain an audience with the Queen. He has already explained

---

[1] Cf. *Constitutionnel*, 21 Nov., 1840; *Figaro*, 22 Nov., 1840 and 23 Sept., 1855; *Siècle*, 18 Nov., 1840; *Moniteur Universel*, 20 Nov., 1840; *Temps*, 18 Nov., 1840; *Journal des Débats*, 25 Nov., 1840.

to her that victory may abandon the allies, that France, well generaled, can still command Europe; but, although Queen Anne agrees with him, her opinions and her will are directed by her favorite. St. John has so far been unable to obtain a hearing for M. de Torcy, as the Duchess of Marlborough commands in the palace and everything is submitted to her jealous and tyrannical control; before St. John can succeed, that obstacle must be overcome.

The young cavalier has noticed in the Queen's jewelry-shop a charming young girl to whom he has promised a place in the royal palace; but, although Anne also has been touched by the grace and the charm of Miss Abigail, not even her desires and the protection of a former minister are sufficient to obtain the smallest position in the palace. It is still necessary to have the consent of the imperious Duchess of Marlborough, which Henry St. John thinks that he can obtain; for he has discovered that the poor, obscure shop-girl is a relative of Marlborough, and intends to threaten the duchess with exposure of this fact. St. John, a former minister, has bought a newspaper; making speeches against Marlborough in Parliament, he writes articles against him in the "Examiner." If the duchess refuses to admit Abigail into Anne's service, he will print in his paper the news that the Duchess of Marlborough, the first lady-in-waiting to the Queen, is cousin to a poor shop-girl. The duchess, fertile in intrigue, and always ready with a reply, threatens to have St. John imprisoned at Newgate, for she has bought a creditor's claim against him. St. John is thus forced to give up this expedient, and hastens to avenge himself in Parliament.

Abigail, who has not been able to obtain a position at court, is struck by another misfortune. Masham, a young officer of the guards with whom she is in love, has had a chance meeting in the park with St. John's cousin, Bolingbroke, a peer of the realm, and as the result of an impertinent remark, is slapped in the face by the nobleman. Infuriated by this insult, Masham challenges the older man to a duel and kills him. The young officer is in a dangerous position, for his offense is to be punished with the most extreme severity. Poor Abigail is in despair: the duchess opposes her entrance to the Queen's service, and still worse, her lover is threatened with execution.

But as a result of the slap which young Masham has received, St. John, badly in debt and consequently without influence in spite of his talents, is heir to the title and the fortune of Bolingbroke. The new Viscount Bolingbroke places his power and wealth at the service of Abigail and Masham. A parliamentary committee now demands vengeance for the murder committed in the park. Masham meanwhile has received an anonymous letter containing an appointment to a captaincy. He tells Bolingbroke of this letter and of the mysterious favor, and Bolingbroke discovers that the secret correspondent, the unknown protector, is a woman, the Duchess of Marlborough herself, who has proved no less susceptible than Abigail and the Queen to Masham's elegant figure and captivating youth. Armed with this secret, he forces the duchess to open the palace to Abigail, who thus finds herself in Anne's service.

Abigail, novice that she is, possesses to a supreme degree the art of fascination, and her candor, her sweet and easy character, charm the Queen, who for the moment has

freed herself from the haughty humor of her favorite.
Abigail's qualities gain by this contrast, and Anne, opening her heart to her, confesses that she is in love with
Masham. It is easy to understand that this mark of confidence is not particularly pleasing to Miss Abigail, who
now knows that she has two rivals — the Queen, and a
duchess more powerful than the Queen.

These two great women, for love of Masham, although
restrained by fear of public opinion and of scandal, do not
long remain inactive. The duchess receives Masham in
her apartments, to give him certain secret dispatches;
the Queen calls him, for she wishes to see her new captain
of the guards. Although these meetings are ostensibly
mere audiences, poor Abigail considers them as amorous
rendezvous, and she is not mistaken. She imparts this
sad news and confesses her grief to Bolingbroke, who
promises to protect her and save Masham for her.

At a court card-party Bolingbroke meets the duchess
and informs her of the Queen's secret love; although he
does not name Masham, he tells her she will soon recognize him by a prearranged signal, as the Queen is to ask
him for a glass of water. In fact, contrary to etiquette,
the Queen does ask the young soldier for a glass of water.
The duchess intervenes and in a haughty tone invokes
court custom and her own rights as a lady of honor. "Eh
bien! donnez-le-moi vous-même!" says the Queen. At
this the duchess protests — the first lady-in-waiting bring
a glass of water! Anne, excited and sustained by Abigail, who urges her to shake off the yoke and to humiliate
the insolent favorite, now commands as a real sovereign.
The Duchess of Marlborough, first lady-in-waiting,
offers the glass. She avenges herself by an intentionally

awkward movement, dropping the tray. Her Majesty is outraged, storms and threatens. The duchess offers her resignation, which Anne accepts.

Although the duchess is now in disgrace, she avenges herself before departing. Knowing of the Queen's love for Masham, she denounces him before the whole court as a murderer, with the result that the Queen is obliged to have her lover arrested. Happily, however, it is Bolingbroke who is charged with his arrest, and the young officer's captivity is not long, for he soon has permission to go to a secret audience with Anne. The duchess, who knows everything and who has kept the keys of the private apartments, appears and interrupts the royal rendezvous. In the process, she stirs up all the courtiers. A young man alone with the Queen in her room! But the duchess is mistaken; Abigail's presence in the room saves the Queen's honor. Bolingbroke intervenes and orders the new favorite to marry Masham, through love for the Queen. Naturally Abigail obeys. The duchess is now hopelessly ruined, Abigail succeeds her in Anne's favor, Bolingbroke is made minister, Marlborough is recalled, and peace is signed: and all these changes have been brought about by a glass of water!

The fall of the Whigs in the person of the Duchess of Marlborough forms the subject, then, of "Le Verre d'Eau." It is easy to imagine Scribe's delight at finding in history an incident which fits in so perfectly with his method as this does. All the contrasts which he loved are to be found in it: great results from small causes, the destinies of states submitted to the caprices of the court, the struggle in Anne between her duty as queen and her passions as a woman. Although several times before,

notably in "Lestocq," he had enjoyed analyzing minutely
this delightful subject, he had never had a more complete
and decisive success than with "Le Verre d'Eau." The
subject of the play is the same as that of a *vaudeville* by
Paul Duport entitled "La Puritaine," and the development of the plot recalls that of Picard's "Les Ricochets."

"Le Verre d'Eau" was doubtless the best five-act
comedy Scribe had so far written. The idea is ingenious
and theatric; the plot skillfully complicated and successfully carried out. The characters of Bolingbroke and
of the duchess are well conceived and developed, although
in Act IV the duchess possibly bears too much resemblance to the *traître* of the boulevard theatres. The
character of the Queen is especially original, and does
great credit to the author: he has succeeded in making a
weak and spineless woman interesting and dramatic.
Possibly, however, Scribe has distorted history too much
in making her young, beautiful, chaste, and languorous,
considering the fact that at the time of the incidents
treated in the play she was a widow nearly fifty years old,
had been pregnant at least a dozen times, and was given
to the pleasures of the cup. In "Marion Delorme" we
see Louis XIII obeying Richelieu, and in "Ruy Blas" a
queen stifling in her flowered prison. The suffering of
these two sovereigns is more comprehensible and more
dramatic than that of Queen Anne, because they are absolute monarchs and for that reason oppressed; whereas
a ruler protected by a constitution and by Parliament, a
ruler whose counsellors may change from one day to another, cannot be dominated against his will by any favorite, no matter how powerful.

Perhaps also Scribe would have done better not to

limit himself to a single fact in proving his theory of great results from small causes; it would have been interesting to see the fortunes of each character, the outcome of each intrigue, each success and each failure, result from very small causes. This idea should have been brought out more vividly and presented more strikingly. The only incident which justifies and strengthens the main idea of the play is the slap which brings on the duel, enriches Bolingbroke, and restores his political fortunes. The various examples cited in the play: the window of Trianon which caused a great war, the saraband which made Bolingbroke a minister, the head cold which deprived him of his portfolio, are merely facts set in amusing speeches, and the real drama derives no profit from them. We are not given to understand very clearly what there is about Masham to explain the love he inspires in three women: a queen, a duchess, and a shop-girl; each of these three women compromises herself for him without the audience being enlightened as to why he merits all this devotion.

Instead of pretending that the coolness between the Queen and the duchess brought about peace between England and France, Scribe could easily have shown that Queen Anne, weary of the duchess's haughtiness, and separated from her by her feelings toward members of the High Church, loved Lady Masham, and that the duchess was ruined by her own bitterness; for after the incident she wrote to the Queen, who was seeking a reconciliation: "I ask only justice, and want no reply."

If we turn to the political side of the situation, we see that neither the dismissal of the duchess, her husband's recall, the destitution of relatives to whom she had given positions, nor the ministerial crisis, would have sufficed to bring England to accept peace with France. Fatigue and exhaustion; the enormous expenditures necessitated by costly victories and ruinous conquests; the death of Joseph I, who left to his brother, in addition to the Empire and all the states of the House of Austria, the immense Spanish succession for which England and France were fighting; the terror inspired by the idea of the reconstruction of the colossal empire of Charles V; the humiliation of Louis XIV; the capture of Minorca and Gibraltar from Spain; the demolition of the port of Dunkirk; the victory of Villars at Denain — these were the real causes of England's determination to seek peace.

The "Figaro," ordinarily so bitter and unjust in its criticisms of Scribe, made the following remark about "Le Verre d'Eau": "M. Scribe vient encore de remporter une victoire éclatante; ' le Verre d'Eau ' est une de ces comédies que les grands critiques échinent avec fureur, traitent de tous leurs noms, transpercent de leurs épigrammes, ce qui n'empêche aucunement les dites comédies de faire leur tour de France, et d'être partout accueillies avec transport."

In "Le Fils de Cromwell, ou une Restauration" (1842),[1] Scribe has treated history as he had treated manners and characters in his *vaudevilles* and in those comedies written before "Une Chaîne," "La Calomnie," and "Le Puff" — remaining on the surface, sketching a number of bright, clever figures, and seasoning the combination with his pungent wit. Previously, however, he had dealt only with what might be called the caprices of history; "Bertrand et Raton" and "Le Verre d'Eau" make no

---

[1] Cf. *Constitutionnel*, 1 Dec., 1842; *Siècle*, 5 Dec., 1842.

pretensions to gravity, and they entertained a public which demanded nothing serious. Here, however, the situation is different, for he has dealt with some of the most solemn and formidable figures of English history, and graciousness and wit will not suffice to paint such men and to revive for us the events with which they are associated.

Four characters dominate the play: Richard Cromwell, son of the Protector; Charles II; and the two generals, George Monk and John Lambert. Richard Cromwell, who, in spite of all his father's efforts, did not have in him the making of a sovereign ruler, accepted a heritage which he would gladly have repudiated. Simple, good, tender-hearted, he had demanded the pardon of Charles II. He assumed authority without pleasure and resigned it without regret. It was said that in the high position assigned to him his virtues were vices. Having meekly and gently received the deputations which came from all parts of the Three Kingdoms to salute him upon his accession to power, and having with great modesty accepted the diplomatic compliments sent to him from all the courts of Europe, he began his protectorate indifferent to his privileges as well as to his duties, a *roi d'Yvetot* following Oliver Cromwell.

Charles II was a double parody, of Francis I and of Henry of Navarre; extremely dissolute, he lacked any conspicuous good qualities to offset the impetuosity of his voluptuous instincts. He prided himself, however, upon his elegance, his magnificent prodigality, his good taste, and his cleverness.

George Monk was one of the generals whom Cromwell had succeeded in winning to his support and who served

the Parliamentary cause most valiantly. After having
had the Protector proclaimed in Scotland, and after dis-
arming the Highlanders, he had withdrawn to the estates
of the Countess of Buccleugh, where he remained five
years. The calm of this retreat having restored him to his
royalist opinions, he fell under Cromwell's suspicion.
However, at the death of the Protector, he accepted the
accession of Richard. It is difficult to ascertain the motives which directed his actions after this initial submis-
sion to Cromwell. A rival of Lambert, who had tried to
subdue and ruin him, he marched victoriously on London
and forced the dissolution of Parliament. Then he turned
royalist and had Charles II proclaimed king. Although
he was at that time the possessor of a great fortune, he
used it so moderately that he left unsettled the question
which divides historians even to-day, whether his course
was dictated by a sincere return to his old convictions, or
whether he merely followed the course of events.

John Lambert, an intrepid soldier, Cromwell's right
arm and agent of the Protector's rise to power, — a
power he later coveted, — was the most formidable of the
Presbyterian chiefs and the most implacable enemy of the
Stuarts. Under Richard Cromwell, he first opposed the
doctrine of the heredity of the Protectorate and then, per-
ceiving the favor with which his rival, Monk, regarded
Charles II, undertook to combat the royalist cause. Under the Restoration, arrested and condemned to death, he
was finally exiled to the Island of Guernsey, where he
died thirty years later.

These characters, who are the soul of the play, have
been entirely altered by Scribe. In his play beautiful
young ladies and gallant old lords are preparing the re-

turn of Charles II to his estates, recruiting against Cromwell and trying to win Monk to the cause of the Restoration. Charles II returns to England, where an interview
is arranged between him and Monk. Pursued by Lambert, the relentless persecutor of his race, he is saved by
one Clark, in reality Richard Cromwell. The latter, in
spite of his disgust at those who surround him, insists
upon retaining authority until he learns that his sweetheart fears this supreme rank, whereupon he gallantly
resigns, and the descendant of the Stuarts mounts the
throne of his fathers. That is how, according to Scribe,
the Restoration was accomplished in England. The characters which should have been kept intact have been
profoundly altered; in this play Richard is endowed with
an energy he never possessed, for Cromwell's son, as
Scribe represents him, would never have renounced the
paternal inheritance. Monk is not only uncertain, but
deceitful. Charles II approaches more nearly the historical truth, although Scribe has overdeveloped vices
which needed no exaggerating, and although he displays
in his conduct a quite unjustifiable imprudence and unreflection. Lambert is still more truthfully portrayed,
but his brusqueness, his cruelty, and his braggadocio are
strained beyond the bounds of good taste.

Although conspiracies, difficult to adapt to the exigencies of comedy, should be left to tragedy and to the
drame, interest in political questions was so widespread
and so lively at the time this play was written that
politics had come to be the great source of comic material and was the subject which absorbed all others.
Hence it was natural that Scribe, like most of his contemporaries, should exploit this mine. And yet, while he

was the mouthpiece of the pacifist bourgeoisie, eager to
avoid civil trouble at any price, he is to be criticized for
using the English Revolution merely for heaping ridicule
on revolutions in general, and for compromising not only
certain historical characters but history itself, in a play
in which reality yields to fantasy. In "Le Fils de Cromwell," as in "Le Verre d'Eau," we find Scribe's theory
of small causes producing great effects. Pascal said:
"Cromwell allait ravager toute la chrétienté, la famille
royale était perdue, la sienne à jamais puissante, sans un
petit de grain de sable qui se mit dans son uretère; Rome
même allait trembler sous lui, mais ce petit gravier qui
n'etait rien ailleurs, mis dans cet endroit le voilà mort, sa
famille abaisée, le roi établi." It is for Helen that Richard abandons the sovereignty of three kingdoms.

Although the love of Adrienne Lecouvreur and the
brilliant Maurice de Saxe had tempted more than one
playwright, these attempts to dramatize the story had
not been successful, for there had as yet appeared no
actress worthy of representing the heroine celebrated by
Voltaire. Scribe, inspired by the genius of Rachel, set to
work to compose his version of Adrienne Lecouvreur's
story. The attempt was a bold one, for it was no small
matter to take Rachel from Greece and Rome and trans-
plant her into the gallant boudoir society of the eighteenth century. At the first reading of the play before
the committee of the Théâtre-Français, Rachel, fearful of
the effect that an appearance in a modern rôle might
have upon her celebrity, begged her comrades, as apprehensive as she, not to accept the play. As everyone interested hesitated to advise the venture, Scribe's drama
was received by the committee with discouraging silence;

whereupon the author withdrew his manuscript, offering
it to the only other woman worthy of playing it, Rose
Chéri. There matters stood for six months until, advised
by various men who had the right to give such counsel,
Rachel and the Comédie came back to Adrienne Lecouvreur as a means of recalling Scribe. The play was
read again, and this time accepted. Rachel's transition
from classical tragedy to modern drama was an event
which created the greatest interest in dramatic and
literary circles, and among the general public as well, and
the excitement and anticipation of public and actors on
the night of the *première* recalled the stormy evening of
the battle of "Hernani."

The construction of "Adrienne" is so typical, and the
arrangement of episodes is so ingenious, that a detailed
analysis of the play may be made here. The love of
Adrienne Lecouvreur and the brilliant Maurice de Saxe,
son of the King of Poland, is the subject, and the jealousy of the Princess de Bouillon, a former mistress of the
Count de Saxe, supplies the motive force of the plot. The
first act, which takes place in the boudoir of the Princess
de Bouillon, makes clear to us that the princess loves
Maurice, who has just returned from his expedition to
Courland; that this dashing young officer now has a new
mistress, whose identity is not yet known; that the
Prince de Bouillon has built and furnished a little house
near the Grange-Batelière for La Duclos, Adrienne's
rival at the Comédie-Française, and that the princess
knows all about this liaison (although the prince does not
suspect this), and has in fact promised her support to
Duclos, provided the latter keeps the prince in subjec-
tion — in this way, the princess is freer and more inde-

pendent herself. It is also made clear to us that the prince, an amateur scientist, a great admirer of the Regent and of Voltaire, a *gentilhomme bourgeois*, as his wife calls him, has had a hand in the manufacture of a terribly poisonous powder, at the Académie des Sciences, of which he is a member, and that one breath of this powder is sufficient to cause violently painful death. A little scandal-mongering priest, in love with Madame de Bouillon, is one of the entertaining figures introduced in this first act.

Act II takes us to the artists' foyer at the Comédie-Française, where Adrienne and Duclos are appearing together for the first time in "Bajazet." Here the feverish life of the actors, with their petty rivalries, their jealousy, their hatred, and their ridiculous pride, forms an effective contrast to the quiet, elegant, and corrupted atmosphere of the first act. The prince thinks he has discovered that Duclos is faithless to him, for he has intercepted a note written by her to Maurice de Saxe, asking him to come to her house at the Grange-Batelière after the performance. In reality, Duclos has written the note at the request of the princess, and it is the latter who is expecting to see Maurice there. The prince and his hanger-on, the little priest, invite all the actors to go with them after the performance to a supper at the Grange-Batelière, planning thus to surprise Duclos and Maurice.

But it is the princess who is waiting at Duclos's house. Here the action is extremely complicated, and the dramatic interest intense; for the two rivals for the love of the Count de Saxe, the actress and the princess, are brought together. Maurice has asked Adrienne to help a certain woman (the princess, of course, who has come

here to meet Maurice) to escape, although he does not tell
her who this woman is. While the other guests are in the
dining-room, Adrienne lowers the light and calls to the
unknown woman — now hiding in the bedroom — to
flee. Before Madame de Bouillon leaves, she and Adrienne talk in the dark, and Adrienne learns (what she
had already feared) that Maurice has another mistress.

As in most tragedies and romantic dramas, the culmen
of the dramatic interest is reached in Act IV. We are
again at the Prince de Bouillon's palace, at a reception
given by the princess, where she has asked Adrienne to
recite for her guests. The princess, since her escapade at
the Grange-Batelière, has been trying to discover the
identity of the woman who had saved her, and who is at
the same time her rival; and when she hears Adrienne
talking with Maurice, she realizes that the actress is the
one Maurice loves. Her insolence to Adrienne reveals to
the actress who *her* rival is, and her anguish at the sight of
the princess's love for Maurice goads the poor girl into
taking revenge in a very satisfying and dramatic manner.
Called upon to recite, she declaims Phèdre's burning lines:

> "Juste ciel! qu'ai-je fait aujourd'hui?
> Mon epoux va paraître, et son fils avec lui.
> Je verrai le témoin de ma flamme adultère
> Observer de quel front j'ose aborder son père!"

And then, as her passion increases, she steps forward on
the stage, points her finger at Madame de Bouillon, who
is whispering affectionately to Maurice, and, continuing
her lines, says:

> "Je sais mes perfidies,
> Œnone, et ne suis point de ces femmes hardies —
> Qui, goûtant dans le crime une honteuse paix,
> Ont su se faire un front qui ne rougit jamais!"

The last act is short, for the princess's revenge has been quick, and fatal. A bouquet given by Adrienne to Maurice, which has fallen into her hands, she fills with the poison powder and sends to the actress. Adrienne, thinking that her lover has spurned her flowers and has returned them to her, kisses them slowly and then throws them into the fire. The poison is quick to act, and when Maurice, who has never really loved Madame de Bouillon, comes to offer his hand to Adrienne, he finds her dying, and she dies without the joy of knowing that Maurice loved her.

In its general construction the play is a series of compromises between the contradictory ideas of the Classicists and those of the Romanticists. For in 1848 those two schools were still struggling, and Scribe must have been incited by the passions of the moment to take into account the renaissance of the classical spirit caused by Rachel's art, and at the same time to cater to the taste developed during the preceding twenty years by the romantic drama. Although the action — as Batchelder, in "Un Dètail de Technique dans Adrienne Lecouvreur," points out — occurs in one city, Paris, to satisfy the Classicists, it moves about in Paris more than is necessary, this to please the Romanticists. As to the unity of action, Scribe threatens several times, in the early part of the play, to break it, for the affair between the prince and Duclos, the priest's love for the princess, Michonnet's love for Adrienne, are all extraneous; but once the real action is engaged, it is of a simplicity rare in modern drama. It is in the duration of the action, in the unity of time, that Scribe has taken the greatest pains to appease both camps and at the same time to interest the audience.

He has exerted all his skill to make the audience expect certain bold innovations, which he does not produce: with very obvious intent he has the time of day given frequently, ten times in all. The action of the play covers thirty-four hours, whereas twenty-four would have been sufficient. Between Acts I and II, it takes the prince six hours to go from his palace on the Quai Malaquais to the Comédie-Française, then situated in the Fossés Saint-Germain des Prés — a walk of scarcely fifteen minutes.

Scribe tried to please the Romanticists by observing no distinction of genres in the play, although here also he makes occasional sacrifices to the demand of the Classicists. Each act except the last begins in a more or less comic tone, while the end of each act is intensely dramatic, even tragic. On the other hand, there are fourteen quotations from classical tragedy: "Bajazet," "Le Cid," "Cinna," "Phèdre," "Psyché," and "Andromaque." And La Fontaine's fable of "Les Deux Pigeons" is made the basis of a very pretty scene. The Romanticists could not fail to approve the mixture of styles and genres: in Act II the elegiac declamation of "Les Deux Pigeons," and the epic movement with the quotation from "Le Cid" — "Paraissez, Navarrais"; in Act III the lyric stanzas sung by the priest to Rameau's music. We find much of the Romantic *impedimentum*, particularly in Act III, which Batchelder calls a "débauche Byronienne dans le genre romantique," with its secret panels, doors, and stairways, its darkness, etc. Batchelder thinks that the characters of the play represent certain important personages of 1848: Maurice de Saxe personifying the military order, and representing Louis Napoleon; the Prince de Bouillon typifying the monarchists, and representing

the Duke de Morny; Adrienne being Rachel, and representing the new school of declamation.

Although several scenes of this play are written with a
care and a finish unusual in Scribe's plays, its dominant
characteristic is mechanical skill carried to its furthest
limits. There is not a single useless phrase or word;
everything foreshadows and prepares for something else.
The dénoûment is prepared for in Act I. No one speaks
or acts haphazardly, everything is accounted for, foreseen, and prepared. And yet what is the real interest of
the drama? What is the rôle of Maurice, placed between
these two women? He does not love Adrienne sufficiently to brave the princess's hatred, and he hesitates
between the woman who may serve his ambitions and
the one who loves him passionately. He is neither ambitious enough to renounce love, nor infatuated enough
to renounce ambition; he is sincere only in the presence
of death. Adrienne, truer, tenderer than Maurice, is still
not as true and tender as she ought to be; it seems that
in order to love Maurice with a really great love she needs
to feel her love sanctioned by the genius of Corneille;
instead of giving herself up freely to the inspirations of
her passion, she seeks counsel from her memory. As to
the Princess de Bouillon, one cannot be interested in her
love for Maurice, as it springs from nothing but vanity;
were he a simple civilian, even handsome and noble-
hearted, she would not have loved him; and had it been
Madame de Noailles who disputed his love, and not
Adrienne, the actress, she would not have been so furious.
The Prince de Bouillon is insignificant and preposterous.

The subject of "Les Contes de la Reine de Navarre"
(1850) is a very pretty one, that of a charming and de-

voted sister employing all the resources of her grace and experience to save her brother, a prisoner. Francis I, taken captive at Pavia, is languishing in his gloomy prison in Madrid, where Marguerite is trying to frustrate the watchfulness of Charles V, and to help her brother escape. This she does by making the Emperor fall in love with her. Then, as she really loves Henri d'Albret, her cousin, the question is to evade her marriage with Charles V. Fortunately, as the Emperor's sister loves Francis I, a marriage between them is secretly arranged as a result of Marguerite's efforts, and by reading one of her celebrated stories, she succeeds in overcoming the Emperor's distrust, and in obtaining first his consent to the marriage and then her brother's liberty. She then marries Henri d'Albret.

In this play, Scribe has made Charles V too insignificant. It is forcing the note to represent the victor of Pavia exposed to the scorn of his own minister, to the violence of his royal prisoner, to the treachery of his fiancée, and to the taunts of his own sister. Francis I is less maltreated than Charles V, first because he is less in evidence, and second because it would have been altogether too daring to ridicule both the conqueror and his prisoner. Scribe's old spirit of opposition is apparent in this play, with its sly and crafty minister, its ridiculous chamberlains, and those bold but inoffensive remarks which have always pleased even the most despotic rulers. Scribe was really always a member of the opposition, liberal under the monarchy, and monarchical under the republic. And in this play he continues the war of masked epigrams he had waged under the preceding governments: "Vous avez pour fiancé un empereur." —

"C'est bien peu de chose." And this phrase, addressed to a below-stairs Figaro: "Il faudrait qu'on te fît ministre." — "Ma foi! il y en a qui ne valent pas mieux que moi." But the play offended no one, abounding as it did in virtuous maxims which the occupants of the *loges* could applaud without reluctance: "Il faut tout faire pour sauver son frère, ou son roi."

Never had Scribe shown a more scrupulous respect for the truth and for exactness of detail than in "La Czarine" (1855),[1] and yet, in spite of this veracity, his play gives an impression of *invraisemblance*. Why? Possibly because there is a truthfulness superior to exactitude of detail, a truthfulness of ensemble, one which the public instinctively feels, which is more important than external verisimilitude—the truthfulness of conception and style. We see Peter the Great writing his will, and hear Catherine relating the episode of her interview on the banks of the Pruth with the vizier from whom she bought the Czar's liberty and the safety of the Muscovite army. But of Peter the Great the author has made a sort of grumbling Almaviva, around whom his family and servants play a variation of the second act of "Le Mariage de Figaro"; for, like Beaumarchais's Spanish grandee, the Czar wants to know what man has entered the women's apartments, and the others league together to deceive him. The Czarine is a hypochondriac Rosine; the Prime Minister a northern Figaro; the Count de Sapieha a corpulent Chérubin; and Admiral Willerbeck more stupid and more cowardly than Antonio, but playing essentially the same rôle. The Catherine of history,

[1] Cf. *Siècle*, 22 Jan., 1855; *Moniteur Universel*, 30 Jan., 1855; *Figaro*, 21 Jan., 1855.

an adventuress of unknown birth; married in Livonia; slave, then mistress, spy and accomplice of Mentschikoff; good-hearted, even-tempered, uproarious and rollicking (the secret of her good-luck and of her influence over the Czar); a lover of *la dive bouteille*, dying two years after her husband as the result of her passion for Tokay — this Catherine has become in Scribe's play one of the honest, old-fashioned adulteresses of the romantic drama; a consumptive Adèle, who, finding the man who has raised her to his own rank too prosaic for her, seeks her ideal in a little counterfeit French marquis. Mentschikoff is no longer the clever buffoon, the pompous parvenu, the courtier accustomed to accepting honors from his master's knout; for Scribe has made of this man, who was in turn valet and hangman, an austere, discontented soldier, whose heart bleeds from the insults heaped upon him in public.

In 1854, a year before the production of the play, Théophile Halley had published the secret memoirs kept by the Sieur de Villebois, aide-de-camp to Peter the Great; and from this publication Scribe could easily have obtained the true story of Catherine's life, had he desired to write a sort of dramatic epic like those that were so popular at the boulevard theatres. This he made no attempt to do, and yet "La Czarine" would have been a better play had he not so disfigured the main characters. The monologue of Act IV is evidence that he had certainly read Philippe de Ségur's "Histoire de Russie et de Pierre le Grand."

Scribe's last historical comedy, "Les trois Maupins" (1858), is a complicated play dealing with the Versailles where "ennui reigns and Madame de Maintenon governs." A fourth act dazzling and bewildering in its complexity, and in the skill with which it is developed, supplies almost the entire interest of the action. This act takes place in a room which resembles the city of Thebes, with its hundred doors: doors to the right, doors to the left, visible doors and secret doors. It is here that Scribe's dexterity triumphs. Imagine a central point in a complicated railway system, which is crossed at intervals of a few moments by trains starting from all points, north, east, south, and west; suppose also that the departure of each train is so calculated that it must reach this crossing absolutely on time to the very second, as an inappreciable delay or advance would be sufficient to cause a catastrophe, or rather a number of them — as many catastrophes as there are trains. Does this comparison suggest sufficiently the swiftness of the grouping and ordering and the precision of the movement which, in the heat of the action, make the scenes and the characters follow each other with lightning rapidity? Only Scribe, with his genius for combinations, his composure before the glare of the footlights, could keep situations, scenes, and actors from colliding as they circulate in the limited space in which the dramatist has confined them.

Alexandre Dumas *père* and Scribe, both of them questionable as historians, although many a Frenchman has learned his history from their novels and plays, resemble each other in one point only, in their extraordinary theatric instinct; in all other points they are at opposite poles. Dumas was an improviser, one of genius, it is true, but of colossal ignorance, an ignorance explained by the circumstances of his early education. Scribe was quite the opposite, a solid, healthy bourgeois of the time of

Louis-Philippe and of Guizot. While Dumas, whose ambition was boundless and who, lacking real love for the truth, had a profound appreciation of the great, was working night and day to repair the defects of his early education, reading entire libraries in his efforts to inform himself, Scribe, writing in his study during the morning, and directing rehearsals in the afternoon and evening, worked regularly for forty years at his trade of dramatist as he would have worked at that of notary. He never took a passionate interest in any of the great questions which divided his contemporaries. The quarrels between the Romanticists and the Classicists, the prodigious development of physical and historical science, Saint-Simonism, the struggle between the bourgeoisie and the proletariat, all those questions which absorbed the great minds about him found him indifferent, and have left only the slightest traces in his works.

The main reason why Scribe did not succeed in this difficult genre is to be found neither in his ignorance nor even in the inadequacy of his psychology, but rather in his indifference and lack of curiosity. The *raison d'être* of the historical drama and novel is that the professional historians do not teach us about the past all that we should like to know. The dramatist and the novelist, whose imaginations come to the aid of science, evoke the men of past ages from their dust, and complete the work of the historian. But in order to succeed in thus filling out the task of the professional chronicler, in bringing the dead age to life, the first condition is that one should take a passionate interest himself in this resurrection. And it is this quality which is radically lacking in Scribe. He wrote historical comedies because it was the fashion to do so, but he had no real interest either in history, or in archæology, or in the philosophy of history, or in any of those things which so absorbed the Romanticists. As a result, his historical plays are the weakest part of his dramatic production.

Petit de Julleville did not hesitate to say that Scribe wrote perhaps the best comedies of the first half of the nineteenth century; Faguet points out that almost every form of dramatic literature treated in the nineteenth century was first perfected by Scribe; and Doumic goes so far as to say that all progress made in the theatre in the nineteenth century starts from Scribe, for, in addition to the fact that for years he reigned as master over authors and public, it was as a reaction against his authority that all later innovations were accomplished, so that, whether followed or attacked, his influence was always felt. What then was his contribution to the dramatic literature of the nineteenth century?

Of Scribe's political and historical comedies the only ones that really justify the name are "Le Solliciteur," "Bertrand et Raton," and "Le Verre d'Eau." In the others the political satire is so completely subordinated to the plot, or is so "special," as to lose its interest; the facts of history are so doctored, and the personages so distorted, that the play fails to reproduce the spirit of the past, giving even a false impression of the essential characteristics of the moment chosen. Lacking a profound interest in and sympathy with the past himself, he was unable to create that interest in his audience. Certain plays which depend for their success upon the interest of topicality lose their value as soon as the interest of the moment is past. "Le Solliciteur" is a clever satire, and, the follies it ridicules being common to all ages and to all people, the play has an intrinsic value different from that of "La Camaraderie," where very special circumstances and characters form the basis of the action. Although "Bertrand et Raton" was undoubtedly written to laugh away the Revolution of 1830, the interests and passions which figure in it are general, and for that reason this comedy would be apposite after any revolution; the fact that the personages represent certain men of 1830 does not alter the general truthfulness. "Le Verre d'Eau," despite a certain infidelity to history, gives a fair idea of the period in question, and successfully develops Scribe's theory of great results from small causes.

It is because of his comedies of manners, whether *vaudevilles* or five-act comedies, that he occupies the important place he does. There are two reasons for this superiority: first, that beyond any other dramatist of the century, the elder Dumas and Sardou not excepted, he was gifted, to an almost incredible degree, with the *instinct du théâtre*, with dramatic inventiveness, and with inexhaustible fertility of imagination; and second, that his plays, especially those written between 1820 and 1850, are a perfect expression of the society of those years. He is certainly the dramatist who for half a century best expressed the intelligence and the feelings of a considerable part of French society; as such he is entitled to esteem as an historian, if not to admiration as a stylist.

The *pièce bien faite* has for some years been in ill-repute. The clever constructions of the younger Dumas and of Augier, and the technical perfection of Sardou, brought the well-made play to a point at which, further improvement being impossible, meaningless virtuosity and barren

imitation caused the system to collapse before the Théâtre Libre. But disorder is no merit, and Sarcey was
eminently right in maintaining that clearness, precision,
and logic constitute essential features of any play, particularly one addressed to a French audience. The interest
of curiosity, when it is the only interest a play possesses,
may not be of any great inherent value; but as the public
of Scribe's time demanded that, and was often satisfied
with nothing else, he cannot be reproached for having
given them what they wanted. The simple fact is that, if
the French drama of the nineteenth century has been able
to accomplish its purpose, either in proving a thesis, in
presenting a *tranche de vie*, or in the painting of manners,
it is because it had at its disposal the most highly perfected technique ever possessed by any dramatic literature, in any country, at any time, and this technique it
received from Eugène Scribe. After Beaumarchais (who
first constructed a complex and, at the same time, com-
pact plot, nervous, brilliant, and bustling), Scribe in his
genre, C. Delavigne in his, utilized and developed this
law of stage motion discovered by Beaumarchais. As
Delavigne lacked the originality and the courage necessary to give this law its fullest development, it is to Scribe
that the modern drama is indebted for its form. Since
Scribe, nothing has been invented in France in the way
of technique, plot-development, or *procédés de théâtre*.
Augier's comedy of manners is constructed upon the
Scribe formula; the thesis play of Alexandre Dumas *fils*,
who so supremely scorned the dramatic "carpenter," is
nothing but an adaptation of the same formula; the
consumptive drama of Octave Feuillet, the vaudevil-
listic comedy and the drama of Sardou, the *vaudeville*

of Labiche, the *comédie de sentiment* of Jules Lemaître, the problem-play of Brieux and of Hervieu, the *comédie d'intrigue et de passion* of Bataille, the comedy of manners of Lavedan, Capus, de Flers — all depend upon the inventions of Scribe for the form they assume to accomplish their purpose.

CHAPTER IV

OPÉRAS-COMIQUES AND OPÉRAS

THE *opéra-comique*, a mixed genre characterized by the alternation of music and of the spoken word, is certainly of ancient French origin, at least in its primitive forms; an indication of the future *opéra-comique* is already to be found in "Aucassin et Nicolette." Its growth and development have been continuous, the musical element constantly acquiring greater importance, with the result that it has tended more and more to resemble the *grand opéra*, from which indeed it differs in modern times only externally and superficially.

We have seen in a previous chapter that as early as the beginning of the eighteenth century the *opéra-comique* appears almost completely constituted, in the form of the comedy with songs, at the fairs of Saint-Laurent and Saint-Germain. "Télémaque," a play written by Lesage and Gilliers in 1714, is the first piece to bear the title *opéra-comique*. The first half of the century was filled with the struggles between this popular genre and the two privileged theatres, the Opéra and the Comédie-Française, both of which, jealous of their prerogatives and justly alarmed by the popularity of the *opéra-comique*, attempted to reduce it to mere pantomime. And in addition to the hostility of these two august institutions, it had to contend with another formidable rival, the troop of Italian actors, whose arrival in 1752 accelerated the movement already begun by Pergolese with his

"Serva Padrona" in 1746, the play which had precipitated the quarrel between those who championed the national French music and those who held for the Italian, one of the noisiest among the latter being Jean-Jacques Rousseau. In this contest between the French and Italian musicians the cause of the national music was championed by Monnet, a man of ambition and intelligence, who in 1752 opened a new and luxurious hall at the fair of Saint-Germain, producing in 1753 "Les Troqueurs," by Vadé and Dauvergne, which may be considered the first real French *opéra-comique*. Although as a result of this competition between the two schools the *opéra-comique*, from its contact with the Italian influence, reached a higher state of musical perfection than it had yet attained, yet even as late as the time of Grétry critics continued to be more concerned with the poems than with the score. However, the interest in dramatic expression was already beginning to give to the musical part a special importance, and the *opéra-comique* could no longer be called a mere *comédie à ariettes;* Monsigny's "Le Déserteur" marks a great transformation, enlarging the frame of the old *comédie à ariettes* and presenting a real lyric drama, poignant and human.

The period which now follows, with Sedaine, Marmontel, Vadé, and Favart as librettists, and Philidor, Gossec, Monsigny, Duni, and Grétry as composers, is one of the most brilliant in the history of the *opéra-comique*, the one in which, definitely constructed, it had the greatest artistic importance, realizing the fusion between French and Italian music, and establishing the definite superiority of the musical element over the spoken. Between 1780 and the opening of the nineteenth century a noticeable evolution took place: the frame was enlarged, the *ariette* became an *air*, the duets, trios, and ensembles received greater musical development, and, in spite of the disorders accompanying the end of the old régime and the appearance of the new, artists were at work applying their genius to the development of a form which was to become one of the greatest glories of French art. It is this period which produced Grétry's "Richard Cœur-de-Lion" (1784) and "L'Epreuve villageoise" (1784), Kreutzer's "Paul et Virginie" (1791), and Méhul's "La Caverne" (1795).

During the Revolution the general tone of the *opéra-comique* had very noticeably become more pretentious, and there had been an attempt at grandeur and an exaggeration of the heroic genre; but with Boïeldieu's "Ma Tante Aurore" in 1803 there is, if not a distinct reaction, at least a return to simplicity, grace, and *sensibilité*. And whereas during the eighteenth century the French public had known only the national music and that of the Italian opera, and had considered dramatic music the only music, there now came, from outside, powerful impulses and beautiful models in the works of Gluck, Mozart, Haydn, and Sacchini. The majority of the writers who were working for the musicians at the beginning of the nineteenth century had no idea of the exigencies of the lyric style, and knew neither how to choose nor how to vary their rhythms. If one wishes to gauge the lack of musical taste in these libretti, he has only to examine the pieces presented during these years at the Opéra-Comique. Many authors of the period 1800–1815 were often mistaken, and took for good libretti what were only more or less interesting comedies with clever dialogue.

It is with "La Dame Blanche," written by Scribe and Boïeldieu in 1825, that the old school of the French *opéra-comique* comes to an end. Henceforth this genre is to evolve with great rapidity. Scribe's first *opéra-comique*, "La Chambre à coucher, ou une Demi-heure de Richelieu" (1813), had been a failure, and it was only with "La Neige," written in 1823, that he began to claim serious attention as a librettist. The story is drawn from the old fables of Charlemagne and his many daughters, and his opposition to their marriage through fear of the possible influence of his sons-in-law; certain features of the play were undoubtedly borrowed from Sir Walter Scott. The librettist, evidently fearing that a hero like Charlemagne would not figure well in an *opéra-comique*, placed the scene in nineteenth-century Germany; possibly also he hesitated to attempt a resurrection of the customs and manners of the eighth century.

"La Neige" is an important work, because it was written conscientiously. Scribe, unlike many of his contemporaries, has done something more than put historical conversations into dialogue form, and divide into scenes, more or less at haphazard, some well-known incident. Neither did he depend upon the musician to save the incorrectness and the weakness of the style by the charm of the music. He worked his material over carefully, endeavored to cast it into a really dramatic mould, attempted to find theatrical combinations, gave to the various characters well-defined physiognomies, and tried, often successfully, the effect of contrasts; in a word, the efforts of the author reveal close study and a knowledge of his art. The critic of the "Journal des Débats" said:

La pièce n'est pas un canevas à musique, ce n'est point un ignoble livret d'opéra prétendu comique ou d'opéra-bouffe; c'est une agréable comédie où la musique n'est appelée que comme auxiliaire. Il est déplorable que ce soit là aujourd'hui une éloge. L'auteur s'est fait reconnaître toujours en faisant ressouvenir quelquefois de Beaumarchais.

"Le Concert à la Cour," produced the following year in collaboration with Auber, called forth equally favorable comment. In choosing Scribe as his collaborator, Auber was sure of pleasing the public he was addressing; the Opéra-Comique was the favorite spectacle of the bourgeoisie, and no dramatic author knew so well as Scribe how to appeal to the middle classes. The innovations and novelties found in his libretti are suggested in the following statement made by the dramatic critic of the "Journal des Débats":

Depuis longtemps on annonce des comédies qui ne sont que des concerts. Tout pour la musique, le public se soucie bien des paroles! Et en effet, le plus souvent l'insipidité des paroles glace l'auditeur. M. Scribe rappelle en ce moment l'opéra-comique à sa véritable destination. Il commence par composer une comédie. Il imagine des situations; il emploie agréablement le temps qu'il dérobe au compositeur; le musicien se tait, l'écrivain nous fait rire ou nous occupe.

In "Fiorella," written with Auber in 1826, Scribe made an attempt at historical exactitude and presentation of local color, for at that time nothing was so attractive to the intelligent part of the public as authenticity of costume and manners.

The musical critics had for some time been insisting that, although the *opéra-comique* as it was then conceived and written was a false, vicious, and ridiculous genre, it would be a very easy matter to remedy the situation, and that the librettists must adopt that dramatic reform of which Sir Walter Scott had given the signal, offering the public a true painting of a period, its manners and usages, and an exact observation of costumes. It was this path which Scribe decided to follow in "La Dame Blanche" (1825),[1] a play which marks a significant date because it characterizes exactly the frame of mind of the spectator at the first performance of this masterpiece; music and poem alike indicated that it belonged to a new order. The musician had found in Scribe the predestined man who, through his collaboration with nearly all the great composers of his time, was to exercise upon the French musical play an immense and, for a time, unrivalled influence.

The scene is laid in Scotland. The Avenels, having sided with the Stuarts, have been proscribed and the last head of the family has died in exile, leaving no heir save a young son, Julien, who had been kidnapped from his cradle some twenty-eight years before, and of whom nothing has been heard since then. Thus the family has died out, or at least is thought to have done so, and Avenel Castle is to be sold at auction to pay the creditors of the estate. The former overseer of the Avenel property, Gaveston, has made his fortune and is desirous of purchasing the castle, and thus of becoming, much to the regret of all the inhabitants of the domain, heir to the property, rank, titles, and prerogatives of the Avenels, who have left the most honorable and cherished memories.

Meanwhile, the White Lady is there, a mysterious being formerly held in great veneration by the inhabitants

[1] Cf. *Journal des Débats*, 12 Dec., 1825; *Constitutionnel*, 12 Dec., 1825; *Moniteur Universel*, 12 Dec., 1825; *Globe*, 13 Dec., 1825.

of this part of Scotland, a marble image of whom has been preserved in the old Gothic manor of the illustrious Avenel family. Although for two centuries the White Lady has been reposing in the shadows of the tomb, yet she still appears from time to time to the terrified mountaineers. At one time in the past she had given some money to a farmer on one of her estates who, had it not been for her, would have been reduced to misery. It is to this farmer that she addresses herself to save the honor and wealth of the house. She writes, asking him to meet her at midnight in one of the buildings attached to the castle, where Gaveston is now living.

This nocturnal rendezvous is very little to the taste of the peasant, or of his wife, and he eagerly accepts the offer to replace him made by a young lieutenant to whom he has offered hospitality. This officer, who is young, courageous, and eager for adventure, goes to the place indicated by the White Lady. At the stroke of midnight she appears. Although the officer can scarcely see her in the heavy shadows, he can hear her very well, and such is the power of the spell which she casts over him that he respects her orders and does not attempt to discover the secret of the mysterious being who speaks to him and urges him to become owner of the castle. He has not a single guinea, but he promises to obey.

The following day the auction sale takes place, and the young officer wins over all the other bidders, including Gaveston, and thus acquires Avenel Castle. The seals are at once lifted, and he takes possession of the ancient dwelling of the lords of the country, receiving the homage of the inhabitants, who are charmed by the kindly manners of their new master. As he roams through the vast galleries of the old Gothic halls, vague, confused memories return to him. It seems to him that he recognizes these spacious rooms and lofty towers, and that he has once before heard these songs which are being sung in celebration of his accession. But soon the five hundred pounds must be paid; where is this huge sum to be found? The White Lady does not desert him in this predicament, but appears and hands him a casket containing an immense treasure, with which he becomes the real possessor of Avenel Castle.

The White Lady is no enchantress. She is none other than a beautiful young girl who has been brought up by the Avenels, and who is attached to them by the deepest gratitude. This young orphan, after the death or disappearance of her benefactors, has become the ward of the overseer, Gaveston. In possession of a precious secret, she has discovered that the statue of the White Lady of Avenel, which stands in the great hall of the castle, contains several millions of pounds, concealed there by the unhappy Avenels to aid the partisans of the Pretender. This treasure could not be reached before the seals were lifted. But immediately after the sale she runs to the statue and, seizing the money, presents it to the young officer, whom she had nursed at one time, in Hanover, where he was wounded, and who is none other than the lost child and heir of the Avenels. As might be expected, the gallant young officer soon marries his charming benefactress.

In writing "La Dame Blanche" Scribe gave one of the best exhibitions of his genius, displaying his ability to treat the romanesque element and to combine gayety and sentimentality in the proper proportions. His adaptation of Sir Walter Scott was most happily inspired, for the Scotch Homer was at that time master of all imaginations. The poem very skillfully combines the melodramatic form with musical situations and details. There is in the subject, in the title itself, a mysterious air which arouses and maintains the curiosity of the spectator. The subject, drawn from Sir Walter Scott, but whether from "The Monastery," "Guy Mannering," or "The Abbott" it would be difficult to say, has two complementary dramatic mainsprings: the amusement excited by the Highlanders' terror of the White Lady of Avenel, and the spectators' desire to know whether she really exists and just who she is. The element of mystery, spectres, and gnomes, in opera, had always proved interesting, as in Quinault's "Armide" and in Grétry's "Zémire et Azor." In this poem, as in "La Neige" and "Une Demi-heure de Richelieu," we find a notable effort to introduce local color — an effort largely successful in spite of certain anachronisms; for instance, though the scene is laid in Scotland, it is hard to tell at just what period, for in the play there is a *young* officer of King William, who died in 1702, and this young officer is represented as having been wounded at the battle of Culloden in 1742.

"La Dame Blanche" is a masterpiece: the play and the music form an exquisite ensemble. To write a work which will weather the caprices of popular taste, the composer of an *opéra-comique* needs not only an ingenious comedy, artfully constructed, and interesting musical situations which will allow him to go naturally from easy prose to rhythmical verses; it is essential also that the subject which inspires him have the qualities necessary to please in all ages. In "La Dame Blanche" the musician identified himself completely with the poet, and both of them were audacious and original enough to impose upon a foreign country the language and customs of their own. On December 16, 1862, at the thousandth performance of this play, the audience applauded enthusiastically these verses recited during one of the entr'actes:

> C'est que Scribe a donné tout ce que le poète
> Peut inventer de mieux pour la lyre interprète;
> Et le maître inspiré prodigua tour à tour
> Le charme que les mots n'ont jamais su décrire,
> L'accent qui fait rêver, l'accent qui fait sourire,
> La gaîté de l'esprit, l'extase de l'amour.

With "La Dame Blanche" Scribe accomplished a genuine revolution in the *opéra-comique*, and affirmed his genius for providing dramatic and musical situations from which the composer could draw the inspiration for his message. His popularity as a librettist was so great at this time that the "Figaro" began to have visions of a dictatorship at the Opéra-Comique similar to that which Scribe already exercised at the Gymnase. "On voit que Monsieur Scribe va jouer un grand rôle à l'Opéra-Comique; ses spirituelles compositions plaisent au public, c'est un fait incontestable, mais il ne faut pas établir en faveur d'un auteur, quel qu'il soit, un monopole qui deviendrait plus tard préjudiciable aux intérêts du théâtre."

After "La Dame Blanche," the old model from which so many copies had been drawn seemed more or less scanty, and talented composers felt the need of working for a larger frame and in more ample proportions.

About the year 1810 there had been an Italian brigand who had terrorized the coast country between Naples and the Papal States with his audacious crimes, and whose exploits had already been adapted to the stage in "Le Brigand napolitain" at the Vaudeville, in "Le Bandit" at the Variétés, and in "Cartouche," a comedy by Overnay and Nézel. Scribe in turn treats it in "Fra Diavolo," written with Auber in 1830, making a new play out of all that had gone before. While there is nothing unusually entertaining in "Fra Diavolo," yet the scene where Zerline, the innkeeper's daughter, is preparing to go to bed, singing happily meanwhile, not knowing that there are two robbers concealed in the room, is most original, and the amusing stupidity of the Englishman and his wife furnishes much gayety. Fra Diavolo is not, as in history, a cruel, ferocious brigand, but an honest robber and gentlemanly rascal, with good drawing-room manners.

"Le Cheval de Bronze" (1835), an *opéra-féerie* [1] based upon an old Chinese legend which corresponds to the story of the apple in the garden of Eden, did not receive a very cordial reception from the critics, who remarked that even a *féerie* needed interest, action, plot, *vraisemblance*, and good sense. It is in this libretto that Scribe says "Voici la nuit, le jour s'enfuit," and farther on, "La nuit sombre répand l'ombre," verses which excited the hilarity of Jules Janin. "L'Ambassadrice" (1836) is the story of one of those popular singers raised for a moment by the caprice of the public to the height of social glory, only to be rejected later by the same public. The treatment of the subject is not very logical, for a man who braves all the rules of society to marry an actress should be sufficiently in love with her not to betray her at the

---

[1] "*Féerie:* Pièce de théâtre à grand spectacle, où figurent les fées, les génies." (Larousse.)

first opportunity; but the action proceeds quickly, gayly, and cleverly; the characters are varied, the dialogue lively. A significant criticism of the play is found in the "Journal des Débats": "Ce petit poème sans prétention mais non sans gaîté a été beaucoup plus goûté du public que tous les poèmes historiques et moyen-âge." "L'Opéra à la Cour" (1840) is a real masterpiece of technical skill and of astounding literary and musical legerdemain. The main idea of "La Dame de Pique" was suggested by a delightful story by Pushkin, translated from the Russian by Mérimée. Although Scribe's libretto bears little resemblance to the original tale, his inventions are more favorable to the music than the Russian story, whose developments might have been more difficult with the supernatural element so frankly admitted.

Of all Scribe's *opéras-comiques* the one which, with "La Dame Blanche," most nearly approaches perfection is "Le Domino noir" (1837). A young embassy clerk in Madrid has met, at a ball given by the Queen of Spain, a domino with whom he has fallen madly in love. At midnight the domino disappears, but not before the young man has seen her getting into a carriage and has caught a glimpse of her face. A year later, to the very day, he finds her again in the same drawing-room; she speaks to him, even removes her mask, gives him reason to think she loves him, and then suddenly departs, saying that an eternal obstacle separates them, and forbidding the disconsolate attaché to try to see her again. Thus ends the first act, and there still remain two before the dénoûment, which in every *opéra-comique* by Scribe and Auber is inevitably the marriage of the two lovers. The second and third acts are marvels of invention. This woman, whom the hero thinks he has lost forever, he finds again for an instant after leaving the ball, but under such circumstances and in such a disguise that he cannot be sure it is really she; through incident after incident she escapes him; his over-excited imagination, his incoherent speech, make his friends think that he is mad, and he himself wonders whether he is not losing his reason. Finally, in a veil-taking service, he hears the voice of his beloved singing a hymn. Is he the victim of an hallucination or, still more incredible, can his domino be a nun? Fortunately, just as he is giving way to despair, everything is explained and all ends happily.

Opéras

The earliest tangible origin of the French *opéra* — leaving aside the "Jeu d'Adam," in which are found already alternance of choral song and declamation in choral form — is to be noticed in "Le Ballet comique de la Reine" (1581), by Baltasarini and La Chesnaie, with music by Beaulieu, a curious and interesting specimen of a new genre, both pompous and comic, with music in all its forms, serious and light, from the *couplet à refrain* [1] to the madrigal for several voices, accompanied by numerous instruments. But as yet there is no dramatic music, properly speaking. After "Le Ballet comique de la Reine" there are a number of plays with music, either mimed ballets, or real comedies, such as "Le Mariage forcé," "Le Sicilien," "Georges Dandin," "Le Bourgeois Gentilhomme"; and before long, tragedy, then in its full glory, called music to its aid and replaced the *ballet de*

---

[1] "*Couplet* — Stance faisant partie d'une chanson." — "*Refrain* — Répétition de mots, de vers ou de strophes, dans le cours ou à la fin des parties d'une pièce de vers lyrique." (Larousse.)

cour by the *opéra* and the *ballet d'action*. Corneille, in his preface to "Andromède," says that music should intervene in tragedy only subordinately, as a more or less useless accessory; and yet with "Psyché" we are very near the lyric tragedy or *opéra*, in respect to the *mise en scène* and especially to the lyricism of the sentiments expressed.

One step now remained to be taken: to find a sung tragedy in which the music should hold the first place. Something of this kind, though less complete and less literary than the lyric tragedy, had been introduced into France from Italy, where opera had received a notable development, beginning with the mysteries and continuing through the dramas, with subjects borrowed from antiquity, mythology, and the Greek tragedies. A good specimen, and one of the earliest, of the Italian operas previous to the seventeenth century, is Rinuccini's "Dafne," although here the literary element is much more important than the musical. It remained for Scarlatti to develop the regular aria and the different forms of the recitative. Peri and Caccini attempted to renew the ancient tragedy of the Greeks and at the same time to produce a lyric tragedy in which the mission of the music should be to render the meaning and even the shading of the words; this was a real innovation. In France, however, something more akin to the national taste was necessary: a music less rich, perhaps, but more vigorous and more expressive, corresponding to the nature of French tragedy. This something, partaking both of the classical tragedy and of the ballet, was found first by Perrin and Cambert, and was then perfected by Lulli, and called *tragédie en musique*, or *opéra français*. Thus with Perrin and Cambert's "Pastorale d'Issy," and later with their

"Pomone," the *opéra* is virtually created in France. It has singers, choruses, an orchestra, an audience, even a royal privilege, indispensable in a country where nothing existed without the king's permission. It still lacked, however, the man of genius to give it its definite form and to make of it a work of art. That man was Lulli.

While Lulli was not the creator of the *opéra* in France, he was its real organizer. Believing that music should take its place also in the *Grand Siècle*, along with the finest form of the art of the period, tragedy, he repudiated his Italian origins, relegated to a secondary place — but without entirely abandoning them — the brilliant *hors-d'œuvre* of the ballet, made the musical language approach the poetic language, sought exact painting of passion and sentiment, and succeeded in pleasing his audience by writing in a musical language comprehensible to the French public. With the tragedy of Corneille and Racine as his model, his ambition was to translate into music the beautiful and noble sentiments expressed by those authors. The libretti of almost all his works were furnished by Quinault.

In the first half of the eighteenth century there were two distinct kinds of *opéras:* the *opéra-ballet*, a development of the old *ballet de cour*, taken generally from mythological allegories, and created by Campra; and the *opéra* properly speaking, or lyric tragedy, which was the musical translation of the classical tragedy. The best librettists of this period were Campistron, Thomas Corneille, Lamotte, and Regnard. "Hippolyte et Aricie" (1723), the first work of Rameau, gave to serious dramatic music a splendor theretofore unknown, and created a revolution in the musical world, arousing the antagonism of the Lullists, sensual dilettanti irritated by this nervous, yet profound, rugged music. As long as Rameau was in the full glory of his genius, the dilettanti had not dared to revolt openly; and even after his death the traditions of the lyric tragedy and of the mythological ballets were continued successfully for some time. But when, in 1752, a troop of Italian actors conducted by Manelli obtained permission to play their répertoire at the Opéra, making their debut in Pergolese's "Serva Padrona," a play well calculated to please a public wearied by the serious and solemn genre which had been in style too long, a new quarrel, *la guerre des bouffons*, broke out. Grimm, favoring the Italian school, opened hostilities with his "Lettre sur Omphale." The King and Madame de Pompadour were for the French school, the Queen for the Italian. Finally, as a result of the quarrel, the Italians were expelled in 1754. Rousseau, later taking up the cause of the foreigners, demanded more dramatic plausibility, and advocated the suppression of the duets, ballets, *fêtes*, and other *divertissements* which suspended the action.

Gluck applied to the great French tragedy his theory of expressive music, the theory that the music should help the poetry by strengthening the expression of feeling and sentiment and the interest of the situations. His efforts resulted in a quarrel between the Italian school of vocalization, represented by Piccini, and that of lyric declamation, in which Gluck overwhelmed his adversary in a contest, both of them writing an "Iphigénie en Tauride." Gluck carried the old musical tragedy of Lulli and Rameau to its culmen of perfection, with the application of his theory that dramatic music can attain its greatest power and beauty only when it is joined to a simple, really poetic libretto expressing natural emotions and true passions. Sacrificing the musical element to the dramatic, he continued the system of the lyric tragedy.

But during the last years of the eighteenth century and the first two decades of the nineteenth, poems such as Gluck demanded were not written. Like the tragedy of those years, the libretti of grand operas were nothing more than a lifeless, stereotyped treatment of the old subjects, — Phèdres and Œdipes succeeding Persées and Andromèdes, — having no charm save that of elegant versification, and giving no inspiration to the composer. This was the situation at the time of the first performance, in 1828, of "La Muette de Portici," by Scribe and Auber.[1] Thenceforth French composers wrote what may be called music of action, or narrative music, the object of the musician being to relate in musical language a dramatic incident, either taken from history or invented; to establish the musical setting without attempting a detailed painting of the picture; to make the characters act without going too deeply into their inner feelings; and, above all, to seek to impress the audience with a clearly outlined musical story.

"La Muette de Portici" is the first *grand opéra* in which Scribe gave any measure of his ability to write dramatic libretti for that genre, since "La Somnambule," though a very pleasing composition, is scarcely more than an arrangement of the comedy of the same name. The

---

[1] Cf. *Journal des Débats*, 2 March, 1828; *Figaro*, 1 March, 1828; *Constitutionnel*, 2 March, 1828; *Globe*, 5 March, 1828; *Courrier des Théâtres*, 2 March, 1828; *Moniteur Universel*, 2 March, 1828; *Revue des Deux Mondes*, Sept., 1879, Blaze de Bury: "Auber et Scribe."

subject of "La Muette" is the same as that of "Masaniello," by Moreau and Lafortelle, an effort to retrace the portrait of the great Masaniello with his strange fate, his power, his pride and ambition, his downfall and his death.

The Neapolitans, under the leadership of the fisherman Masaniello, have resolved to free themselves from the yoke of their Spanish oppressors. Alphonso, son of the Duke of Arcos, the Spanish viceroy in Naples, has seduced Masaniello's sister Fenella, a dumb girl, who does not know the identity of her lover until she sees him marching to the cathedral to his marriage with Elvire. Infuriated by this insult to his sister, Masaniello summons his companions, and arousing the fishermen, the fruit-sellers, and the other members of the conspiracy, hastens with the crowd to the royal palace, where a fierce struggle ensues between the insurrectionists and the royal troops, the Spanish forces being defeated. Masaniello's victory, his triumphal entry into Naples, and his leniency toward the Spanish prisoners, arouse the jealousy and hatred of a band of malcontents headed by Pietro, who betray him to the forces raised by the foreigners. Attacked in his palace during a festive celebration, deserted by his followers who, terrified by a violent eruption of Mt. Vesuvius which they consider the presage of a great disaster, leave him alone to face his enemies, Masaniello falls beneath the blows of his assailants. Fenella in despair casts herself from the balcony into the waves of glowing lava which are pouring down from Vesuvius.

It had been a long time since such magnificence and good taste, such fidelity of costume, so scrupulous an ob-

servance of local color, so perfect an ensemble, had been
seen on the stage of the Opéra. And yet, in spite of the
exactitude of detail, the real story of Masaniello has been
completely altered, to the advantage of the opera, one
may say — for the romanesque combinations with which
it has been decorated serve to raise into relief the living
portrait of the period and of the place; and such an appeal to the eye is particularly important in an opera. The
Bay of Naples is placed before us in all its splendor;
pages and fishermen, lords and ruffians, ladies of the
court and peasant girls, despatch-bearers and magis-
trates, pass before us in their varied costumes, assemble,
pass back and forth, and disperse, with the grace and
freedom of nature, their movements directed by an invisible but consummate art.

It would be unjust to accord all the praise to the musician; the poet deserves his share as well, for the libretto
of "La Muette" marks an immense progress in the structure of the musical drama. Not only is the language
sufficiently rhymed for the melody, but it is measured,
cadenced, and set into a rhythmical form which furnishes
the musician with verses which he can easily sing. For
several years musical critics had reproached Scribe for
being, as it were, the great tyrant of dramatic music,
oppressing it with his wit; but in "La Muette" it is clear
that he realized that each art should be lord and master in
its own domain. He has left the composer an open field
for his inspiration. The libretto abounds in musical
situations, and in verses well arranged for the rhythm,
yet never aspiring to create an effect by their own beauty;
there are no long metaphors, no tirades, but an extraordinary clearness, a concision in all the explanations of

the plot, which obviates the necessity of interminable recitatives.

All circumstances conspired for the success of the piece — a success which, in spite of the revolutionary tone of the play, never for a moment alarmed the Restoration government; for, although the spirit of the times is to be found entire in "La Muette," at first no one suspected it. Not until two years later did the Revolution of 1830 uncover the volcano hidden under the flowers. At the time of the appearance of the play, the storm was not yet threatening, although its muffled rumblings sufficed to inspire a musician already fascinated by his subject. From this point of view alone, "La Muette" would deserve a special place in the history of the modern opera. Never before had a musical drama been given such an ovation. The uninterrupted succession of pictures representing the life of a people, seemed to the public absolutely original; for, as to landscape and setting, lyric art was still governed by the traditions of the French classical tragedy, and everyone knows what the Racinian tradition was worth from the point of view of picturesqueness. The public was charmed by this warm, poetic painting of the southern sky, by this dramatic symphony, as highly colored as a Veronese, in which nothing is omitted, neither character-study, nor movement, nor passion, nor the azure of the Bay of Naples, nor Vesuvius with its flames — all executed with moderation and sobriety in accordance with the precepts of an art which has the sincerity of ignorance, innocent of all theory and of all system.

The year 1830 was a time of transformation for "La Muette," the patriotic fervor of the subject breaking through the romanticism which had been the first charm of the opera, stirring singers and public alike to enthusiasm. On Friday, July 23, there had been a performance of "La Muette"; the 24th and 25th were days of rest; for Monday the 26th the bills had announced "Guillaume Tell," but the agitation manifested by the public at the royal decrees signed at Saint-Cloud on the 25th did not allow the performance of this opera. Fighting began on the 27th and did not finish until the 29th. Closed for two weeks, the Opéra was not reopened until the 4th of August, and on that date "La Muette" offered on the stage a faithful picture of the barricades, the revolt, and the battles which had just been seen in the streets of Paris. Two months later, after serving as propaganda in France, "La Muette" was taken to Belgium, where it took a no less active part in the incidents of September there; and from those days this opera took on the revolutionary character which it has always had since. Knowing the rôle which was attributed to "La Muette" during the stormy period that served as a prelude to the events of 1870, we are not surprised that after the disasters of 1870 and 1871 a work which was guilty of having sung victory so convincingly should fall into a disfavor lasting for years.

"La Muette" did not break openly with the past; this opera which changed the future of the genre kept in touch with the old school by a number of traditions worth preserving, and even by some that might better have been discarded. It is, for instance, rather curious to find at the very beginning of the first modern French opera the last of the confidantes of classical tragedy. "De Fenella quel est le sort?" the prince asks his companion; and the latter replies, as Arcas, Théramène, or Corosmin might have done:

Seigneur, je l'ignore, et mon zèle
Pour découvrir sa trace a fait un vain effort.

Yet Scribe and Auber have the honor of being the first to take their place in the new school, and to break with the traditions of the old classical style. For the first time the chorus takes part in the action and is really a hero itself, a hero in a drama in which theretofore it had served only as a supernumerary. The Greek and Roman mobs of Sacchini and Spontini have been removed from the abstraction in which they had formerly been placed, and have come to life; when they move about on the stage, singing the morning hymn on the sunny beach, or evoking the god of battles to the sound of the tocsin, they are no longer mere automata, but real men. The common people have taken possession of the stage so long reserved to the descendants of Æneas and Dardanus; fishermen and beggars appear before a public accustomed to seeing mitred pontiffs, princesses, and warriors with their golden helmets. There is a new realism in the costumes and the stage movement.

Scribe's next opera, "Le Philtre" (1831), is not significant enough to merit discussion, but an interesting innovation at its first appearance may be worth mentioning. From March 15, 1671, to October 13, 1831, the curtain at the Opéra, raised at the last measures of the overture, was not lowered until the end of the performance, the stage remaining uncovered throughout the play, and all the changes taking place in sight of the audience. Special curtains, called *rideaux de service*, lowered after each of the first four acts, were followed by the great curtain, which, falling at the last chords of the opera, solemnly announced the conclusion of the play. At the end of the first act of "Le Philtre," the curtain was lowered, allowing the stage-hands to change the setting without the help of machinery.

What "La Dame Blanche" had been in the history of the *opéra-comique*, "Robert le Diable" was in the history of the *opéra*.[1] The novelty and the innovation were at once recognized by the critics, as the following lines from the "Constitutionnel" well show:

> Enfin, voici du nouveau; ce ne sont plus ces anciens palais ébran-lés par les dernières lueurs d'un quinquet qui s'éteint, ces antiques débris, ces vieilles colonnes qui tremblent au seul attouchement d'une Vénus en papillottes ou d'un Amour en escarpins; ce n'est plus un héros criant son amour en *la mi la*, une princesse s'époumonant à rendre le dernier soupir, une bergère se mirant dans une fontaine.

The subject of "Robert le Diable" is to be found in an old Norman legend, according to which a maid of noble birth married a beautiful knight, by whom she had a son named Robert, who was so wicked, malicious, and inclined to evil from early youth that everyone called him Robert le Diable. In those times of superstition, it was not long before people began to say that he was really the son of the devil. The same subject is to be found in a German novel called "Petit Pierre"; one of the situations is found in "Faust," that in which the singing of religious songs makes the principal character change his projects; and the great seduction scene was already in "Robin des Bois."

---

[1] Cf. *Journal des Débats*, 23 Nov., 1831 and 18 July, 1836; *Constitutionnel*, 23 Nov., 1831; *Revue des Deux Mondes*, 29 Nov., 1831; *Moniteur Universel*, 25 Nov., 1831.

In Act I we see in the background the city of Palermo, and in the foreground a seashore where knights from all nations, among them Robert, Duke of Normandy, have gathered for a tournament being given by the Duke of Messina. Before breaking lances the knights have gathered round the table to drink, and have urged a Norman pilgrim named Raimbaud to enliven the festival with some new ballad. Raimbaud says he will sing the adventures of one Robert, surnamed the Devil, a prince whose title is justified by his birth and by his actions; for, born of Bertha, a Norman princess who had been seduced by a demon whom she later married, this son is dominated by two passions which incline him now to good, now to evil.

Infuriated by the pilgrim's tale, Robert orders him to be hanged, but Raimbaud implores his pardon so touchingly in the name of his pretty fiancée, that Robert forgives him on condition that the beautiful maid be brought to him at once. This maid is none other than Alice, Robert's own foster-sister, who has come to him bearing a pious message, a letter addressed to him by his dying mother, which he is to read only when he becomes worthy to do so. Since he admits his unworthiness, Alice must continue to keep the letter for some time. She has meanwhile gained his confidence, and he tells her of his troubles and sorrows, and of his love for the Princess of Sicily, whom he has lost through his impetuosity — for, thinking that Isabelle shared his love, he had tried to steal her from her father. While fleeing with her he had been attacked by a number of knights, and was about to succumb when a knight named Bertram took his defense, felled his most valiant assailants, and saved him. Alice advises him to write to the Princess beseeching her pardon, and promises that she herself will carry the letter to her.

At that moment Bertram appears. At the sight of him Alice shudders, for he bears a terrifying resemblance to the Satan in the picture in her village church. She and Raimbaud now withdraw, having obtained permission to marry and continue on their pilgrimage. Bertram is delighted to learn that Robert, his protégé, had received Alice merely with the intention of seducing her, for he had feared Alice's virtuous influence on the duke. After the repast Robert, with Bertram's encouragement, takes part in a game of dice between the knights, and loses everything — money, jewels, silver-plate, equipment, horses, even his arms.

The second act takes place in the palace of Isabelle, Princess of Sicily, where she is giving audience to young women presenting petitions. Among these suppliants is Alice, with Robert's letter. As the Princess really loves Robert, she consents to see him, forgives his wrongs and his follies, and allows him to fight for her in the tournament, in which the victor is to be her husband. Armed and accoutred by the Princess, and preparing to hasten to the combat, he is stopped by a herald who, in the name of the Prince of Granada, one of Isabelle's suitors, challenges him to a duel, telling him that the Prince is awaiting him in a neighboring forest. Robert leaves the tournament and follows the herald, and the other knights joust without him.

In Act III Raimbaud is seen wandering among the cliffs and rocks of Sainte-Irène, where he has a rendezvous with Alice. Instead of Alice, however, he finds Bertram, who casts a purse of gold at him, advising him to lead a joyous life and to abandon Alice, so poor and so unworthy of him. Bertram has come to this deserted savage spot on an important errand — it is here that the king of the fallen angels holds his court, and already we hear their screams and their infernal shouts of joy. This Bertram is in reality Robert's father, and it is for love of his son that he urges Robert to crime, so that they may be damned together and never separated from each other. He goes into the cavern where the demons are making merry, and just at this moment Alice arrives at the meeting-place. Failing to find Raimbaud, but hearing horrible shrieks in which she distinguishes the name of Robert, she approaches the cavern and sees the mysteries of Satan and his associates. Drawing back in terror, she falls at the foot of a cross placed at the other side of the scene, kisses it, and faints.

Bertram now reappears, in despair, for Hell has pronounced the irrevocable decree that, if Robert does not give himself to him before midnight, the struggle is finished and he must lose his son forever. Alice hears him and recognizes him; and when he realizes that she has heard everything, he threatens to kill her lover, her father, and all her family if she reveals the slightest detail of what she has just seen and heard. Meanwhile, Robert, having lost everything in the dice game, is in the depths of despair. Bertram had reduced him to this extremity in order to increase his own powers of seduction over him, and now promises his son he will recover everything, mistress, power, and fortune, if he will go to the statue of Sainte-Rosalie and take from it a twig of cypress which she holds in her hand. This will of course be a sacrilege, but his crime will be well rewarded. Robert consents, and

takes the road to the cloister where Sainte-Rosalie re-
poses, surrounded by wicked nuns whom celestial justice
has condemned to the flames of Hell.

The scene now changes to represent a cloister, part of
which is in ruins, allowing the pale moonlight to pene-
trate the broken arches. The statues of the nuns repose
upon their tombs, and as Bertram evokes the spirits of
these sinful women their statues slowly come to life, arise,
and, as the lights begin to glow, gather under the dark
arches. Bertram now promises to give them back their
life for an hour on condition that they persuade Robert
to pluck the cypress twig, forcing him by their charms to
carry out his imprudent promise. At once the instinct of
passion returns to these bodies which only a moment
before had been lifeless; the nuns seek cups and dice,
drink, play, and, to be freer in their movements, take off
their long robes. Some of them make offerings to an idol
representing Satan. This *ronde de sabbat* gradually becomes wilder and wilder, and finally ends in a bacchana-
lian orgy. At the height of the dance Robert appears,
and the nuns by their seductions entice him to Sainte-
Rosalie's tomb, where he plucks the fatal twig. At this,
songs of victory arise from the bowels of the earth.

Act IV brings us back to the apartments of the Princess
of Sicily, who is in her bedroom, receiving the presents
sent her by her fiancé, the Prince of Granada. Robert
enters, holding in his hand the cypress twig. As this is a
talisman which causes everyone to fall asleep, Isabelle
yields to the magic charm. She is soon awakened, however, by Robert, trying to take advantage of her leth-
argy. She resists, and breaks the twig. The courtiers

and guards, awakening, recognize Robert and carry him
out.

The fifth act opens with a very beautiful chorus of
monks, introducing penitents into the cathedral of Palermo, the vestibule of which is represented on the stage.
Robert, who has been saved once more by Bertram, this
time from the anger of Isabelle's father, comes seeking
shelter and safety in this church. Bertram follows him,
and with the intention of taking advantage of Robert's
despair proposes to him that he sign a pact. Robert first
consents, and then hesitates, for at this moment hymns
with solemn organ accompaniment recall memories of his
childhood and the days when his mother used to pray for
him. Repulsed as an enemy, Bertram now makes himself
known to his son, who despairingly resigns himself to
sharing his father's fate. Alice is watching over him, however, and opposes maternal solicitude to the father's
power by reading Bertha's letter, that mystic will left in
her hands. Robert, implored both by his father and by
Alice, is afraid to decide. He hesitates so long that midnight rings, and Hell, receiving Bertram, delivers Robert
from his father's ardent supplications. The curtain of the
vestibule rises and discloses the interior of the immense
cathedral, lighted by thousands of lamps, and the organ
peals forth, accompanying the chants. The Princess, at
the foot of the altar, is awaiting Robert, her fiancé. The
curtain falls upon this magnificent scene.

The fundamental idea of the poem is, of course, the
struggle between Heaven and Hell for the soul of Robert
le Diable, and it is this thought which has directed all the
work of the composer. The libretto abounds in striking
contrasts, which Meyerbeer, with powerful imagination,

has employed in such a way as to produce the most brilliant effects. The disposition of the libretto is of a sort to give great inspiration to the composer; the infernal choir is striking and horrible; there is a delightful trio; and the religious chorus with organ accompaniment inspires quiet meditation. The third act, with the infernal chorus, which is Victor Hugo's *sabbat* and Boulangé's drawing put into action, is beautiful both as to music and as to *mise en scène*. Romanticism, then in all the charm of its novelty, has inspired both author and composer: the infernal waltz, the appearance of the nuns and their ballet, are typically romantic scenes. By appealing especially to the intelligence of the public, by learning from Scribe the importance of accessories and the theory of small causes producing great results, by taking advantage of the religious idea, a source of endless meditation and perpetual conflicts of opinion, Meyerbeer succeeded in winning over the French public. Moreover, the Norman legend of Robert was skillfully chosen, for with its romantic coloring it appealed to popular taste and dramatized the eternal struggle between good and evil in the human soul. "Robert le Diable" may be said to have overcome the July Revolution and to have sustained French opera during the public tempests. Castil-Blaze, generally so unwilling to admit Scribe's talent, said of this opera: "Le livret est au moins pour moitié dans la fortune de la partition."

"La Juive" (1835) [1] deals with a beautiful period of European history: the time when the communes were

---

[1] Cf. *Journal des Débats*, 25 Feb., 1835; *Revue de Paris*, March–April, 1835; *Quotidienne*, 27 Feb., 1835; *Revue des Deux Mondes*, Feb., 1835; *Moniteur Universel*, 28 Feb., 1835; *Figaro*, 27 Feb., 1835.

building their cathedrals; when, in order to appear at a
tournament properly dressed himself, and with his horses
and his servants fittingly accoutred, a baron did not
hesitate to engage and sometimes alienate his barony;
when, in order to receive a papal legate or some foreign
king, a city would spend in advance ten years' revenue;
when Charles the Bold, Duke of Burgundy, ordered a
costume woven with gold and embroidered with pearls.
In those days, should the most insignificant prince present himself at the gates of a city, at once the provost-
ship, the sheriffship, and all the guilds were thrown into
excitement, and to honor the guest the whole bourgeoisie donned costumes of flowered satin, velvet robes
trimmed with sable, with embroideries and decorations
of gold. "La Juive" is a resurrection of those centuries
of magnificence, and a restoration of those splendid costumes.

In Act I we see the portal of a beautiful cathedral, surrounded by picturesque Gothic buildings. The crowd is
pouring out of the holy place to the sound of the great
organ and is gathering at the entrance, for this is the day
when Sigismund, Emperor of Germany, accompanied by
a multitude of sovereigns of all Christendom, comes to his
city of Constance to open the council. The Emperor's
solemn entry takes place on Christmas Eve; the churches
and inns are crowded; wine flows freely, and all work is
suspended. And yet the clanking of a hammer is heard,
in the house of Eleazar, a Jew, who, with his daughter
Rachel, is dragged from his house, insulted, and threatened with death. Leopold, married to the Emperor's
niece Eudoxie, loves Rachel and has assumed the disguise
of a Jew in order to see her.

Act III takes place in a garden, at the end of which is a beautiful rustic vista; at one end, under a tapestried tent surmounted by a daïs in red velvet, and raised above the others, is the Emperor's table. In this scene the descriptions of the most magnificent banquets of the Middle Ages have been carried out with scrupulous precision. The banqueters are served by mounted knights, who, receiving the plates from the varlets, pass them to the pages and nobles, who place them upon the imperial table. The buffets are covered with magnificent silverplate, in which an antiquarian might recognize a careful study of the times. According to the customs of those years the *entremets*, a sort of pantomime, takes place between the courses. A fortress, crowned with towers and battlements, guarded by turbaned infidels, and propelled by a machine concealed in the interior, advances and is summoned to surrender; at the refusal of the unbelievers, the armed Christians prepare to attack, but suddenly the fortress is transformed into an imposing Gothic edifice, from which step beautiful maidens, who perform a ballet before the Emperor.

In Act IV, where the simplest setting would have sufficed, the scene is one of the greatest luxury, representing a Gothic hall, furnished and decorated in the finest taste. Lighted by an effect of sunlight, beautiful stained-glass windows cast a rich glow upon the Flemish tapestries which adorn the wall. Eleazar, who has yielded to Leopold's entreaties that he be allowed to remain with Rachel, learns that his daughter's lover is a Gentile; and when Leopold refuses to renounce his faith and marry the young Jewess, — which he cannot do, being already married to Eudoxie, — Eleazar drives the Gentile from

his home. Rachel follows him and sees him enter the
palace, spends the night lying at the entrance, and then,
sure that Leopold has not come out, forces her way in,
for a secret instinct seems to reveal the frightful truth
to her. Once within, she succeeds in being admitted to
Eudoxie's service, where nothing escapes her sight. She
swears vengeance upon her betrayer, for in her ulcered
heart vengeance has replaced love.

Leopold also is unhappy. Torn as he is with remorse,
he is only irritated by Eudoxie's tenderness, and it is with
regret that he is obliged to yield to her entreaties and
that, accompanied by the Emperor and his procession of
kings, prelates, princes, and princesses, he sits down to a
splendid banquet given in honor of his victories over the
Hussites. The slave who fills his cup is none other than
Rachel, who even yet does not know of the union that
binds him to another woman. In a moment, however,
Eudoxie, receiving from the hand of Eleazar a beautiful
gold chain which she had had him make, puts it around
Leopold's neck. "Non," cries Rachel, snatching the
chain from the prince, "cet homme est indigne d'un tel
honneur; c'est un lâche; il est coupable et il mérite la
mort selon les lois des Chrétiens, car quoique Chrétien, il a
eu commerce avec une maudite, avec une Juive, et cette
maudite, cette Juive, sa complice, c'est moi."

Cardinal Brogni pronounces anathema and maledic-
tion upon the prince and his accomplices, requesting the
council to pass sentence upon them. Yet, as Rachel is the
only one who has spoken, she can save Leopold by retract-
ing her word. If Eleazar will abjure his faith, renounce
the creed of his fathers, and bow in humiliation to foreign
idols, he can save himself and Rachel. This he haughtily

refuses to do, and declares that before dying he will strike some Christian with his vengeance.

Lequel? Toi, Brogni. Te souviens-tu du jour où les Napolitains entrèrent dans Rome, promenant partout le fer et la flamme? Ton palais fut réduit en cendres, ta femme expira; près d'elle sa fille, qu'elle venait de mettre au monde, restait mourante, tu la crus perdue; eh bien! un de ces Juifs que tu proscris encore, cédant à la compassion, se précipite à travers les ruines fumantes et enlève cet enfant. Sa retraite, tu l'ignoreras toujours; son libérateur, tu ne le connais pas; j'emporterai ce double secret dans la tombe. Va maintenant, prêtre du dieu des Chrétiens, prononcer votre sentence.

Although the old Cardinal throws himself at the Jew's feet, beseeching him to reveal the mystery, Eleazar remains silent. Leopold, whom Rachel has declared innocent, has already fled from Constance.

In the last act the crowd has gathered to enjoy the spectacle of the torture of Rachel and Eleazar. In the foreground of an immense public square, surrounded by Gothic buildings and crowded with soldiers and civilians, has been erected a tent from which the principal members of the council may watch the *auto-da-fe*. All the lugubrious pomp displayed by Catholicism under such circumstances is faithfully reproduced; the condemned Jew and his daughter advance to the sound of the funeral knell, tolled from the belfry, in the midst of a procession of torch-bearing penitents whose funeral costumes are in painful contrast with the brilliant suits of armor. This melancholy scene, under the blue and radiant sky, in the pomp which surrounds the dignitaries of the church, is striking and produces a wonderful effect. At this supreme moment, Eleazar beseeches Rachel to accept the Cardinal's offer, abjure her faith, and spare herself. She refuses and rushes toward the torture instruments, where the flames are already crackling. Just as the girl throws herself into the boiling oil, Cardinal Brogni learns that she is his daughter. And thus Eleazar has his revenge on the Christians.

The author of this drama, and of "Robert le Diable," was neither Alexandre Dumas nor Victor Hugo, but Eugène Scribe, and he was yet to write "Les Huguenots" and "Le Prophète."

The dramatic critic of the "Moniteur Universel," speaking of "La Juive," said:

Ordinairement on fait peu d'attention aux paroles d'un grand opéra, à ces lignes plus que négligemment rimées, à ces canevas indigents que, par ironie sans doute, on est convenu d'appeler des poèmes. Il y en a bien peu sur lesquelles la critique ne passe dédaigneuse ou indifférente. Monsieur Scribe a voulu venger le genre du peu d'estime où on le tient, et le remettre en honneur. Il faut reconnaître que cet opéra affecte souvent, avec un rare bonheur, les formes entraînantes et énergiques du drame largement compris. De belles situations, des scènes empreintes d'un intérêt puissant se succèdent; de ce nombre on remarque surtout celle du deuxième acte, où Eléazar et sa fille se réfugient sur le parvis de la cathédrale, chassés par la fureur populaire; au troisième acte la situation fortement dramatique, où le Juif, vaincu par les prières de sa fille, consent à lui donner un Chrétien pour epoux; plus tard celle où Rachel se perd en dénonçant Léopold; la terrible révélation d'Eléazar au Cardinal Brogni; enfin la position non moins pénétrante d'Eudoxie implorant de sa rivale la grâce de Léopold.

"La Juive" is a splendid example of the lyric drama.

"Les Huguenots" (1836) [1] is based upon the Massacre of St. Bartholomew, an incident which had already been treated several times on the stage. Before the "Charles IX" of Chénier, there had been two plays dealing with the events of the night of August 24, 1572: one by Arnaud

---

[1] Cf. *Journal des Débats*, 7 March, 1836; *Quotidienne*, 2 March, 1836; *Revue des Deux Mondes*, March, 1836; *Moniteur Universel*, 7 March, 1836.

Baculard, often played at the amateur theatricals at the
Hôtel de France where Lekain was developing his talent;
the other by a certain Chevalier de Chantelouve, published toward the end of the sixteenth century, in which
the author, a zealous Catholic, depicts Admiral Coligny
as a prey of the furies, planning horrible massacres of the
Catholics. Melodrama also, in its turn, was to utilize the
subject; and Mérimée put it into fiction form in his
"Chronique de Charles IX." It remained for Scribe to
treat it in an opera, although in its heat, its passion and
color, this libretto is more of a melodrama than a tragedy:
the septet of the duel, the benediction of the daggers,
and the final trio are melodramatic scenes of the highest
order.

History tells us that toward the end of the year 1340
Alfonso, King of Castile, had conceived for Leonora de
Guzman so violent a passion that, in order to marry this
woman, remarkable both for her beauty and for her wit,
he had formed the project of repudiating his queen. This
story had already served as the basis of a tragedy by
Arnaud Baculard, "Le Comte de Comminges," before
Scribe utilized it in "La Favorite," in collaboration with
Donizetti, in 1840. Going back to the Middle Ages, to the
picturesque period when the Crescent was struggling
with the Cross for the fertile soil, the marvelous palaces,
and the blue sky of Spain, he has studied the institutions,
the customs, the physiognomy, and the costumes of
the time. The libretto suggests certain reminiscences.
"Guido et Ginevra" furnished the romance in the first
act; "Robert le Diable" the religious songs with organ
accompaniment in Act V; the anathema scene is found in
Act III of "La Juive"; and the dénoûment reproduces

that of "Le Comte de Comminges." Yet these criticisms of detail are amply answered by qualities rare, but essential, in literary composition of this genre: clear and rapid action, an ever-increasing interest, dramatic situations musically presented.

The subject treated in "Le Prophète" (1849), for which Meyerbeer wrote the music, is one that in itself would not seem to offer many dramatic or musical situations; yet of all of Scribe's operas it is perhaps the one in which he most successfully united all the conditions essential in an opera libretto, and made interesting and dramatic the incidents furnished by history, skillfully combining them into an action as simple as it is moving. While love plays a very small rôle in this poem, so many other strong and tender passions replace it that the interest of the spectator does not fail for a single instant.

Fidès, the mother of Jean de Leyde, is by far the most interesting character in "Le Prophète." This pious woman, tenderhearted yet energetic, kneeling in the cathedral of Münster and praying to the God of her fathers for a son whom she believes to be lost, is a noble creation. "Le Prophète" is both an opera and an oratorio, striking a new note in the history of the lyric drama; pastoral and almost demi-genre in the first part, it rises in the second to lyricism and even to the epic. Along with large pictures, such as the finale of Act III, with its inspiring religious and martial vigor, and the immense musical fresco of the cathedral scene, there are intimate, profound expressions in the rôle of Fidès and in the arias of the first act. It can be said that, if "Guillaume Tell" is the last beautiful work of one school, "Le Prophète" is the first opera of one just appearing.

Scribe's last opera, "L'Africaine," written in collaboration with Meyerbeer, was not produced until 1865, four years after his death. Scribe has transformed the Vasco da Gama of history, who until the day of his death knew nothing but the favors of men and fortune and is here made to be a second Christopher Columbus, suffering the persecutions of which the Genoese navigator was the victim, pursued by the Inquisition and by the King.

"Un musicien est responsable du sujet qu'il traite, et vous ne vous imaginez pas peut-être qu'on mette un libretto dans la main d'un compositeur comme dans celle d'un enfant l'on met une pomme." Already, at the time when Weber pronounced these words, the music alone was no longer sufficient to assure the interest and success of an opera. Some have claimed that Scribe, even more than Auber, Rossini, and Meyerbeer, was the real author of the modern opera. And although such a claim may be excessive, it cannot be denied that this writer, so keen, so alert, so inventive in his *comédies de genre*, showed in his operas a sense of the most dramatic romanticism and an art, unknown until then, of speaking and appealing to the masses.

If there is one part of Scribe's work which I should willingly believe immortal, it is that in which he has effaced himself before others greater than he; where he has been the ingenious, adroit, and yet discreet collaborator of men like Boïeldieu, Auber, Halévy, Meyerbeer. It was Scribe who for more than thirty years furnished poems for *opéras* and *opéras-comiques* to the most celebrated composers of his time. Although he doubtless thought that he was accomplishing a task of secondary importance, they are his most durable titles to glory.

"Les Huguenots" and "La Dame Blanche" having had
more than a thousand performances, "Robert le Diable,"
"La Juive," "Le Prophète," "Fra Diavolo," "Les Diamants de la Couronne" having been played not only in
France but throughout the world, the librettist is entitled
to a share of this glory; those who do not know him even
by name know by heart the words which Meyerbeer set
to music, and the author of the poem can claim a small
part of the success of the composer.

What was it that won for Scribe the first place among
the librettists of his time? Certainly not his talent as a
poet. Théodore de Banville said:

De même que certains hommes ont reçu du ciel le don de rimer,
d'autres hommes ont reçu du ciel, en naissant, le don de ne pas rimer.
Don surnaturel et inexplicable comme l'autre. Scribe, par exemple
(après Voltaire), avait reçu le don de ne pas rimer; il le possède
jusqu'au miracle: aussi faut-il admirer chez lui cette faculté sans
vouloir l'expliquer, non plus qu'un miracle.

No, Scribe was not a poet, at least in this sense, and his
association with Auber had nothing in common with that
which was the glory of Quinault and Lulli. Poetry in an
opera libretto is superfluous. Quinault was a real poet,
indeed, but it was not for that reason that he rendered
Lulli such inestimable services; it was because he knew
thoroughly his business as a librettist. One can be worse
than mediocre as a writer and still succeed in this difficult
genre, if one has other qualities which it is rare to find
united in one man and which Scribe possessed to the
highest degree. The first of all is to be able to imagine
musical situations; by that is not meant necessarily
dramatic situations, what Sarcey called *les scènes à faire*
(for instance that of Horace and Curiace at the moment
when they are going to fight), but situations that poetry

is insufficient to render, that music alone is capable of expressing. Situations of this kind abound in Scribe's libretti, and it is partly for that reason that some of them are masterpieces. The duet between Raoul and Valentine in the fourth act of "Les Huguenots," is one of the most celebrated. The idea is borrowed from Mérimée's "Chronique de Charles IX": the young Huguenot noble-man is with his mistress, the Countess de Turgis, a good Catholic, at the moment of the beginning of the Massacre of St. Bartholomew. Scribe, however, has given a much more dramatic character to the scene by supposing that his hero, Raoul de Nangis, hidden in Valentine's apart-ment shortly after her marriage to the Count de Nevers, has just heard her father tell of the danger threatening the Protestants. He rushes to join his brethren, at that moment being massacred. The situation is too violent to allow the development of ideas and sentiments that one expects in a drama. The moment of rapture, when Raoul forgets the whole world, his duty, and even the massacre of his brothers, as Valentine confesses her love for him, would produce a pitiful effect were it a scene from trag-edy, where our thought and imagination are appealed to, and not in an opera, where the most logical criticisms are helpless against the music, just as the hero's conscience is powerless to resist the voice of the woman he loves.

Another scene, eminently musical as well as dramatic, is the famous cathedral scene in "Le Prophète," in which Jean de Leyde, at the height of his triumph, sees his old mother stretching out her arms to him. If he recognizes and embraces her, not only will his prestige disappear, — for it is as the son of God that he is acclaimed by the mul-titude, — but his mother will fall beneath the daggers of

the three Anabaptists. To save both himself and his
mother, Jean de Leyde, pretending to call divine inspiration to his help, obliges Fidès to kneel before him, as
before a prophet, and to declare that she has lied, that he
is not her son. It is one of the most beautiful musical
situations imaginable; musical more than dramatic, for
a tragic poet who would attempt to treat it without the
help of music would find himself helpless at the outset.
The scene is so conceived that Jean de Leyde cannot express aloud the sentiments which are struggling in his
soul; we have to guess them, and it is the beautifully
pathetic recitative which Meyerbeer puts into the mouth
of his hero and the wonderful orchestral accompaniment
supporting this recitative which help us to understand
and to feel what a dramatist would have been unable to
express with the means at his disposal. Metastasio, who
was the Scribe of his time, gave all his attention to the
form, to the plasticity of the poem, which was a sort of
scaffolding for the composer's edifice. In Scribe's poems,
on the contrary, it is the situation which dominates, and
the form does not count; the work is negligible as to
style and color, but admirable as material for contrasts,
as a programme for the music. It is easy to see what great
help Meyerbeer, artist and critic, could get from such a
collaborator.

It will be noticed furthermore that Scribe, so antipa-
thetic to romanticism in his dramas and comedies, is on
the contrary a Romanticist in his *opéras*. Is there anything more romantic, more mediæval, than "Robert le
Diable"? "Les Huguenots" is full of reminiscences of
Vitet's "Scènes historiques" and Mérimée's "Chronique," two works of the advance-guard of Romanticism.

As a matter of fact, there is not much local color in Scribe's verses, since it was the musician who was to take care of that, provided the librettist gave him the occasion; and this Scribe did, knowing so well what his public demanded. In "La Muette," the Neapolitan fishermen with their red bonnets and their nets; in "Le Prophète," the black-robed sectarians wandering over the plains of Westphalia preaching revolt; in "La Juive," the tournament and the stately procession of cardinals passing through the streets of Constance — all this reminds us that Scribe is a contemporary of Delacroix as well as of Victor Hugo. He really bears very little resemblance to them, and I dare say cared very little for them; but with his commercial instinct he realized that the picturesque was a mine to be exploited. And he exploited it most profitably.

The qualities which distinguish Scribe's comedies — skill and clarity of composition — are found in his *opéras*, adapted to the exigencies of the genre in which he is writing. One of the most important things in a lyric drama is the necessity of making oneself easily understood by the spectator, who must be able to follow the story easily and without fatigue. But as only the best singers can make themselves understood, as indifferent artists fail to convey more than half of their words, and as choruses are practically unintelligible, it is absolutely necessary that the action be clear and simple if one is to enjoy a really dramatic pleasure at the performance of an opera. And so, when writing for Auber, Halévy, or Meyerbeer, Scribe avoids the complications which are found in his comedies, realizing that such finesse would not only be lost, but that it would obscure the very thing that in an opera can never be too clear.

These are some of the reasons which make Scribe the greatest French *opéra* librettist. But although his talent in that genre is unquestioned, his real titles to glory are his *opéra-comique* libretti. The poems of "La Muette" and of "Le Prophète" prove that he was skillful and understood clearly the taste of his period and the conditions of the genre in which he was working; but "La Dame Blanche," "Le Domino noir," "Fra Diavolo," "L'Ambassadrice," are original works, perfect in their genre, which would be worth reading and studying, even were Boïeldieu's and Auber's music forgotten. The *opéra-comique* is a genre more truly French than the *opéra*, with its vague, profound sentiments; for the clearness of the *opéra-comique* and its cleverness appeal more to the French public. The composers of French *opéras-comiques* were almost all French, while, from Lulli to Meyerbeer, three fourths of the great musicians whose *opéras* were represented in France were Italians or Germans. Scribe and Béranger have in common the fact that they are both of real French tradition and owe nothing to the foreign geniuses who inspired and directed the Romanticists, often more than was reasonable. The origins of the *opéra-comique* relate it both to the *vaudeville* and to comedy, two genres in which French writers have produced numerous masterpieces. Scribe did not find at once the form best suited to the genre; "La Chambre à coucher" (1813) is scarcely more than a *vaudeville;* and while in "Le Maçon" (1825) there is gayety and a good portrayal of popular manners, it is not until 1825, with "La Dame Blanche," that he showed what he could do. The play marks a date in the history of the theatre as well as in that of music, for librettist and musician have both found what Sarcey called *un monde nouveau*. There is nothing in the repertoire of Favart, Sedaine, or of Marmontel in just this genre. "La Dame Blanche" is a romantic opera. The sombre, mysterious, and poetic features of Sir Walter Scott's novel have given place to a modernized, humanized charm; the hero is a real Frenchman, an intrepid, heedless lieutenant of the Empire; and yet Scribe was too clever not to keep the local Scotch color that was to contribute so much to the success of the play. "Le Domino noir," "Les Diamants de la Couronne," and "Fra Diavolo" are masterpieces of their kind. It is probably safe to say that Scribe's *opéras-comiques* will outlive not only his comedies and most of his *vaudevilles*, but many other works perhaps more literary, certainly more pretentious. While in comedy Scribe was skillful, in the *opéra*, and especially in the *opéra-comique*, he was superior.

CHAPTER V

CONCLUSION

IT is possible that Scribe's plays, particularly his *comédies-vaudevilles* and his comedies of manners, are more important in the history of the French theatre in the nineteenth century than has generally been admitted. And not merely as specimens of dramatic technique: all question of style and literary value aside, they have a documentary interest as pictures of the society of those days. Moreover, it is undeniable that such plays as "Le Mariage d'Argent," "Le Mariage de Raison," "Une Chaîne," "La Camaraderie," "Bertrand et Raton," and "Le Verre d'Eau," influenced very markedly the growth, the form, and the function of the comedy of manners, of the historical and the political comedy. Practically every innovation, every reform, every novelty found in the drama of the nineteenth century originated with Scribe, and the highest point in the development of the main genres of dramatic literature was reached in his plays.

As early as the middle of the eighteenth century an effort had been made to revivify French comedy by the creation of new, mixed genres, and by the use of hitherto untried devices. The *drame bourgeois* of Diderot; the *comédie larmoyante* of Nivelle de La Chaussée; Sedaine's "Le Philosophe sans le savoir"; Nepomucène Lemercier's "Pinto," the first of the series of historic dramas which led through Duval to the historic drama of the eighteen-thirties, and which reached its culmen in Scribe's ingenious hands — all these are compositions essentially different from the comedy of the seventeenth and early eighteenth centuries. Picard, profiting by Beaumarchais's brilliant success, enlarged the scope of the comedy of manners, varying the theatrical devices, multiplying the episodic, or secondary rôles, and complicating the construction of the plot. Classical tragedy was by the end of the eighteenth century in a state of rapid decadence, — cold, artificial, and stereotyped imitation of Corneille, Racine, and Voltaire, — and was daily losing ground before a new, bastard form, the melodrama of Guilbert de Pixérécourt, which was to prepare the way for the glorified melodrama of Hugo and Dumas. Along with all these new forms, the older ones — classical comedy in verse or in prose, and classical tragedy — persisted, however, although constantly losing popularity and interest, until by the middle of the nineteenth century they were definitely supplanted by the new comedy, and by the *drame*.

Scribe made his first appearance as a dramatist at the Théâtre du Vaudeville and at the Théâtre des Variétés. Recognizing the intrinsic interest of the lighter forms of comedy, then called *vaudeville*, or *comédie-vaudeville*, realizing at the same time their artificiality, and seeing the possibilities they offered to a keen observer and lively writer, he began writing little plays which, while conforming in essential respects to the contemporary *comédie-vaudeville*, offered certain novel features which revived and eventually transformed it. This transformation of the *comédie-vaudeville* was effected between 1811 and 1820; "Une Nuit de la Garde Nationale," "Les Montagnes russes," "L'Hôtel des Quatre Nations," and the other plays written during this period, are much better

constructed than the *vaudevilles* which until then had
been presented at the secondary theatres.

Nor was this the only difference. The interest of
Scribe's plays, their originality — which was at once
recognized — lay chiefly in the fact that, as well as being farcical or sentimental, they were sufficiently topical
and apposite to be entertaining as dramatizations of current events and as sketches of contemporary manners.
After the opening of the Théâtre du Gymnase in 1820, his
comédies-vaudevilles began to present on the stage other
figures than those that had theretofore appeared at the
Vaudeville and at the Variétés. Instead of watching
"Les Désespoirs de Jocrisse," the audience found entertainment in pictures of middle-class life such as "La
Demoiselle à marier," "La Charge à payer," and "Le
Budget d'un jeune Ménage." Stockbrokers, notaries,
and retired officers replaced "Fanchon la Vielleuse" and
"Cadet Roussel." In place of a nonsensical plot, absurdly
put together, the spectators were offered a carefully and
logically constructed story which, improbable as it might
be in detail, nevertheless seemed plausible. The coarse
lubricity, the obscene and frequently scatological language of "Esturgeon," "Madame Angot," and "Jérôme
Pointu," were replaced by a clever, sparkling dialogue,
sometimes frankly farcical, often sentimental, always
amusing. The public, quick to appreciate the change, had
been won over at once; after a few initial failures the
young dramatist was almost uniformly successful, and by
the last years of the Restoration had become by far the
most popular playwright of the French capital.[1]

[1] The longer favor of Victor Hugo, the notoriety of *Hernani* and of
Antony, the greater literary beauty of the plays of de Musset, have kept us

The transition from this renewed *comédie-vaudeville* to real comedy was as easy as it was logical. Suppression of the *couplet*, enlargement of the scene, extension of the frame, addition of more important figures and characters, intensification of the satire, reduction of the buffoonery (already attenuated), complication of the plot by increasing the number and the complexity of the *procédés de théâtre* — all this resulted in such plays as "Une Chaîne," "Bertrand et Raton," and "La Calomnie." A witty article by Jules Janin in the "Journal des Débats" gives such an entertaining and at the same time so sound a description of the earlier plays at the Gymnase, those that preceded the five-act comedies in prose at the Thé-

from realizing that with the contemporary public Scribe was more popular than any of the Romanticists. The following figures from Joannidès's interesting book on the Théâtre-Français, showing the number of performances of plays by modern writers, are suggestive. In 1816 Andrieux led with 25 performances, Collin d'Harleville had 11, and Picard 8; in 1820 Duval headed the list with 27, Andrieux had 10; in 1823 Scribe led with 48 performances, Duval had 19, and C. Delavigne, 10; in 1827 Picard had 81, Mazères 60, Duval 52, Scribe 17; in 1830 (the year of *Hernani*) Picard had 60, Hugo 39, Andrieux 38; in 1833 C. Delavigne had 72, Scribe 32, Picard 29, Hugo none; in 1834 Scribe led with 135 performances (more than any one author had had, since 1816, at least), Duval came second with 63, Delavigne third with 46; in 1835 Delavigne had 83, Hugo (the year of *Angelo*) 36, Scribe 22; in 1840 Scribe led with 90, Delavigne came second with 32, Dumas had 18, Vigny 18, Hugo 9; in 1842 Scribe led with 152, Dumas having 40, Delavigne 31, Hugo 5; in 1844 Scribe again led with 53, Dumas having 20, Hugo 4; in 1846 Augier, with *La Ciguë*, led with 47, Scribe coming second with 35, Dumas having 18, and Hugo 8; in 1848 Musset had 143, Scribe 55, Augier 29, Hugo 8; in 1851 Scribe led with 100, Musset had 44, Dumas 33, Augier 29, Hugo 8; in 1860 Scribe led with 47, Barrière coming second with 45, Musset having 39, and Augier 35. Between 1823 and 1900 Scribe had 2798 performances with 24 plays; Augier, 2616 performances with 18 plays; Musset, 1841 performances with 14 plays; the younger Dumas, 1427 performances with 12 plays; and Hugo, 1163 performances with 7 plays.

âtre-Français, that I cannot refrain from quoting from it in spite of its length:

La comédie du Gymnase c'est un vieux soldat en moustaches qui pleure au lieu de jurer. C'est un jeune colonel qui met de l'eau de Cologne à son mouchoir. C'est une petite fille en tablier vert qui sourit en même temps à sa poupée et à son petit cousin. Dans cette comédie tout le monde se fait mignon, se fait petit et joli; tout le monde s'y fait grande dame et grand seigneur; Chérubin y joue un aussi grand rôle qu'Agnès; Mondor se change en marquis, et Mme. Durcevet en duchesse; le vieux monde dramatique se dénature dans le petit théâtre, il se rabaisse d'une coudée, il est à genoux! C'est à peine au Gymnase si un paysan parle patois, à peine si une femme fait une faute d'orthographe; on n'y fume pas un seul cigare, on n'y boit pas un verre d'eau-de-vie, et c'est à grand'peine si les marins eux-mêmes se permettent de prendre du tabac.

Voilà pour la conduite générale des héros et des héroïnes du Gymnase. Quant à leur conduite particulière, elle n'est pas moins étrange, pas moins romanesque. Toutes ces petites filles élevées dans un monde tout positif, monde de banquiers qui calculent, monde de grands seigneurs qui intriguent, monde d'ambitieux qui se poussent, se conduisent pourtant avec la frivole légèreté de jeunes filles de grande maison qui n'ont rien à faire ni rien à perdre. Elles aiment, elles haïssent, elles se marient, elles se livrent, elles s'enfuient, elles montent à cheval souvent, elles ont des pères veufs qu'elles traitent en esclaves, elles ont toutes sortes de volontés bizarres; jamais sur le théâtre d'aucune époque, on n'avait vu tant d'attaques de nerfs, tant de spasmes, tant de lettres d'amour, tant de déclarations improvisées, tant de promenades au bois de Boulogne; voilà pour les femmes. Et pour les hommes jamais on n'avait vu tant de duels, tant de gants jaunes, tant de pertes au jeu, tant de moustaches et d'éperons; comme aussi jamais sur aucun théâtre, on n'avait vu tant de châteaux, cascades, jardiniers, chœurs de paysannes.

Eh bien! il faut en convenir, toute la Restauration qui s'est amusée de cette espèce de drame avec transport, devait en effet s'amuser. La société de la Restauration qui avait adopté le Gymnase pour son théâtre, était un mélange singulier de passé, de présent, et d'avenir qui avait besoin d'une comédie ainsi faite pour lui plaire, sans être chagrinée ni dans son passé, ni dans son présent, ni dans son avenir. Cette société à part, dont tous les éléments étaient indécis et vermoulus, et qui n'a duré qu'un jour, avait à se ménager beau-

coup comme Empire, comme noblesse, comme fortune. L'Empire
tenait à ses vieux soldats, à ses anciens généraux, à ses grognards
aussi fidèles domestiques qu'intrépides soldats. M. Scribe, en homme
habile, a conservé les soldats et les généraux de l'Empire. Il a fait du
grognard qui jurait toujours aux Variétés et qui disait force sottises
aux Anglais et aux Russes, un vieux militaire sentimental et poussant
de gros soupirs auprès d'une jeune fille qui l'écoute en souriant; la
métamorphose n'a pas déplu au grognard, et il a coupé un peu de sa
moustache pour faire plaisir à sa maîtresse et à M. Scribe. Quant au
vieux général, M. Scribe ne l'a pas moins relevé que son camarade le
grognard. Il lui a donné une jolie terre, un château moderne, une
nièce à marier qu'il épouse presque toujours, des tableaux et une
livrée, et quelquefois un titre honorifique, comte ou baron. Livrée,
tableaux, nièce qu'il épouse, titres honorifiques, le vieux général a
pris tout cela pour faire plaisir à M. Scribe. Et dans le fait, l'empereur ne faisait-il pas des barons? pourquoi M. Scribe ne ferait-il
pas quelques comtes par-ci, par-là?

Mais l'émigration et la véritable cour voient M. Scribe distribuer
ainsi en plein théâtre ses titres. Et elle pouvait se récrier à l'insolence! Qu'avons-nous fait à M. Scribe, nous laissons ses lauriers à
l'Empire, qu'il nous laisse nos titres! Et le courroux de ces messieurs était grand et légitime: aucun laurier, aucune gloire ne valent
à leurs yeux ces vieux parchemins que tout le sang, tout le feu, toute
la gloire et tous les progrès d'une révolution n'avaient pu anéantir.

A ceux-là M. Scribe répondait poliment, et d'autant plus poliment qu'il comptait beaucoup sur eux pour son théâtre: "Messieurs, pardonnez-moi si l'Empire n'est pas mort encore; et tant
qu'il vivra, je dois le représenter dans mes pièces, ainsi le veulent
le *Constitutionnel* et M. Béranger. Mais laissez-moi faire et vous
aurez justice. Remarquez d'abord que, si par hasard je fais baron ou
comte, tout au plus, un vieux général, je ne lui donne jamais un rang
plus élevé. Il n'y a pas un duc dans mes pièces, pas un vicomte, pas
un marquis; je ne puis pas faire marquis, moi qui vous parle, puisque
Bonaparte n'en a pas fait! Ainsi, d'abord, vous avez pour vous le
duché, la pairie héréditaire, la cour; le petit et le grand lever; vous
seuls, commes chez Louis XVIII, vous serez chez moi gentilshommes
de la chambre, menins, gentilshommes ordinaires, dévots, pension-
naires, cordons bleus, si vous voulez, mais rarement, parce qu'il faut
être vraisemblable, et qu'en France il n'y a qu'une chose de laquelle
on n'abuse pas, c'est le cordon bleu. Vous serez donc toujours dans
mes pièces des gentilshommes de droit divin. Si je donne quelques

châteaux à de vieux généraux, vous aurez mieux que cela, vous
autres: vous aurez les dettes, les lettres de change, les chapeaux
neufs, les chevaux anglais, les belles passions; je ferai pour vous tout
ce que peut désirer une bonne nourrice à son nourisson, et à la fin de
mon drame, quand vous vous serez bien battus en duel, comme vous
êtes pauvres et ruinés par la Révolution, je vous ferai épouser une
fille de banquier, si vous daignez y consentir."

Mais d'autre part, les banquiers, les financiers, la Chaussée-
d'Antin, monde de luxe, monde puissant, éclairé, qui lisait les journaux, qui savait à fond la charte constitutionnelle, qui fait que tous
sont égaux, et la valeur de l'argent, qui fait que personne n'est égal
à un autre, venaient sur M. Scribe comme la noblesse lui était
venue. — "Mais vous en parlez bien à votre aise, mon petit monsieur? Marier nos filles à vos gentilshommes, de quel droit? Si nous
vous laissons faire, vous les aurez bientot mariées à un officier de
fortune! Apprenez, monsieur, que tous les hommes sont égaux
devant la loi. Or, nous sommes les maîtres, puisque nous sommes les
gens riches!" Ce qui etait puissamment raisonné.

A quoi M. Scribe répondait: "Mais, messieurs, qui vous cha-
grine? Donnez-moi quelques mariages à faire entre vos jeunes filles
et mes gentilshommes. Accordez-moi une contribution d'une ving-
taine de millions de dot à distribuer, laissez-moi les faire riches et en
revanche ils vous feront nobles. En revanche, vous mesdames, vous
irez à Saint-Sulpice comme des duchesses; vous aurez votre banc à
l'église et votre loge à l'Opéra; vous ferez des aumônes et des lec-
tures; vous ferez tout ce qu'on fait à la cour; cela ne vaut-il pas un
peu de l'or que vous avez gagné si facilement!" Or, M. Scribe l'a
fait comme il l'a dit; il a jeté la noblesse à pleines mains sur la
roture; il a jeté la fortune à pleines mains sur la noblesse; la noblesse
et la finance ont été les deux héroïnes de ses pièces; seulement, pour
tempérer l'orgueil de l'une et de l'autre, il les a entremêlées d'un peu
d'histoire militaire; il les a assaisonées de vieux soldats et de vieux
généraux, ingrédient qui a réussi beaucoup dans les premiers temps
de la comèdie de M. Scribe, mais dont l'effet se perdait chaque jour;
c'était à peine si M. Scribe l'employait encore quand est venu la
révolution de juillet.

Ainsi, la comédie du Gymnase a réussi et devait réussir par cela
même que c'était une comédie à double face, une comédie à deux
tranchants, qui ménageait tout ce qui était à ménager, qui flattait
tout ce qui était à flatter, c'est-à-dire qui flattait tout le monde,
l'Empire et la Restauration, le soldat et le financier, le vieillard et le

jeune homme, le passé et le présent. Il n'aurait pas mieux demandé que de flatter l'avenir, mais qui songeait à prévoir l'avenir?[1]

The originality of Scribe's comedies of manners lies in the fact that, while they are more or less faithful portraits of the men and women about him and while they picture the society of the July Monarchy, they are developed by means which are the direct antithesis to those employed by his predecessors. Whereas before him dramatists had always shown youth triumphant over age, passion and sentiment surmounting calculation and prudence, Scribe portrays society as he saw it about him, seeking material comfort instead of chasing rainbows; a society blasé and practical, opposed to romance and fantasy. Common sense thus took the place of sentiment, and really rejuvenated French comedy, almost poetizing it, for there is a certain poetry in the dramatic imitation of reality.

This society which occupies the centre of the stage in Scribe's plays was the mixed society which the Revolution of 1830 had placed at the head of affairs and which had put on the throne a king after its own heart; it was composed partly of the old legitimist aristocracy of the Faubourg Saint-Germain, partly of the Napoleonic nobility of the Faubourg Saint-Honoré, with a large admixture of the *noblesse d'argent* of the Chaussée-d'Antin. Scribe's plays, "too refined to interest the masses, too commonplace and too prosaic to appeal to the really aristocratic public, offered the middle-classes the mixture of temperate ambition and decent vulgarity which they could appreciate."[2] Unable to appeal to the intellectual

[1] *Journal des Débats*, 29 July, 1832.
[2] Petit de Julleville, *Le Théâtre en France*.

and artistic élite, Scribe was worshipped by the masses;
neither too idealistic nor too cynical, shrewd, practical,
and clear-minded, he was in direct spiritual touch with
the spectators who formed his public. Marriage, not
love, is the theme of most of his plays; love as preparatory and incidental to marriage is found in many of his
prettiest pictures, but it seldom constitutes the real interest of the play. No such figures as Antony, Adèle, or
Hernani, are found in Scribe's repertoire. It is here that
Scribe breaks most completely with the romanesque stage
traditions. Although he had against him the sentimental
and the imaginative, he was supported by the great majority of the people.

A society so materialistic as that of 1830 to 1850 was
certain to enjoy the spectacle of the dramatization of
money, and in Scribe's plays money takes the place of the
fatum of Greek tragedy. Probably in no other dramatic
literature does one find so many discussions of bank accounts, investments, loans, mortgages, dividends, and
business failures. And just as Scribe succeeded in renew-
ing the old love themes by going counter to the conventions existing before him, so does he present an innovation in the way in which he uses money: it is a real motive
force in the plot, and it is this which makes his plays dif-
fer from classical comedy and from that of the eighteenth
century, in which money is usually nothing more than a
dramatic device, a feature of the plot.

Lenient would place Scribe midway between the two
great currents which the literature of the first half of the
nineteenth century followed: the one idealistic, trans-
cendental, and vague, starting with Goethe, Chateau-
briand, and Byron, and leading to Victor Hugo, George

Sand, and de Musset; the other positivist and realist, starting from Balzac. I should place Scribe in the second group; for although, as Lenient says, he was always temperate and moderate, his writings are positivistic and materialistic. There is no romance in them, and nothing romanesque, and if there is occasionally a dose of sentiment, it is not real sentiment, but clever sentimentality. That he was not always a realistic observer like Balzac is certain; the reproach of unreality and artificiality so often brought against his plays is justified; but that does not mean that they have any of the fantasy of de Musset, any of the idealism of George Sand, any of the grandeur of Victor Hugo.

Scribe was frequently reproached for his lack of interest in the great movements with which he was contemporary. This criticism is scarcely just. While indeed he was moderate in his political opinions, as in everything else, he was honest and even courageous. Throughout the Restoration he was undoubtedly more in sympathy with the Liberals than with the Conservatives, and many of his plays of this period are markedly insurgent in general tone and in detail. After the fall of the Bourbons in 1830 he gave whole-hearted support to the King and to the constitutional government, as best able, he thought, to control the republican and Bonapartist tendencies which might constitute a menace to peace and order. "Avant, Pendant, et Après," written just before the downfall of the Restoration government, really opens the way for genuine political comedy, which had never, because of the restrictions of the old régime, been able to attain to any importance, and which in "Bertrand et Raton" became a real, dignified dramatic genre. He could not, in spite of his approval of the government, fail to see the vices inherent in the parliamentary régime, and it is thus that we find him ridiculing the mania for power which he had occasion to see personified in the Guizots, Molés, and Thiers, and which is the theme of "L'Ambitieux"; it is thus that in "La Calomnie" he exposes the pettiness, even the immorality, of the means often employed in political struggles.

Lacking Hugo's and Dumas's real love for the past and their ability to evoke it poetically, he succeeded nevertheless, through diligence and painstaking effort, in bringing historical drama to its highest point of development. What he lacked in poetic divination he made up in dramatic intuition. His "local color" is at least as impressive as Dumas's, and his historic dramas, as dramatic compositions, are far superior to those of either of the great Romanticists; their structure is much firmer and far more logical, they show a greater knowledge of stage optics, and they contain fewer absurdities. As history, "Le Verre d'Eau" is equal to "Marie Tudor" and to "Henri III et sa Cour"; inferior to them in poetic inspiration, it surpasses them in intelligence of construction. The success of the historic drama of the later nineteenth century, that of Sardou, was due largely to its strong, highly-developed framework, which it inherited from Scribe.

The greatest misunderstanding between Scribe and the dramatic critics arose from the fact that many of the latter demanded of a play one quality which Scribe's plays rarely possessed, and which he esteemed not only of little importance on the stage but positively to be avoided — literary style. A writer should probably be judged accord-

ing to the success with which he accomplishes what he
attempts to do; to deplore the lack of poetry and style in
Scribe's plays is as much beside the point as it would be to
berate Racine for not having written as brilliant comedies
as Beaumarchais, or Beaumarchais for not having produced such masterpieces of poetry as "Phèdre" and
"Andromaque." Scribe's most implacable enemies, Jules
Janin, Théophile Gautier, and Théodore de Banville,
were so offended by the prosiness and insipidity of his
style that they could not see the very evident qualities of
what he wrote. After several years of bitter attacks
upon the popular playwright, Gautier finally realized the
futility of his criticisms.

La critique se trouve à l'endroit de M. Scribe dans une singulière
position. Il est certain que ces pièces réussissent. Non au public
blasé et dédaigneux des premières, mais bien aux honnêtes bourgeois
plus ou moins père de famille qui, sans se préoccuper d'art, de style,
de poétique, vont se délasser le soir au théâtre des travaux de la
journée.

On ne peut nier les succès de M. Scribe. — Voilà bientôt quinze
ans qu'il défraie à lui tout seul tous les théâtres de Paris, de la ban-
lieue, de la province, de l'Europe et autres parties du monde. Voilà
certainement beaucoup de titres au respect de la critique; et cependant, nul auteur n'a été plus rudement morigéné que M. Scribe par la
critique. M. Scribe a beaucoup d'esprit, de finesse, d'entente de la
scène; sa merveilleuse facilité d'improvisation suffit à toutes les
besognes; il n'a ni grands défauts ni grandes qualités (ce qui est la
plus excellente condition de réussite); il est commun, mais rarement
trivial; sa manière d'écrire, courante et négligée, se fait accepter
facilement de tout le monde; rien ne fait angle, rien n'accroche
l'esprit au passage. L'absence de style et de correction ne choque
aucunement les spectateurs, inquiets seulement de savoir si l'on
épousera ou non à la fin de la pièce.

Une autre raison de la vogue de M. Scribe c'est qu'il n'a pas la
moindre étincelle de poésie, car si les poètes chantent avec Horace:
"Odi profanum vulgus et arceo," le vulgaire le leur rend bien. La
poésie et la forme, voilà ce que le public ne peut souffrir.[1]

[1] Gautier, *La Presse*, 25 Nov., 1840.

And a year later in the same journal:

Il est assez ennuyeux de contredire sans cesse des succès irrécu-
sables, aussi abdiquons-nous, à l'égard de M. Scribe, notre rôle de
critique. On ne peut le nier, ses pièces réussissent, ont des représentations nombreuses, font beaucoup d'argent et amusent une infinité
d'honnêtes gens. Quant à nous, quatre à cinq années de feuilletons,
etc., nous ont amené à cette idee, confirmée par les succès de M.
Scribe, que le théâtre n'avait rien de littéraire, et que la pensée n'y
était que pour fort peu de choses. La poésie, la philosophie, l'étude
du cœur, l'analyse des passions et des caractères, le caprice, la
fantaisie, le style, ces qualités, les plus hautes de l'art, causeraient
assurément la chute d'un ouvrage.[1]

Uninteresting as they are when criticized from the
stylistic point of view, his plays possess certain qualities
much more important in dramatic compositions, without
which, in fact, a piece is not dramatically well written, no
matter what other merits it may possess. The fertility
and the ubiquity of Scribe's talent, applied as it was to so
many different dramatic forms, presuppose an ensemble
of qualities, inferior by themselves, but which, taken together, make up a very effective equipment: an instinc-
tive and unerring aptitude for ascertaining the taste and
the desires of the public; an exceptional understanding of
stage optics; skillfulness in exploiting *l'actualité morale;*
facility in arranging his material so as to give an appearance of novelty even to time-worn themes and combinations; unparalleled ability in fabricating complications of
plot and in bringing the resulting entanglement to a
predictable and satisfying dénoûment; a disposition of
amusing lines and piquant situations so happy that they
never seem to have been hunted for. With all these gifts,
Scribe seldom develops into a mere virtuoso of technique
as Sardou so often does, for the reason that the effective

[1] Gautier, *La Presse*, 8 Dec., 1841.

arrangement of dramatic material is usually of secondary importance with the elder dramatist, while with Sardou the mechanics of the play is often the end as well as the means. Probably the features of Scribe's work most criticized by people of taste are just those which appealed most to the public: the prodigious *tours de force* which are so frequent in his plays. I doubt whether any dramatist excels him in the ability to give an air of plausibility to improbable situations, and in the ease with which he overcomes inherent difficulties. Of course, this breathless rush to a clever dénoûment, through a series of brilliant exhibitions of legerdemain, results in paleness of characterization; his characters get their personality more from the actors' interpretation than from the play itself.

I know of no juster estimate of Scribe's contribution to the dramatic literature of the nineteenth century than that printed in the "Figaro" on the occasion of Scribe's retirement, in 1860:

Oui, M. Scribe manque d'idéal, de style, et de profondeur; il voit petit et peint mesquinement; dans ses pièces l'argent joue le rôle de la fatalité antique; il pousse jusqu'à l'absurde une théorie empruntée à Voltaire: "Les petites causes produisent de grands effets"; s'il touche à une idée consacrée c'est invariablement pour en exploiter l'envers; voilà ce qu'on a eu raison de crier sur les toits; puis en voyant la Comédie-Française réaliser péniblement trois cents francs avec des chefs-d'œuvre et encaisser le maximum des recettes avec *les Contes de la Reine* ou *les Doigts de fée*, je reconnais qu'il était du droit, et peut-être du devoir du feuilleton, de déclarer que tous les succès de M. Scribe ne valaient pas une scène de Molière, un acte de Regnard, de Lesage ou même de Beaumarchais. Mais je sais tant d'esprit à M. Scribe, je lui soupçonne tant de bon sens, que je ne crois pas que sur ce point et sur les autres, il ait jamais pensé autrement que les gens de goût. Il ne se compare même pas à Destouches, il se reconnaît inférieur à Marivaux; enfin il appelle Collin d'Harleville, Andrieux et Picard ses maîtres, et là sa modestie l'entraîne trop loin, il leur est très supérieur.

Ici, je vous renvoie à son répertoire. Lisez, et quand vous aurez fini, vous ne me ferez pas de reproche. Ce n'est jamais ennuyeux, et c'est presque toujours fort amusant. Hors du théâtre cela vit parce que cela est très spirituel. L'esprit de M. Scribe est de garde comme le bon champagne. On a dit de cet esprit qu'il le prenait un peu partout; je le veux bien, mais il en trouve beaucoup dans son propre fonds, et, comme dit M. de Loménie, "Indépendamment de l'esprit qu'il prend aux autres, il en a à lui tout seul une provision énorme, qu'il dépense et prodigue sans jamais l'épuiser."

Que de délicieuses pièces dans ce répertoire: *Une Visite à Bedlam, la Somnambule, l'Ours et le Pacha, Michel et Christine, le Charlatanisme, la Demoiselle à marier, l'Héritière, le plus beau Jour de la Vie, les premières Amours, Héloïse et Abélard.* En comédies: *Valérie, le Mariage d'Argent* (presque une œuvre de première ordre), *Bertrand et Raton, la Camaraderie, le Verre d'Eau.* Des opéras-comiques impossibles mais ravissants: *le Domino noir, la Part du Diable, la Dame Blanche, les Diamants de la Couronne.* Pour les trouver charmants, il n'est même pas besoin de les comparer aux libretti des "jeunes." Hélas! M. Scribe ne leur barrera plus le passage. Enfin, les opéras: *la Muette, Robert le Diable, la Juive, les Huguenots,* et tant d'autres dont on a avec raison beaucoup critiqué la "poésie," mais si bien coupés pour la mélodie, si empoignants, si adroitement charpentés, que sans musique, et à la seule condition de les récrire, ils deviendraient des drames fort intéressants et à grand succès. "Le secret de votre prospérité théâtrale, c'est d'avoir heureusement saisi l'esprit de votre siècle et fait le genre de comédie dont il s'accommode le mieux, et qui lui ressemble le plus." (Villemain, en recevant Scribe à l'Académie.) C'était et c'est encore la vérité, mais ce ne l'est pas toute entière. M. Scribe a fait plus, il a été et il continue d'être le maître de tous ceux qui, après lui, ont abordé la scène. Tous les auteurs dramatiques à une exception près, (M. T. Barrière), procèdent de lui et ne vivent que par ses procédés, il leur a appris à mêler et à démêler des incidents, à nouer et à dénouer une intrigue, à faire pivoter une pièce sur une idée comme un miroir à alouettes sur son axe. C'est M. Scribe qui a créé le dénoûment et en a fait quelque chose d'imprévu, quoique toujours attendu, comme le bouquet d'un feu d'artifice.

Encore une fois, tout le théâtre actuel se résume en Scribe, et cela est si vrai qu'à part trois exceptions vous ne me citerez pas un grand succès qui ne soit une pièce à la Scribe. Gabrielle, le mari poète — procédé Scribe, l'opinion générale prise à rebrousse poils. Il en est de même de Philiberte: Gabrielle et Philiberte, c'est du Scribe alcoolisé avec de l'Augier. *Le Duc Job* (Léon Laya), c'est autre chose, c'est du Scribe tempéré par de l'eau claire. Mais *l'Honneur et l'Argent*? Dame! M. Ponsard fait du cidre avec ses pommes. Je ne parle pas de *Mlle. de la Seiglière*, tout le monde sait que c'est une belle nièce de M. Scribe. Quant à M. Octave Feuillet, c'est M. Scribe ayant bu le restant de la cave d'Alfred de Musset, jusqu'à en perdre son adresse merveilleuse, et sa science du théâtre. Je me fais fort de trouver du Scribe dans tous les ouvrages que le public honore de ses suffrages.

Je voudrais bien ne pas avoir l'air de jouer au paradoxe, mais je ne puis m'empêcher de dire que M. Scribe a été le premier réaliste au théâtre. Eh! quoi, vous riez? Je maintiens mon dire, et le colonel, l'avoué, la jeune veuve de la Restauration ont été dans leur temps de vraies photographies (pardon pour l'anachronisme); j'en conviens avec vous, maintenant ce sont des gravures de modes antédilu-viennes. Ces types n'en ont pas moins été étudiés sur nature. Des croquis faits à la hâte, je le sais; mais, en attendant les Rubens et les Raphaël, laissez-moi, je vous prie, me plaire avec Gavarni.

APPENDICES

APPENDIX A

THE DENTU EDITION OF THE COMPLETE WORKS OF EUGÈNE SCRIBE (PARIS, 1875)

THE name of the collaborator is indicated for each play, as is the date of the first performance. In the list of *opéras*, *opéras-comiques*, and *ballets* the first name following the title is that of the collaborator, the second that of the composer.

ABBREVIATIONS

Vaud.	*Vaudeville* or *vaudevilles*
Com.-vaud.	*Comédie-vaudeville*
Com.	*Comédie*
Com. hist.	*Comédie historique*
Opéra-com.	*Opéra-comique*
Th. du Vaud.	Théâtre du Vaudeville
Th. des Var.	Théâtre des Variétés
Th. du Gym.	Théâtre du Gymnase
Th. Fran.	Théâtre-Français
Th. de l'Op.	Théâtre de l'Opéra
Th. de l'Op.-Com.	Théâtre de l'Opéra-Comique

The description of the plays is given in French, as in the Dentu edition.

COMÉDIES-VAUDEVILLES

Les Dervis. Vaud. en 1 acte. Germain Delavigne. Th. du Vaud., 2 Sept., 1811.

L'Auberge, ou les Brigands sans le savoir. Vaud. en 1 acte. G. Delavigne. Th. du Vaud., 19 May, 1812.

Thibaut, Comte de Champagne. Vaud. historique en 1 acte. G. Delavigne. Th. du Vaud., 27 Sept., 1812.

Le Bachelier de Salamanque. Com. en 1 acte, mêlée de vaudevilles. H. Dupin and G. Delavigne. Th. des Var., 18 Jan., 1815.

La Mort et le Bûcheron. Folie-vaud. en 1 acte. Poirson. Th. du Vaud., 4 Nov., 1815.

Encore une Nuit de la Garde Nationale, ou le Poste de la Barrière. Tableau-vaud. en 1 acte. Poirson. Théâtre de la Porte-Saint-Martin, 15 Dec., 1815.

Flore et Zephyre. A propos-vaud. en 1 acte. Poirson. Th. du Vaud., 8 Feb., 1816.

Farinelli, ou la Pièce de Circonstance. Vaud. en 1 acte. H. Dupin. Th. du Vaud., 25 July, 1816.

Gusman d'Alfarach. Com.-vaud. en 2 actes. H. Dupin. Th. du Vaud., 22 Oct., 1816.

Les Montagnes russes, ou le Temple à la mode. Vaud. en 1 acte. Poirson and Dupin. Th. du Vaud., 31 Oct., 1816.

La Jarretière de la Mariée. Com.-vaud. en 1 acte. H. Dupin. Th. des Var., 12 Nov., 1816.

Le Comte Ory, anecdote du XIe siècle. Vaud. en 1 acte. Poirson. Th. du Vaud., 16 Dec., 1816.

Le Nouveau Pourceaugnac. Com.-vaud. en 1 acte. Poirson. Th. du Vaud., 18 Feb., 1817.

Le Solliciteur, ou l'Art d'obtenir des Places. Com. en 1 acte, mêlée de couplets. Ymbert and Varner. Th. des Var., 17 April, 1817

Wallace, ou la Barrière Montparnasse. A propos-vaud. en 1 acte. Dupin and Poirson. Th. du Vaud., 8 May, 1817.

Les Deux Précepteurs, ou l'Asinus Asinum. Com. en 1 acte, mêlée de couplets. Moreau. Th. des Var., 19 June, 1817.

Le Combat des Montagnes, ou la Folie-Beaujon. Folie-vaud. en 1 acte. H. Dupin. Th. des Var., 12 July, 1817.

Le Café des Variétés. Epilogue en vaud. H. Dupin. Th. des Var., 5 Aug., 1817.

Tous les Vaudevilles, ou Chacun chez soi. A propos-vaud. en 1 acte. Désaugiers and Poirson. Th. du Vaud., 18 Sept., 1817.

Le Petit Dragon. Com. en 2 actes, mêlée de vaud. Poirson and Mélesville. Th. du Vaud., 18 Sept., 1817.

Les Comices d'Athènes, ou les Femmes Agricoles. Com.- vaud. en 1 acte, imitée du grec d'Aristophane. Varner. Th. du Vaud., 7 Nov., 1817.

Les Nouvelles Danaïdes. Vaud. en 1 acte. H. Dupin. Th. des Var., 3 Dec., 1817.

La Fête du Mari, ou Dissimulons. Com.-vaud. en 1 acte, mêlée de vaud. H. Dupin. Th. de la Gaîté, 24 Dec., 1817.

Chactas et Atala. Drame en 4 actes et en style mêlé. H. Dupin. Th. des Var., 9 March, 1818.

Les Dehors Trompeurs, ou Boissy chez Lui. Com.-vaud. en 1 acte. Poirson and Mélesville. Th. des Var., 6 April, 1818.

Une Visite à Bedlam. Com. en 1 acte, mêlée de vaud. Poirson. Théâtre du Vaud., 23 April, 1818.

Les Vélocipèdes, ou la Poste aux Chevaux. A propos-vaud. en 1 acte. Dupin and Varner. Th. des Var., 2 May, 1818.

La Volière de Frère Philippe. Com.-vaud. en 1 acte. Poirson and Mélesville. Th. du Vaud., 15 June, 1818.

Le Nouveau Nicaise. Com.-vaud. en 1 acte. H. Dupin. Th. des Var., 15 Oct., 1818.

L'Hôtel des Quatre-Nations. A propos en 1 acte, mêlé de vaud. Dupin and Brazier. Th. des Var., 7 Nov., 1818.

Le Fou de Péronne. Com. en 1 acte, mêlée de vaud. Th. du Vaud., 18 Jan., 1819.

Les Deux Maris. Com. en 1 acte, mêlée de vaud. Varner. Th. des Var., 3 Feb., 1819.

Le Mystificateur. Com.-vaud. en 1 acte. Poirson and Cerfbeer. Th. du Vaud., 22 Feb., 1819.

Caroline. Com.-vaud. en 1 acte. Ménissier. Th. du Vaud., 15 March, 1819.

Les Bains à la Papa. Folie-vaud. en 1 acte. Dupin and Varner. Th. du Vaud., 9 Oct., 1819.

Les Vêpres Siciliennes. Parodie-vaud. en 1 acte. Mélesville. Th. du Vaud., 17 Nov., 1819.

La Somnambule. Com.-vaud. en 2 actes. Th. du Vaud., 6 Dec., 1819.

L'Ennui, ou le Comte Derfort. Com.-vaud. en 2 actes. Dupin and Mélesville. Th. des Var., 2 Feb., 1820.

L'Ours et le Pacha. Folie-vaud. en 1 acte. Saintine. Th. des Var., 10 Feb., 1820.

Le Spleen. Com. en 1 acte, mêlée de vaud. Poirson. Th. des Var., 20 March, 1820.

Le Chat Botté. Féerie-vaud. en 2 actes. Mélesville and Poirson. Th. du Vaud., 19 April, 1820.

Marie Jobard. Imitation burlesque en 6 actes et en vers. Dupin and Carmouche. Th. des Var., 11 April, 1820.

L'Homme Automate. Folie-parade, mêlée de couplets. Varner and Ymbert. Th. des Var., 10 May, 1820.

Le Vampire. Com.-vaud. en 1 acte. Th. du Vaud., 15 June, 1820.

L'Eclipse Totale. Tableau-vaud. en 1 acte. H. Dupin. Th. des Var., 6 Sept., 1820.

Le Témoin. Com.-vaud. en 1 acte. Mélesville and Saintine. Th. des Var., 28 Sept., 1820.

Le Déluge, ou les Petits Acteurs. Vaud. en 1 acte. Mélesville and Saintine. Th. des Var., 12 Oct., 1820.

L'Homme Noir. Enigme en 1 acte, mêlée de vaud. H. Dupin. Th. du Vaud., 18 Nov., 1820.

L'Hôtel des Bains. Tableau-vaud. en 1 acte. H. Dupin. Th. des Var., 22 Nov., 1820.

Le Beau Narcisse. Vaud. en 1 acte. Saintine and de Courcy. Th. de la Porte-Saint-Martin, 9 Dec., 1820.

Le Boulevard Bonne-Nouvelle. Prologue en vaud. (Inauguration du Gymnase Dramatique.) Moreau and Mélesville. Th. du Gym., 28 Dec., 1820.

L'Amour Platonique. Com. mêlée de vaud. Mélesville. Th. du Gym., 18 Jan., 1821.

Le Secrétaire et le Cuisinier. Com.-vaud. en 1 acte. Mélesville. Th. du Gym., 18 Jan., 1821.

Frontin Mari-Garçon. Com.-vaud. en 1 acte. Mélesville. Th. du Vaud., 18 Jan., 1821.

Le Colonel. Com.-vaud. en 1 acte. G. Delavigne. Th. du Gym., 29 Jan., 1821.

L'Intérieur de l'Étude, ou le Procureur et l'Avoué. Com.-vaud. en 1 acte. H. Dupin. Th. des Var., 1 Feb., 1821.

Le Gastronome sans Argent. Vaud. en 1 acte. Brulay. Th. du Gym., 10 March, 1821.

Le Ménage de Garçon. Com.-vaud. en 1 acte. H. Dupin. Th. du Gym., 27 April, 1821.

La Campagne. Com.-vaud. en 1 acte. Dupin and Mélesville. Th. des Var., 7 May, 1821.

La Petite Sœur. Com.-vaud. en 1 acte. Mélesville. Th. du Gym., 6 June, 1821.

Le Mariage Enfantin. Com.-vaud. en 1 acte. G. Delavigne. Th. du Gym., 16 Aug., 1821.

Les Petites Misères de la Vie Humaine. Com.-vaud. en 1 acte. Mélesville. Th. du Gym., 20 Oct., 1821.

L'Amant Bossu. Com.-vaud. en 1 acte. Mélesville and Vaudière. Th. du Gym., 22 Oct., 1821.

L'Artiste. Com.-vaud. en 1 acte. Perlet. Th. du Gym., 23 Nov., 1821.

Michel et Christine. Com.-vaud. en 1 acte. H. Dupin. Th. du Gym., 3 Dec., 1821.

Philibert Marié. Com.-vaud. en 1 acte. Moreau. Th. du Gym., 26 Dec., 1821.

Le Plaisant de Société. Folie-vaud. en 1 acte. Mélesville. Th. du Gym., 18 Feb., 1822.

Mémoires d'un Colonel de Hussards. Com. en 1 acte, mêlée de vaud. Mélesville.

La Demoiselle et la Dame, ou Avant et Après. Com.-vaud. en 1 acte. Dupin and de Courcy. Th. du Gym., 11 March, 1822.

La Petite Folle. Drame en 1 acte, mêlé de couplets. Mélesville. Th. du Gym., 6 May, 1822.

Le Vieux Garçon et la Petite Fille. Com.-vaud. en 1 acte. G. Delavigne. Th. du Gym., 24 May, 1822.

Les Nouveaux Jeux de l'Amour et du Hasard. Com.-vaud. en 1 acte. G. Delavigne. Th. du Gym., 21 June, 1822.

Les Eaux du Mont-Dore. Vaud. en 1 acte. De Courcy and Saintine. Th. du Gym., 25 July, 1822.

La Veuve du Malabar. Vaud. en 1 acte. Mélesville. Th. du Gym., 19 Aug., 1822.

La Nouvelle Clary, ou Louise et Georgette. Com.-vaud. en 1 acte. H. Dupin. Th. du Gym., 11 Nov., 1822.

L'Ecarté, ou un Coin du Salon. Tableau-vaud. en 1 acte. Mélesville and Saint-Georges. Th. du Gym., 14 Nov., 1822.

Le Bon Papa, ou la Proposition de Mariage. Com.-vaud. en 1 acte. Mélesville. Th. du Gym., 2 Dec., 1822.

La Loge du Portier. Tableau-vaud. en 1 acte. Mazères. Th. du Gym., 14 Jan., 1823.

L'Intérieur d'un Bureau, ou la Chanson. Com.-vaud. en 1 acte. Ymbert and Varner. Th. du Gym., 25 Feb., 1823.

Trilby, ou le Lutin d'Argail. Vaud. en 1 acte. Carmouche. Th. du Gym., 13 March 1823.

Le Plan de Campagne. Com.-vaud. en 1 acte. Dupin and Mélesville. Th. du Gym., 14 April, 1823.

Le Menteur Véridique. Com.-vaud. en 1 acte. Mélesville. Th. du Gym., 24 April, 1823.

La Pension Bourgeoise. Com.-vaud. en 1 acte. Dupin and Dumersin. Th. du Gym., 27 May, 1823.

La Maîtresse au Logis. Com.-vaud. en 1 acte. Th. du Gym., 9 June, 1823.

Partie et Revanche. Com.-vaud. en 1 acte. Francis and Brazier. Th. du Gym., 16 June, 1823.

L'Avare en Goguettes. Com.-vaud. en 1 acte. G. Delavigne. Th. du Gym., 12 July, 1823.

Les Grisettes. Vaud. en 1 acte. H. Dupin. Th. du Gym., 8 Aug., 1823.

La Vérité dans le Vin. Com.-vaud. en 1 acte. Mazères. Th. du Gym., 10 Oct., 1823.

Le Retour, ou la Suite de Michel et Christine. Com.-vaud. en 1 acte. H. Dupin. Th. du Gym., 17 Oct., 1823.

Un Dernier Jour de Fortune. Com.-vaud. en 1 acte. Dupaty. Th. du Gym., 11 Nov., 1823.

Rossini à Paris, ou le Grand Dîner. A propos-vaud. en 1 acte. Mazères. Th. du Gym., 29 Nov., 1823.

L'Héritière. Com.-vaud. en 1 acte. G. Delavigne. Th. du Gym., 20 Dec., 1823.

Le Coiffeur et le Perruquier. Vaud. en 1 acte. Mazères. Th. du Gym., 15 Jan., 1824.

Le Fondé de Pouvoirs. Vaud. en 1 acte. Carmouche. Th. du Gym., 18 Feb., 1824.

La Mansarde des Artistes. Com.-vaud. en 1 acte. H. Dupin and Varner. Th. du Gym., 2 April, 1824.

Les Trois Genres. Prologue en 1 acte. Th. de l'Odéon, 27 April, 1824.

Le Leicester du Faubourg, ou l'Amour et l'Ambition. Vaud. grivois en 1 acte. Saintine and Carmouche. Th. du Gym., 1 May, 1824.

Le Baiser au Porteur. Com.-vaud. en 1 acte. Gensoul et de Courcy. Th. du Gym., 9 June, 1824.

Le Dîner sur l'Herbe. Tableau-vaud. en 1 acte. Mélesville. Th. du Gym., 2 July, 1824.

Les Adieux au Comptoir. Com.-vaud. en 1 acte. Mélesville. Th. du Gym., 9 Aug., 1824.

Le Château de la Poularde. Com.-vaud. en 1 acte. Dupin and Varner. Th. de Madame, 4 Oct., 1824.

Le Bal Champêtre, ou les Grisettes à la Campagne. Tableau-vaud. en 1 acte. H. Dupin. Th. de Madame, 21 Oct., 1824.

Coraly, ou la Sœur et le Frère. Com.-vaud. en 1 acte. Mélesville. Th. de Madame, 19 Nov., 1824.

Monsieur Tardif. Com.-vaud. en 1 acte. Mélesville. Th. de Madame, 1 Dec., 1824.

La Haine d'une Femme, ou le Jeune Homme à marier. Com.-vaud. en 1 acte. Th. de Madame, 14 Dec., 1824.

Vatel, ou le Petit-fils d'un Grand Homme. Com.-vaud. en 1 acte. Mazères. Th. de Madame, 18 Jan., 1825.

La Quarantaine. Com.-vaud. en 1 acte. Mazères. Th. de Madame, 3 Feb., 1825.

Le Plus Beau Jour de la Vie. Com.-vaud. en 2 actes. Varner. Th. de Madame, 22 Feb., 1825.

La Charge à payer, ou la Mère intrigante. Com.-vaud. en 1 acte. Varner. Th. de Madame, 13 April, 1825.

Les Inséparables. Com.-vaud. en 1 acte. H. Dupin. Th. de Madame, 2 May, 1825.

Le Charlatanisme. Com.-vaud. en 1 acte. Mazères. 10 May, 1825.

Les Empiriques d'autrefois. Com.-vaud. en 1 acte. Alexandre. Th. de Madame, 11 June, 1825.

Les Premières Amours, ou les Souvenirs d'Enfance. Com.-vaud. en 1 acte. Th. de Madame, 12 Nov., 1825.

Le Médecin des Dames. Com.-vaud. en 1 acte. Mélesville. Th. de Madame, 17 Dec., 1825.

Le Confident. Com.-vaud. en 1 acte. Mélesville. Th. de Madame, 5 Jan., 1826.

La Demoiselle à marier, ou la Première Entrevue. Com.-vaud. en 1 acte. Mélesville. 18 Jan., 1826.

Le Testament de Polichinelle. Com.-vaud. en 1 acte. Moreau an. Lafortelle. Th. de Madame, 17 Feb., 1826.

Les Manteaux. Com.-vaud. en 2 actes. Varner and Dupin. Th. de Madame, 20 Feb., 1826.

La Belle-Mère. Com.-vaud. en 1 acte. Bayard. Th. de Madame, 1 March, 1826.

L'Oncle d'Amérique. Com.-vaud. en 1 acte. Mazères. Th. de Madame, 14 March, 1826.

La Lune de Miel. Com.-vaud. en 2 actes. Mélesville and Carmouche. Th. de Madame, 31 March, 1826.

Simple Histoire. Com.-vaud. en 1 acte. De Courcy. Th. de Madame, 26 May, 1826.

L'Ambassadeur. Com.-vaud. en 1 acte. Mélesville. Th. de Madame, 10 July, 1826.

Le Mariage de Raison. Com.-vaud. en 2 actes. Varner. Th. de Madame, 10 Oct., 1826.

La Chatte Métamorphosée en Femme. Folie-vaud. en 1 acte. Mélesville. Th. de Madame, 3 March, 1827.

Les Élèves du Conservatoire. Tableau-vaud. en 1 acte. Saintine. Th. de Madame, 28 March, 1827.

Le Diplomate. Com.-vaud. en 2 actes. G. Delavigne. Th. de Madame, 23 Oct., 1827.

La Marraine. Com.-vaud. en 1 acte. Lockroy and Chabot. Th. de Madame, 27 Nov., 1827.

Le Mal du Pays, ou la Batelière de Brienz. Tableau-vaud. en 1 acte. Mélesville. Th. de Madame, 28 Dec., 1827.

Le Prince Charmant, ou les Contes de Fée. Folie-vaud. en 1 acte. Poirson et Dupin. Th. de Madame, 14 Feb., 1828.

Yelva, ou l'Orpheline Russe. Vaud. en 2 parties. Devilleneuve and Desvergiers. Th. de Madame, 18 March, 1828.

Le Vieux Mari. Com.-vaud. en 2 actes. Mélesville. Th. de Madame, 2 May, 1828.

La Manie des Places, ou la Folie du Siècle. Com.-vaud. en 1 acte. Bayard. Th. de Madame, 19 June, 1828.

Avant, Pendant, et Après. Esquisses historiques en 3 parties. De Rougemont. Th. de Madame, 28 June, 1828.

Le Baron de Trenck. Com.-vaud. en 2 actes. G. Delavigne. Th. de Madame, 14 Oct., 1828.

Les Moralistes. Com.-vaud. en 1 acte. Varner. Th. de Madame, 22 Nov., 1828.

Malvina, ou un Mariage d'Inclination. Com.-vaud. en 2 actes. Th. de Madame, 8 Dec., 1828.

Théobald, ou le Retour de Russie. Com.-vaud. en 1 acte. Varner. Th. de Madame, 12 Feb., 1829.

Madame de Sainte-Agnès. Com.-vaud. en 1 acte. Varner. Th. de Madame, 20 Feb., 1829.

Aventures et Voyages du Petit Jonas. Pièce romantique en 3 actes. Dupin. Th. des Nouveautés, 28 Feb., 1829.

Les Héritiers de Crac. Vaud. en 1 acte. Mélesville. Th. de Madame, 21 Aug., 1829.

La Famille du Baron. Vaud. épisodique en 1 acte. Mélesville. Th. de Madame, 21 Aug., 1829.

Les Actionnaires. Com.-vaud. en 1 acte. Bayard. Th. de Madame, 22 Oct., 1829.

Louise, ou la Réparation. Com.-vaud. en 2 actes. Mélesville et Bayard. Th. de Madame, 16 Nov., 1829.

La Cour d'Assises. Tableau-vaud. en 1 acte. Varner. Th. de Madame, 28 Dec., 1829.

La Seconde Année, ou à Qui la Faute? Com.-vaud. en 1 acte. Mélesville. Th. de Madame, 12 Jan., 1830.

Zoé, ou l'Amant Prêté. Com.-vaud. en 1 acte. Mélesville. Th. de Madame, 16 March, 1830.

Philippe. Com.-vaud. en 1 acte. Mélesville and Bayard. Th. de Madame, 19 April, 1830.

Le Foyer du Gymnase. Prologue, mêlé de couplets. Th. du Gym., 17 Aug., 1830.

Une Faute. Drame en 2 actes, mêlé de couplets. Th. du Gym., 17 Aug., 1830.

La Protectrice. Com.-vaud. en 1 acte. Varner. Th. du Gym., 2 Nov., 1830.

Jeune et Vieille, ou le Premier et le Dernier Chapitre. Com.-vaud. en 2 actes. Mélesville and Bayard. Th. du Gym., 18 Nov., 1830.

La Famille Riquebourg, ou le Mariage mal assorti. Com.-vaud. en 1 acte. Th. du Gym., 1 Jan., 1831.

Les Trois Maîtresses, ou une Cour d'Allemagne. Com.-vaud. en 2 actes. Bayard. Th. du Gym., 24 Jan., 1831.

Le Budget d'un Jeune Ménage. Com.-vaud. en 1 acte. Bayard. Th. du Gym., 4 March, 1831.

Le Quaker et la Danseuse. Com.-vaud. en 1 acte. Th. du Gym., 28 March, 1831.

La Favorite. Com.-vaud. en 1 acte. Th. du Gym., 16 May, 1831.

Le Comte de Saint-Ronan, ou l'École et le Château. Com. en 2 actes, mêlée de vaud. H. Dupin. Th. du Palais-Royal, 21 June, 1831.

Le Suisse de l'Hôtel: Anecdote de 1816. Vaud. en 1 acte. De Rougemont. Th. du Gym., 14 Nov., 1831.

Le Soprano. Com.-vaud. en 1 acte. Mélesville. Th. du Gym., 30 Nov., 1831.

Le Luthier de Lisbonne. Anecdote contemporaine en 2 actes, mêlée de vaud. Bayard. Th. du Gym., 7 Dec., 1831.

La Vengeance Italienne, ou le Français à Florence. Com.-vaud. en 2 actes. Poirson et Desnoyers. Th. du Gym., 23 Jan., 1832.

Le Chaperon. Com.-vaud. en 1 acte. Duport. Th. du Gym., 6 Feb., 1832.

Le Savant. Com.-vaud. en 2 actes. Monvel. Th. du Gym., 22 Feb., 1832.

Schahabaham II, ou les Caprices d'un Autocrate. Folie-vaud. en 1 acte. Saintine. Th. du Gym., 2 March, 1832.

L'Apollon du Réverbère, ou les Conjectures du Carrefour. Tableau populaire en 1 acte. Mélesville and Saintine. Th. des Var., 21 March, 1832.

Le Premier Président. Drame en trois actes, mêlé de vaud. Mélesville. Th. du Gym., 21 Aug., 1832.

Une Monomanie. Com.-vaud. en 1 acte. Duport. Th. du Gym., 31 Aug., 1832.

Le Paysan Amoureux. Com.-vaud. en 2 actes. Bayard. Th. du Gym., 17 Sept., 1832.

La Grande Aventure. Com.-vaud. en 1 acte. Varner. Th. du Gym., 2 Nov., 1832.

Toujours, ou l'Avenir d'un Fils. Com.-vaud. en 2 actes. Varner. Th. du Gym., 13 Nov., 1832.

Camilla, ou la Sœur et le Frère. Com.-vaud. en 1 acte. Bayard. Th. du Gym., 12 Dec., 1832.

Le Voyage dans l'Appartement, ou l'Influence des Localités. Com.-vaud. en 5 tableaux. Duport. Th. des Var., 18 Jan., 1833.

Les Malheurs d'un Amant Heureux. Com.-vaud. en 2 actes. Th. du Gym., 29 Jan., 1833.

Le Gardien. Com.-vaud. en 2 actes, tirée du roman d'Indiana. Bayard. Th. du Gym., 11 March, 1833.

Le Moulin de Javelle. Com.-vaud. en 2 actes. Mélesville. Th. du Gym., 8 July, 1833.

Jean de Vert. Pièce-féerie en 5 tableaux, mêlée de vaud. Mélesville and Carmouche. Th. du Vaud., 19 Aug., 1833.

Un Trait de Paul I, ou le Czar et la Vivandière. Com.-vaud.-anecdote en 1 acte. Duport. Th. du Gym., 12 Sept., 1833.

La Dugazon, ou le Choix d'une Maîtresse. Com.-vaud. en 1 acte. Duport. Th. du Gym., 30 Oct., 1833.

Le Lorgnon. Com.-vaud. en 1 acte. Th. du Gym., 21 Dec., 1833.

La Chanoinesse. Com.-vaud. en 1 acte. Francis-Cornu. Th. du Gym., 31 Dec., 1833.

Salvoisy, ou l'Amoureux de la Reine. Com.-vaud. en 2 actes. De Rougemont and de Camberousse. Th. du Gym., 18 April, 1834.

La Frontière de Savoie. Com.-vaud. en 1 acte. Bayard. Th. du Gym., 20 Aug., 1834.

Estelle, ou le Père et la Fille. Com.-vaud. en 1 acte. Th. du Gym., 7 Nov., 1834.

Etre aîmé, ou Mourir. Com.-vaud. en 1 acte. Th. du Gym., 10 March, 1835.

Une Chaumière et son Cœur. Com.-vaud. en 2 actes et trois parties. Th. du Gym., 12 May, 1835.

La Pensionnaire Mariée. Com.-vaud. en 1 acte. Varner. Th. du Gym., 3 Nov., 1835.

Valentine. Drame en 2 actes, mêlé de couplets. Mélesville. Th. du Gym., 4 Jan., 1836.

Chut! Com.-vaud. en 2 actes. Th. du Gym., 26 March, 1836.

Sir Hugues de Guilfort. Com.-vaud. en 2 actes. Bayard. Th. du Gym., 3 Oct., 1836.

Avis aux Coquettes, ou l'Amant Singulier. Com.-vaud. en 2 actes. De Camberousse. Th. du Gym., 29 Oct., 1836.

Le Fils d'un Agent de Change. Com.-vaud. en 1 acte. H. Dupin. Th. des Var., 30 Nov., 1836.

Les Dames Patronnesses, ou à Quelque-chose Malheur est Bon. Proverbe, mêlé de couplets, en 1 acte. Arvers. Th. du Gym., 15 Feb., 1837.

César, ou le Chien du Château. Com.-vaud. en 2 actes. Varner. Th. du Gym., 4 March, 1837.

L'Étudiant et la Grande Dame. Com.-vaud. en 2 actes. Mélesville. Th. des Var., 30 March, 1837.

Le Bout de l'An, ou les Deux Cérémonies. Com.-vaud. en 1 acte. Varner. Th. du Palais-Royal, 2 June, 1837.

Clermont, ou une Femme d'Artiste. Com.-vaud. en 2 actes. Vander-Burch. Th. du Gym., 30 March, 1838.

Cicily, ou le Lion Amoureux. Com.-vaud. en 2 actes. Th. du Gym., 8 Dec., 1840.

Le Veau d'Or. Com. en 1 acte, mêlée de couplets. H. Dupin. Th. du Gym., 26 Feb., 1841.

Les Surprises. Com.-vaud. en 1 acte. Roger. Th. du Gym., 31 July, 1844.

Babiole et Joblot. Com.-vaud. en 2 actes. Saintine. Th. du Gym., 1 Oct., 1844.

Rebecca. Com.-vaud. en 2 actes. Th. du Gym., 2 Dec., 1844.

L'Image. Com.-vaud. en 1 acte. Sauvage. Th. du Gym., 17 April, 1845.

Jeanne et Jeanneton. Com.-vaud. en 2 actes. Varner. Th. du Gym., 29 April, 1845.

La Loi Salique. Com.-vaud. en 2 actes. Th. du Gym., 30 Dec., 1845.

Geneviève, ou la Jalousie Paternelle. Com.-vaud. en 1 acte. Th. du Gym., 30 March, 1846.

La Protégée sans le savoir. Com.-vaud. en 1 acte. Th. du Gym., 5 Dec., 1846.

Maître Jean, ou la Comédie à la Cour. Com.-vaud. en 2 actes. H. Dupin. Th. du Gym., 14 Jan., 1847.

Irène, ou le Magnétisme. Com.-vaud. en 2 actes. Lockroy. Th. du Gym., 2 Feb., 1847.

D'Aranda, ou les Grandes Passions. Com.-vaud. en 2 actes. Th. du Gym., 6 April, 1847.

Une Femme qui se jette par la Fenêtre. Com.-vaud. en 1 acte. Le-moine. Th. du Gym., 19 April, 1847.

La Déesse. Com.-vaud. en 3 actes. Saintine. Th. du Gym., 30 Oct., 1847.

O Amitié! ou les Trois Epoques. Com.-vaud. en 3 actes. Varner. Th. du Gym., 14 Nov., 1848.

Les Filles du Docteur, ou le Dévouement. Com.-vaud. en 2 actes. Masson. Th. du Gym., 10 Feb., 1849.

Héloïse et Abélard, ou à Quelque-chose Malheur est Bon. Com.-vaud. en 2 actes. Masson. Th. du Gym., 22 April, 1850.

Madame Schlick. Com.-vaud. en 1 acte. Varner. Th. du Gym., 9 Feb., 1852.

COMÉDIES-DRAMES

Le Valet de son Rival. Com. en 1 acte. G. Delavigne. Th. de l'Odéon, 19 March, 1816.

Les Frères invisibles. Mélodrame en 3 actes. Mélesville and Delestre-Poirson. Th. de la Porte Saint-Martin, 10 June, 1819.

Le Parrain. Com. en 1 acte. Delestre-Poirson and Mélesville. Th. du Gym., 23 April, 1821.

Valérie. Com. en 3 actes. Mélesville. Th. Fran., 21 Dec., 1822.

Rodolphe, ou Frère et Sœur. Drame en 1 acte. Mélesville. Th. du Gym., 20 Nov., 1823.

Le Mauvais Sujet. Drame en 1 acte. Camille. Th. du Gym., 16 July, 1825.

Le Mariage d'Argent. Com. en 5 actes. Th. Fran., 3 Dec., 1827.

La Bohêmienne, ou l'Amérique en 1775. Drame historique en 5 actes. Mélesville. Th. du Gym., 1 June, 1829.

Les Inconsolables. Com. en 1 acte. Th. Fran., 8 Dec., 1829.

Dix Ans de la Vie d'une Femme, ou les Mauvais Conseils. Drame en 5 actes et 9 tableaux. Terrier. Th. de la Porte Saint-Martin, 17 March, 1832.

Bertrand et Raton, ou l'Art de conspirer. Com. en 5 actes. Th. Fran., 14 Nov., 1833.

La Passion Secrète. Com. en 3 actes. Th. Fran., 13 March, 1834.

L'Ambitieux. Com. en 5 actes. Th. Fran., 27 Nov., 1834.

La Camaraderie, ou la Courte Echelle. Com. en 5 actes. Th. Fran., 19 June, 1837.

Les Indépendants. Com. en 3 actes. Th. Fran., 20 Nov., 1837.

La Calomnie. Com. en 5 actes. Th. Fran., 20 Feb., 1840.

La Grand'mère, ou les Trois Amours. Com. en 3 actes. Th. du Gym., 14 March, 1840.

Japhet, ou la Recherche d'un Père. Com. en 2 actes. Vanderburch. Th. Fran., 20 July, 1840.

Le Verre d'Eau, ou les Effets et les Causes. Com. en 5 actes. Th. Fran., 17 Nov., 1840.

Une Chaîne. Com. en 5 actes. Th. Fran., 29 Nov., 1841.

Oscar, ou le Mari qui trompe sa Femme. Com. en 3 actes. Duveyrier. Th. Fran., 21 April, 1842.

Le Fils de Cromwell, ou une Restauration. Com. en 5 actes. Th. Fran., 20 Nov., 1842.

La Tutrice, ou l'Emploi des Richesses. Com. en 3 actes. Duport. Th. Fran., 29 Nov., 1843.

Le Puff, ou Mensonge et Vérité. Com. en 5 actes. Th. Fran., 22 Jan., 1848.

Adrienne Lecouvreur. Com.-drame en 5 actes. Legouvé. Th. Fran., 14 April, 1849.

Les Contes de la Reine de Navarre, ou la Revanche de Pavie. Com. en 5 actes. Legouvé. Th. Fran., 15 Oct., 1850.

Bataille de Dames, ou un Duel en Amour. Com. en 3 actes. Legouvé. Th. Fran., 17 March, 1851.

Mon Étoile. Com. en 1 acte. Th. Fran., 6 Feb., 1854.

La Czarine. Drame en 5 actes. Th. Fran., 15 Jan., 1855.

Feu Lionel, ou Qui vivra verra. Com. en 3 actes. Potron. Th. Fran., 23 Jan., 1858.

Les Doigts de Fée. Com. en 5 actes. Legouvé. Th. Fran., 29 March, 1858.

Les Trois Maupins, ou la Veille de la Régence. Com. en 5 actes. Boisseaux. Th. du Gym., 23 Oct., 1858.

Rêves d'Amour. Com. en 3 actes. De Biéville. Th. Fran., 1 March, 1859.

La Fille de Trente Ans. Com. en 4 actes. Emile de Najac. Th. du Vaud., 15 Dec., 1859.

La Frileuse. Com. en 3 actes. Th. du Vaud., 6 Sept., 1861.

Opéras and Ballets

La Somnambule, ou l'Arrivée d'un Nouveau Seigneur. Ballet-pantomime en 3 actes. Aumer. Hérold. Th. de l'Op., 19 Sept., 1827.

La Muette de Portici. Opéra en 5 actes. G. Delavigne. Auber. Th. de l'Op., 29 Feb., 1828.

Le Comte Ory. Opéra en 2 actes. Delestre-Poirson. Rossini. Th. de l'Op., 20 Aug., 1828.

La Belle au Bois Dormant. Ballet-Pantomime-Féerie en 3 actes. Aumer. Hérold. Th. de l'Op., 27 April, 1829.

Alcibiade. Opéra en 2 actes. Haussens. Bruxelles, Grand-Théâtre, 30 Oct., 1829.

Manon Lescaut. Ballet-pantomime en 3 actes. Aumer. Halévy. Th. de l'Op., 3 May, 1830.

Le Dieu et la Bayadère, ou la Courtisane Amoureuse. Op.-ballet en 2 actes. Auber. Th. de l'Op., 13 Oct., 1830.

Le Philtre. Opéra en 2 actes. Auber. Th. de l'Op., 20 June, 1831.

L'Orgie. Ballet-pantomime en 3 actes. Corallé. Carafa. Th. de l'Op., 18 July, 1831.

Robert le Diable. Opéra en 5 actes. G. Delavigne. Meyerbeer. Th. de l'Op., 21 Nov., 1831.

Le Serment, ou les Faux-Monnayeurs. Opéra en 3 actes. Mazères. Auber. Th. de l'Op., 11 Oct., 1832.

Gustave III, ou le Bal Masqué. Opéra historique en 5 actes. Auber. Th. de l'Op., 27 Feb., 1833.

Ali-Baba, ou les Quarante Voleurs. Opéra en 4 actes, précédé d'un prologue. Mélesville. Chérubini. Th. de l'Op., 22 July, 1833.

La Juive. Opéra en 5 actes. Halévy. Th. de l'Op., 23 Feb., 1835.

Les Huguenots. Opéra en 5 actes. Meyerbeer. Th. de l'Op., 29 Feb., 1836.

Guido et Ginevra, ou la Peste de Florence. Opéra en 5 actes. Halévy. Th. de l'Op., 5 March, 1838.

La Volière, ou les Oiseaux du Bocage. Ballet-pantomime en 1 acte. Mlle Thérèse Essler. Gide. Th. de l'Op., 5 May, 1838.

Le Lac des Fées. Opéra en 5 actes. Mélesville. Auber. Th. de l'Op., 1 April, 1839.

La Tarentule. Ballet-pantomime en 2 actes. Corallé. Gide. Th. de l'Op., 24 Jan., 1839.

La Xacarilla. Opéra en 1 acte. Marliani. Th. de l'Op., 28 Oct., 1839.

Le Drapier. Opéra en 3 actes. Halévy. Th. de l'Op., 6 Jan., 1840.

Les Martyres. Opéra en 4 actes. Donizetti. Th. de l'Op., 10 April, 1840.

La Favorite. Opéra en 4 actes. Royer and Vaëz. Donizetti. Th. de l'Op., 2 Dec., 1840.

Carmagnola. Opéra en 2 actes. Ambroise Thomas. Th. de l'Op., 19 April, 1841.

Dom Sébastien, roi de Portugal. Opéra en 5 actes. Donizetti. Th. de l'Op., 13 Nov., 1843.

Jeanne la Folle. Opéra en 5 actes. Clapisson. Th. de l'Op., 6 Nov., 1848.

Le Prophète. Opéra en 5 actes. Meyerbeer. Th. de l'Op., 16 April, 1849.

La Tempête. Opéra en 3 actes, précédé d'un prologue. Halévy. Londres, Théâtre de la Reine, 8 June, 1850. Paris, Th.-Italien, 25 Feb., 1851.

L'Enfant Prodigue. Opéra en 5 actes. Auber. Th. de l'Op., 6 Dec., 1850.

Zerline, ou la Corbeille d'Oranges. Opéra en 3 actes. Auber. Th. de l'Op., 16 May, 1851.

Florinde, ou les Maures en Espagne. Opéra en 4 actes. Debillemont. Londres, Théâtre de la Reine, 3 July, 1851.

Le Juif Errant. Opéra en 5 actes. Saint-Georges. Halévy. Th. de l'Op., 23 April, 1852.

La Nonne Sanglante. Opéra en 5 actes. G. Delavigne. Gounod. Th. de l'Op., 18 Oct., 1854.

Les Vêpres Siciliennes. Opéra en 5 actes. Duveyrier. Verdi. Th. de l'Op., 13 June, 1855.

Marco Spada, ou la Fille du Bandit. Ballet-pantomime en 3 actes. Mazillier. Auber. Th. de l'Op., 1 April, 1857.

Le Cheval de Bronze. Opéra-ballet en 4 actes. Auber. Th. de l'Op., 21 Sept., 1857.

L'Africaine. Opéra en 5 actes. Meyerbeer. Th. de l'Op., 28 April, 1865.

Opéras-Comiques

La Chambre à coucher, ou une Demi-Heure de Richelieu. Opéracom. en 1 acte. Guénée. Th. de l'Op.-Com., 29 April, 1813.

La Meunière. Opéra-com. en 1 acte. Mélesville. Garcia. Th. du Gym., 16 May, 1821.

Le Paradis de Mahomet, ou la Pluralité des Femmes. Opéra-com. en 3 actes. Mélesville. Kreutzer and Kreubé. Th. de l'Op.-Com., 23 March, 1822.

La Petite Lampe Merveilleuse. Opéra-com.-féerie en 3 actes. Mélesville. Piccini. Th. du Gym., 29 July, 1822.

Leicester, ou le Château de Kenilworth. Opéra-com. en 3 actes. Mélesville. Auber. Th. de l'Op.-Com., 25 Jan., 1823.

Le Valet de Chambre. Opéra-com. en 1 acte. Mélesville. Carafa. Th. de l'Op.-Com., 16 Sept., 1823.

La Neige, ou le Nouvel Eginhard. Opéra-com. en 4 actes. G. Delavigne. Auber. Th. de l'Op.-Com., 8 Oct., 1823.

Concert à la Cour, ou la Débutante. Opéra-com. en 1 acte. Mélesville. Auber. Th. de l'Op.-Com., 3 June, 1824.

Léocadie. Drame lyrique en 3 actes. Mélesville. Auber. Th. de l'Op.-Com., 4 Nov., 1824.

Le Maçon. Opéra-com. en 3 actes. G. Delavigne. Auber. Th. de l'Op.-Com., 3 May, 1825.

La Dame Blanche. Opéra-com. en 3 actes. Boïeldieu. Th. de l'Op.-Com., 10 Dec., 1825.

La Vieille. Opéra-com. en 1 acte. G. Delavigne. Fétis. Th. de l'Op.-Com., 14 March, 1826.

Le Timide, ou le Nouveau Séducteur. Opéra-com. en 1 acte. Saintine. Auber. Th. de l'Op.-Com., 30 May, 1826.

Fiorella. Opéra-com. en 3 actes. Auber. Th. de l'Op.-Com., 28 Nov., 1826.

Le Loup-Garou. Opéra-com. en 1 acte. Mazères. Mlle Bertin. Th. de l'Op.-Com., 10 March, 1827.

La Fiancée. Opéra-com. en 3 actes. Auber. Th. de l'Op.-Com., 10 June, 1829.

Les Deux Nuits. Opéra-com. en 3 actes. Bouilly. Boïeldieu. Th. de l'Op.-Com., 20 May, 1829.

Fra Diavolo, ou l'Hôtellerie de Terracine. Opéra-com. en 3 actes. Auber. Th. de l'Op.-Com., 28 Jan., 1830.

La Marquise de Brinvilliers. Drame lyrique en 3 actes. Castil-Blaze. Musique de Auber, Batton, Berton, Blangini, Boïeldieu, Carafa, Cherubini, Hérold et Paer. Th. de l'Op.-Com., 31 Oct., 1831.

La Médecine sans Médecin. Opéra-com. en 1 acte. Bayard. Hérold. Th. de l'Op.-Com., 17 Oct., 1832.

La Prison d'Edimbourg. Opéra-com. en 3 actes. De Planard. Carafa. Th. de l'Op.-Com., 20 July, 1833.

L'Estocq, ou l'Intrigue et l'Amour. Opéra-com. en 4 actes. Auber. Th. de l'Op.-Com., 24 May, 1834.

Le Fils du Prince. Opéra-com. en 2 actes. De Feltre. Th. de l'Op.-Com., 28 Aug., 1834.

Le Châlet. Opéra-com. en 1 acte. Mélesville. Adam. Th. de l'Op.-Com., 25 Sept., 1834.

Le Cheval de Bronze. Opéra-féerie en 3 actes. Auber. Th. de l'Op.-Com., 23 March, 1835.

Le Portefaix. Opéra-com. en 3 actes. Gomis. Th. de l'Op.-Com., 16 June, 1835. .

Actéon. Opéra-com. en 1 acte. Auber. Th. de l'Op.-Com., 23 Jan., 1836.

Les Chaperons Blancs. Opéra-com. en 3 actes. Auber. Th. de l'Op.-Com., 9 April, 1836.

Le Mauvais Œil. Opéra-com. en 1 acte. G. Lemoine. Mlle Puget. Th. de l'Op.-Com., 1 Oct., 1836.

L'Ambassadrice. Opéra-com. en 3 actes. Saint-Georges. Auber. Th. de l'Op.-Com., 21 Dec., 1836.

Le Domino Noir. Opéra-com. en 3 actes. Auber. Th. de l'Op.-Com., 2 Dec., 1837.

Le Fidèle Berger. Opéra-com. en 3 actes. Saint-Georges. Adam. Th. de l'Op.-Com., 11 Jan., 1838.

Marguerite. Opéra-com. en 3 actes. De Planard. Boïeldieu. Th. de l'Op.-Com., 18 June, 1838.

La Figurante, ou l'Amour et la Dame. Opéra-com. en 3 actes. Dupin. Clapisson. Th. de l'Op.-Com., 24 Aug., 1838.

Régine, ou Deux Nuits. Opéra-com. en 2 actes. Adam. Th. de l'Op.-Com., 17 Jan., 1839.

Les Treize. Opéra-com. en 3 actes. Duport. Halévy. Th. de l'Op.-Com., 15 April, 1839.

Polichinelle. Opéra-com. en 1 acte. Duveyrier. Montfort. Th. de l'Op.-Com., 14 June, 1839.

Le Shérif. Opéra-com. en 3 actes. Halévy. Th. de l'Op.-Com., 2 Sept., 1839.

La Reine d'un Jour. Opéra-com. en 3 actes. Saint-Georges. Adam. Th. de l'Op.-Com., 19 Sept., 1839.

Zanetta, ou Jouer avec le Feu. Opéra-com. en 3 actes. Saint-Georges. Auber. Th. de l'Op.-Com., 18 May, 1840.

L'Opéra à la Cour. Opéra-com. en 4 parties. Saint-Georges. Grisars and Boïeldieu. Th. de l'Op.-Com., 16 July, 1840.

Le Guitarrero. Opéra-com. en 3 actes. Halévy. Th. de l'Op.-Com., 21 Jan., 1841.

Les Diamants de la Couronne. Opéra-com. en 3 actes. Saint-Georges. Auber. Th. de l'Op.-Com., 6 March, 1841.

La Main de Fer, ou un Mariage Secret. Opéra-com. en 3 actes. De Leuven. Adam. Th. de l'Op.-Com., 26 Oct., 1841.

Le Diable à l'Ecole. Légende en 1 acte. Boulanger. Th. de l'Op.-Com., 17 Jan., 1842.

Le Duc d'Olonne. Opéra-com. en 3 actes. Saintine. Auber. Th. de l'Op.-Com., 4 Feb., 1842.

Le Codex Noir. Opéra-com. en 3 actes. Clapisson. Th. de l'Op.-Com., 9 June, 1842.

Le Kiosque. Opéra-com. en 1 acte. Duport. Mazos. Th. de l'Op.-Com., 2 Nov., 1842.

La Part du Diable. Opéra-com. en 3 actes. Auber. Th. de l'Op.-Com., 16 June, 1843.

Le Puits d'Amour. Opéra-com. en 3 actes. De Leuven. Balfe. Th. de l'Op.-Com., 20 April, 1843.

Lambert Simnel. Opéra-com. en 3 actes. Mélesville. Monpon. Th. de l'Op.-Com., 14 Sept., 1843.

Cagliostro. Opéra-com. en 3 actes. Saint-Georges. Adam. Th. de l'Op.-Com., 10 Feb., 1844.

Oreste et Pylade. Opéra-com. en 1 acte. Dupin. Thys. Th. de l'Op.-Com., 28 Feb., 1844.

La Sirène. Opéra-com. en 3 actes. Auber. Th. de l'Op.-Com., 26 March, 1844.

La Barcarolle, ou l'Amour et la Musique. Opéra-com. en 3 actes. Auber. Th. de l'Op.-Com., 22 April, 1845.

Le Ménétrier. Opéra-com. en 3 actes. Labarre. Th. de l'Op.-Com., 9 Aug., 1845.

La Charbonnière. Opéra-com. en 3 actes. Mélesville. Montfort. Th. de l'Op.-Com., 13 Oct., 1845.

Ne touchez pas à la Reine. Opéra-com. en 3 actes. Vaëz. Boisselot. Th. de l'Op.-Com., 16 Jan., 1847.

Le Sultan Saladin. Opéra-com. en 1 acte. Dupin. Bordèse. Th. de l'Op.-Com., 8 Feb., 1847.

Haÿdée, ou le Secret. Opéra-com. en 3 actes. Auber. Th. de l'Op.-Com., 28 Dec., 1847.

La Nuit de Noël, ou l'Anniversaire. Opéra-com. en 3 actes. Reber. Th. de l'Op.-Com., 9 Feb., 1848.

La Fée aux Roses. Opéra-com.-féerie en 3 actes. Saint-Georges. Halévy. Th. de l'Op.-Com., 1 Oct., 1849.

Giralda, ou la Nouvelle Psyché. Opéra-com. en 3 actes. Adam. Th. de l'Op.-Com., 20 July, 1850.

La Chanteuse Voilée. Opéra-com. en 1 acte. De Leuven. Victor Massé. Th. de l'Op.-Com., 26 Nov., 1850.

La Dame de Pique. Opéra-com. en 3 actes. Halévy. Th. de l'Op.-Com., 28 Dec., 1850.

Mosquita la Sorcière. Opéra-com. en 3 actes. Vaëz. Boisselot. Th. de l'Opéra-National, 27 Sept., 1851.

Les Mystères d'Udolphe. Opéra-com. en 3 actes. G. Delavigne. Clapisson. Th. de l'Op.-Com., 4 Nov., 1852.

Marco Spada. Opéra-com. en 3 actes. Auber. Th. de l'Op.-Com., 21 Dec., 1852.

La Lettre au Bon Dieu. Opéra-com. en 2 actes. De Courcy. Duprez. Th. de l'Op.-Com., 28 April, 1853.

Le Nabab. Opéra-com. en 3 actes. Saint-Georges. Halévy. Th. de l'Op.-Com., 1 Sept., 1853.

L'Étoile du Nord. Opéra-com. en 3 actes. Meyerbeer. Th. de l'Op.-Com., 16 Feb., 1854.

La Fiancée du Diable. Opéra-com. en 3 actes. Romand. Victor Massé. Th. de l'Op.-Com., 5 June, 1854.

Jenny Bell. Opéra-com. en 3 actes. Auber. Th. de l'Op.-Com., 2 June, 1855.

Manon Lescaut. Opéra-com. en 3 actes. Auber. Th. de l'Op.-Com., 23 Feb., 1856.

La Chatte Métamorphosée en Femme. Opéra-com. en 1 acte. Mélesville. Offenbach. Th. des Bouffes-Parisiens, 19 April, 1858.

Broskovano. Opéra-com. en 2 actes. Boisseaux. Deffès. Th. Lyrique, 29 Sept., 1858.

Les Trois Nicolas. Opéra-com. en 3 actes. Lopez and De Leuven. Clapisson. Th. de l'Op.-Com., 16 Dec., 1858.

Les Petits Violons du Roi. Opéra-com. en 3 actes. Boisseaux. Deffès. Th. Lyrique, 30 Sept., 1859.

Yvonne. Opéra-com. en 3 actes. Limmander. Th. de l'Op.-Com., 29 Nov., 1859.

Le Nouveau Pourceaugnac. Opéra-com. en 1 acte. Delestre-Poirson. Hignard. Th. des Bouffes-Parisiens, 14 Jan., 1860.

Barkoaf. Opéra-bouffe en 3 actes. Boisseaux. Offenbach. Th. de l'Op.-Com., 24 Dec., 1860.

La Circassienne. Opéra-com. en 3 actes. Auber. Th. de l'Op.-Com., 2 Feb., 1861.

Madame Grégoire. Opéra-com. en 3 actes. Boisseaux. Clapisson. Th. Lyrique, 8 Feb., 1861.

La Beauté du Diable. Opéra-com. en 1 acte. De Najac. Alary. Opéra-Com., 28 May, 1861.

La Fiancée du Roi de Garbe. Opéra-com. en 3 actes et 6 tableaux. Saint-Georges. Auber. Th. de l'Op.-Com., 11 Jan., 1864.

L'Ours et le Pacha. Opéra-bouffe en 1 acte. Saintine. Bazin. Th. de l'Op.-Com., 21 Feb., 1870.

ROMANS. NOUVELLES. PROVERBES

Un Ministre sous Louis XV, ou le Secret de rester en place. Historiette en action. *Revue de Paris*, April, 1829.

Le Jeune Docteur, ou le Moyen de Parvenir. Historiette en action. *Revue de Paris*, May, 1829.

La Tête-à-Tête, ou Trente Lieues en Poste. Proverbe. *Revue de Paris*, July, 1830.

La Conversion, ou à l'Impossible nul n'est tenu. Proverbe. *Revue de Paris*, Oct., 1830.

Potemkin, ou un Caprice Impérial. Anecdote de la Cour de Russie. *Revue de Paris*, April, 1831.

Le Prix de la Vie. Historiette tirée des mémoires d'un gentilhomme de Bretagne. *Europe Littéraire*, March, 1833.

Judith, ou la Loge d'Opéra. Historiette contemporaine. *La Presse,* Feb. and March, 1837.

Le Roi de Carreau. Nouvelle. *Revue de Paris,* July, 1837.

La Maîtresse Anonyme. Nouvelle. *Le Constitutionnel,* June–July, 1838.

Carlo Broschi. Nouvelle historique. *Journal des Débats,* Aug.–Sept., 1839.

Maurice. Historiette contemporaine. *Le Siècle,* Dec., 1844–Jan., 1845.

Piquillo Alliaga, ou les Maures sous Philippe III. Roman. *Le Siècle,* March–Sept., 1846.

Les Malheurs Heureux. Proverbe en 3 parties. *Le Constitutionnel,* April, 1851.

Le Filleul d'Amadis, ou les Amours d'une Fée. Roman de Chevalerie. *Le Constitutionnel,* Nov.–Dec., 1855.

Noélie. Nouvelle. *Le Constitutionnel,* March–April, 1859.

La Jeune Allemagne, ou les Yeux de ma Tante. Roman. *Le Constitutionnel,* Jan.–March, 1857.

Fleurette. Histoire d'une Bouquetière. Roman. *Le Constitutionnel,* Oct.–Dec., 1860.

APPENDIX B

LIST OF BOOKS AND ARTICLES RELATING TO SCRIBE, THE FRENCH DRAMA, AND PARISIAN THEATRES

SCRIBE

Batchelder, J. *Un détail de technique dans le drame d'Eugène Scribe, "Adrienne Lecouvreur," et les Influences de* 1848. Paris, Société française d'imprimerie et de librairie. In-8. 1909.

Benoist, A. "Le Théâtre de Scribe: les comédies historiques." *Revue des Cours et Conférences*, 14 Feb., 1895, p. 417, and 21 Feb., 1895, p. 449.

Brunetière, F. "Scribe et Musset." *Revue Bleue*, vol. XLIX, 5 March, 1892, pp. 289–296.

Epagny, Jean d'. *Molière et Scribe*. Paris, A. Durand. In-18. 1865.

Lecigne, C. *Scribe et son théâtre*. Paris, Sueur-Charruey. In-8. 1906.

Kaufmann, Michael. *Zur Technik der Komödien von Eugène Scribe*. Hamburg, Lutcke und Wulff. 1911.

Larroumet, G. "Le Centenaire de Scribe." (In Noël, Ed., *Les Annales du théâtre et de la musique*, vol. XVIII. Paris, 1876–1893.)

Legouvé, Ernest. *Eugène Scribe*. Paris, Didier et Cie. In-8. 1874.

Matthews, Brander. *French Dramatists of the Nineteenth Century*. New York, 1901.

Mirecourt, Eugène de. *Scribe*. Paris, J. P. Roret et Cie. In-16. 1854.

Rolland, J. *Les Comédies politiques d'Eugène Scribe*. Paris, E. Sansot et Cie. In-12. 1912.

THE FRENCH DRAMA

Auger, H. *La Question du théâtre au point de vue social*. Paris, Tresse. In-8. 1848.

Banville, Th. de. *Mes Souvenirs*. Paris, Charpentier. In-12. 1882.

Bonassies, J. *La Censure dramatique*. Paris, Librairie Lagnier. In-8. 1873.

Brisson, A. *Le Théâtre et les Mœurs*. Paris, Flammarion. In-16. 1906.

Claretie, J. *La Vie moderne au théâtre*. Paris, G. Barba. 2 vols. in-12. 1869–1875.

Doumic, R. *De Scribe à Ibsen*. Paris, Delaplane. In-12. 1893.

Dumas, A. *Souvenirs dramatiques*. Paris, C. Lévy. 2 vols. in-18. 1881.

Faguet, E. *Propos de théâtre*. Paris, Société française d'imprimerie et de librairie. 3 vols. in-16. 1903–1906.

—— *Notes sur le théâtre contemporain*. Paris, H. Lecène et H. Oudin. 3 vols. in-18. 1889–1891.

—— *Drame ancien, drame moderne*. Paris, A. Colin. In-12. 1898.

Formentin, Charles. *Essai sur les origines du drame moderne en France*. Paris, Pedone-Lauriel. In-8. 1879.

Gautier, T. *Histoire de l'art dramatique depuis vingt-cinq ans*. Paris, Magnin, Blanchard et Cie. 6 vols. in-12. 1858–1859.

Des Granges, C. M. *La Comédie et les mœurs sous la Restauration et la Monarchie de Juillet* (1815–1848). Paris, Fontemoing. In-8. 1904.

Guex, J. *Le Théâtre et la société française de 1815 à 1848*. Paris, Fischbacher. In-8. 1900.

Guillemot, J. *L'Evolution de l'idée dramatique chez les maîtres du théâtre, de Corneille à Dumas fils*. Paris, Perrin. In-16. 1910.

Hallays-Dabot, V. *Histoire de la censure théâtrale en France*. Paris, E. Dentu. In-12. 1862.

Janin, J. *Histoire de la littérature dramatique*. Paris, Michel-Lévy frères. 6 vols. in-12. 1853–1858.

Larroumet, G. *Nouvelles études d'histoire et de critique dramatiques*. Paris, Hachette et Cie. In-16. 1899.

—— *Etudes de critique dramatique*. Paris, Hachette et Cie. 2 vols. in-16. 1906.

Legouvé, E. *Soixante ans de souvenirs*. Paris, Hetzel et Cie. 2 vols. in-8. 1886–1887.

Lenient, C. *La Comédie en France au 18e siècle*. Paris, Hachette et Cie. 2 vols. in-18. 1888.

Muret, Th. *L'histoire par le théâtre*, 1789–1851. Paris, Amyot. 3 vols. in-12. 1865.

Pergameni, H. *Le Théâtre politique en France depuis 1789*. Brussels, Moreau. In-8. 1903.

Sarcey, F. *Quarante ans de théâtre*. Paris, F. Didot et Cie; Bibliothèque des Annales politiques et littéraires. 8 vols. in-12. 1900.

Weiss, J. J. *Trois années de théâtre*, 1883–1885. Paris, Calmann-Lévy. In-12. 1894.

REFERENCES ON THE OPÉRA AND THE OPÉRA-COMIQUE

Aubin, L. *Le Drame lyrique; histoire de la musique dramatique en France*. Paris, Fischbacher. In-8. 1908.

Blaze de Bury. *Meyerbeer et son temps*. Paris, Michel-Lévy frères. In-18. 1865.

Castil-Blaze. *De l'opéra en France*. Paris, Janet et Cotelle. 2 vols. in-8. 1820.

Chouquet, G. *Histoire de la musique dramatique en France depuis les origines jusqu'à nos jours*. Paris, Firmin Didot. In-8. 1873.

Desarbres, N. *Deux siècles à l'Opéra*. Paris, E. Dentu. In-18. 1868.

Font, Aug. *Favart, l'opéra-comique et la comédie-vaudeville au 17ᵉ et au 18ᵉ siècles*. Paris, Fischbacher. In-8. 1894.

Nuitter, Ch. et Thoinan, E. *Les Origines de l'opéra français*. Paris, Plon-Nourrit et Cⁱᵉ. In-8. 1886.

Pougin, A. *Molière et l'opéra-comique*. Paris, J. Baur. In-8. 1882.

—— *L'opéra sous l'ancien régime et sous la Révolution*. Paris, Fischbacher. In-8. 1914.

Regnard, A. *La Renaissance du drame lyrique: 1660–1876; Essai de dramaturgie musicale*. Paris, Fischbacher. In-18. 1895.

Soubies, A. et Malherbe, Ch. *Précis de l'histoire de l'opéra-comique*. Paris, Dupret. In-16. 1887.

PARISIAN THEATRES

Albert, M. *Les Théâtres de la foire*. Paris, Hachette et Cⁱᵉ. In-12. 1900.

—— *Les Théâtres des boulevards* (1789–1848). Paris, Lecène et Oudin. In-12. 1902.

Beaulieu, H. *Les Théâtres du boulevard du Crime* (1752–1862). Paris, Daragon. In-8. 1905.

Bernardin, N. M. *La Comédie italienne en France et les théâtres de la foire et du boulevard* (1570–1791). Paris, Revue Bleue. In-12. 1902.

Bonassies, J. *Les Spectacles forains et la Comédie-Française; le droit des pauvres avant et après 1789; les auteurs dramatiques et la Comédie-Française au 19ᵉ siècle*. Paris, E. Dentu. In-12. 1875.

Boutet de Monvel, Roger. *Les Variétés* (1850–1870). Paris, Plon-Nourrit et Cⁱᵉ. In-12. 1905.

Brazier, N. *Chronique des Petits-théâtres de Paris*. Paris, Allardin. 2 vols. in-8. 1837. Reprinted by D'Heylli (Rouveyre et Blond). 2 vols. in-12. 1883.

Cain, Georges. *Anciens théâtres de Paris*. Paris, Fasquelle. In-12. 1906.

Chabrol, W. *Histoire et description du Palais-Royal et du Théâtre-Français*. Paris, Plon-Nourrit et Cie. In-8. 1883.

Descombes, Ch. M. *Le Théâtre-Français*. Paris, Garnier frères. In-8. 1859.

Ginisty, P. *Choses et gens de théâtre*. Paris, Perrin. In-16. 1892.

Goncourt, Ed. et Jules de. *Mystères des théâtres*. Paris, Librairie Nouvelle. In-8. 1853.

Joannidès, A. *La Comédie-Française*, 1680–1900; 1901; 1902; 1903; 1904. Paris, Plon-Nourrit et Cie. In-8.

Michaux, L. *Histoire et description du théâtre de la Gaîté*. Paris, Plon et Cie. In-8. 1884.

—— *Histoire et description du Théâtre du Vaudeville*. Paris, Plon et Cie. In-8. 1884.

Vauthier, G. *L'Opéra sous la Restauration*. Paris, La Revue Musicale. In-8. 1910.

INDEX

INDEX